Clergy and Christian Educators comment on *The Baby Boomer Bible Study*:

"Excellent material. I love the work-book format...that's the way to learn. The charts are superior...better than any I have found. A great piece of work...avoids the pitfalls and moves right ahead with the wonderful story of the Bible. *The Baby Boomer Bible Study* has the positive 'ring of truth.'"

> *-- Reverend Frank Warden, M.Th., Perkins School of Theology,*
> *J.D., Vanderbilt Law School, author of Trinity Bible Study*

"A book of this nature comes along on rare occasions. This study can take a person who may have only a beginner's perspective on Scripture, and give them a clear picture of how the Bible is put together. It can be used again and again through the adult education program of a church. Because our church constantly attracts adults who do not have any Bible background, this program brings them 'up to speed' in a short period of time. It could also serve as a 'refresher course' for adults of all ages from time to time. Any church could benefit from this as a part of their education program."

> *-- Dr. Charles R. Wade, President of the Texas Baptist Convention,*
> *Senior Pastor, First Baptist Church, Arlington, Texas*

"The challenge the church faces as we move into the twenty-first century is how to translate the faith we hold dear into a language that can be understood and believed by persons who may not share our traditions, our literature, our music or our icons. *The Baby Boomer Bible Study* takes a quantum leap in that direction. I am grateful for it."

> *-- Dr. Tom Graves, District Superintendent,*
> *North Texas Annual Conference, The United Methodist Church*

"Since launching our new Presbyterian Church in October 1996, I've been searching for a Bible 101 course. Our 200 current participants include many people who have not attended church in their adult lives. Our young median age also means we have a visual/computer generation of Christians. *The Baby Boomer Bible Study* is the answer to my prayers. The simple, yet excellent maps, graphics and charts make this a very visual tool. This incredibly user-friendly workbook is one of those 'keepers' to which my parishioners will return time and again for the rest of their Christian adventure on earth."

> *-- The Reverend Joe Gossett, Trinity Presbyterian Church,*
> *College Station, Texas*

"The *Baby Boomer Bible Study* is proving to be an excellent tool for teaching people to open their Bibles and claim the 'Faith Story' as their own."

> *-- Lisa L. Ray, Director of Christian Education,*
> *Mt. Bethel United Methodist Church, Marietta, Georgia*

"*The Baby Boomer Bible Study* is an excellent resource for churches wanting to give their members a panoramic survey of the Bible. Joe White's engineering background is refreshing and his use of tables, maps, glossaries, flow charts, and other helps, makes the Scriptures much easier to understand for all of us."

> *-- John Williams, Director of Youth and Adult Education,*
> *Christ the King Lutheran Church, Kingwood, Texas (Houston area)*

"Joseph White has done the Christian community a great service by writing *The Baby Boomer Bible Study*. It is not a theological treatise involving exhaustive, scholarly research. This book is an introduction to the Bible. It was written by a layman for lay persons. It is an excellent beginning point for serious Bible students. This book deserves wide readership."

-- *L. H. Coleman, Th.D., Southwestern Baptist Theological Seminary,*
President of Coleman Stewardship Services

"We haven't even begun *The Baby Boomer Bible Study* and we've already filled the class because of the appealing concept of it all. Many of our congregation have decided that such a simplified program is just what they have been waiting for, and have jumped on board with enthusiasm. The format you have devised appears more 'user friendly' than any we've attempted before and we're anxious to begin! Thank you for your creative approach to teaching God's Word!"

-- *The Reverend Richard E. Grant, and Amy,*
St. Thomas Episcopal Church, Wharton, Texas (Houston area)

Media comments on The Baby Boomer Bible Study:

"Includes maps, graphs and charts about such things as the content of the books of the Bible ... Valuable and informative." Hopefully, "a first step in luring many people into Bible study."

-- *Jim Jones, religion editor for the Fort Worth Star Telegram*

"Offers a concise method for presenting basic Bible information ... Serviceable and informative ... The flow charts, tables, lists, maps, and diagrams present a great deal of information in readily accessible formats."
-- *Book Review, Religion Section, the Dallas Morning News*

"Brings new meanings to scriptures for baby boomers ... Easy to follow because of its simple language, visual aids, and mounds of information ... Ideal for new Bible readers."

-- *The Arlington Morning News*

"Targets people with no previous knowledge of the Bible, [and provides] insights into major themes and characters ... Writing style is concise, and the material rarely strays into areas of theological speculation or controversy."

-- *The Arlington Star-Telegram*

"The Baby Boomer Bible Study makes it easy for individuals to fill in their gaps in Bible knowledge, or for groups to begin a first-time introduction to the Bible."

-- *Christian Family Magazine*

The BABY BOOMER BIBLE Study

Written by: Joseph A. White

Technical Editor: Jerry Chism, *Doctor of Ministry*

Published by:
White Diversified Engineering Inc.
Arlington, Texas

All Scripture except in Chapter 8 (Poetry)

Scripture taken from the HOLY BIBLE, NEW INTERNATIONAL
VERSION. Copyright © 1973, 1978, 1984 International Bible Society.
Used by permission of Zondervan Bible Publishers.

Chapter 8 (Poetry)

Scripture taken from the NEW AMERICAN STANDARD BIBLE (R),
(C) Copyright The Lockman Foundation 1960, 1962, 1963, 1968,
1971, 1972, 1973, 1975, 1977
Used by permission.

Library of Congress Catalog Card Number: 96-90414

ISBN 0-9636278-4-8

Published by
White Diversified Engineering Inc.
P.O. 171084
Arlington, Texas 76003

Cover by
Kee brook studios of Arlington, Texas

Printed in the United States of America
by
Gilliland of Arkansas City, Kansas

10 9 8 7 6 5 4

Table of Contents

List of Tables

x

List of Maps

List of Diagrams

The What, How, Who & Why of the Baby Boomer Bible Study
questions and answers

What is the Baby Boomer Bible Study?
It is an introductory Bible study that can be used in group Bible study, individual study or for Sunday School class.

How much Bible background do I need to do the study?
None. This is your starting place.

How much additional Bible reading is required to answer the questions?
No additional Bible reading is required; its all in the book. The study is self-contained and the answers are in the back of the book.

How long does the study take?
Group study is recommended to last for 14 sessions of 1 ½ hour length with everyone reading the lesson and answering the questions prior to class.

Individual study is completely self-paced.

Sunday School classes can progress through the entire study or simply focus on specific areas of the Bible.

Can children and youth use the study?
Absolutely. Older elementary children and certainly junior and senior high are adept at this type of simplified format.

Who wrote this Bible study?
A layperson (i.e. not a minister or preacher). Joe is an engineer and likes to refer to the study as "an engineering report on the Bible."

Why did he write it?
Joe taught junior and senior high Bible study for 17 years and introductory adult Bible study for the past 7 years. He constantly pursued a clear concise method to introduce the Bible. After many years of developing his own teaching methods and material, students and clergy suggested that Joe formalize his work and share it.

What is in the book?
- **66** step by step tables that lead you through the Scripture.
- **19** maps that are clear and concise.
- **15** computer type flow diagrams which graphically represent the main text.
- **21** "*Theologically Speaking*" boxes written by a minister that provide pertinent yet understandable comments concerning the theology of the subject at hand.
- **486** questions (390 with answers) which are divided into 3 levels of difficulty.
- **21** chapter and subject icons, original artwork, lists of tables, maps and diagrams
- **444** entries in a glossary written especially for the study.

Do I need a Bible to complete the study?
The answer is no and yes.

Technically to complete the study - No.

Practically - Yes, of course you need a Bible. Invariably your curiosity will get the best of you. You will want to scan through and familiarize yourself with the layout and text of the Bible. Hopefully you will use one of the many excellent study Bibles available today.

When I complete the study what will I have gained?
Upon completion of the study you will have two things:

Number one, you will have a general overview of the Bible. In other words, the big picture, how it all fits together.

Number two, you will have your own Bible reference book with which you are very familiar and comfortable.

What are the ultimate objectives of the study?
- To introduce you to the Bible.
- To give you confidence in your Bible knowledge and ability.
- To instill in you a desire to go on to more in-depth Bible study.

About the Author

Joe White was raised on a small farm in Arkansas and is a lifelong United Methodist. He is a graduate of the University of Arkansas, a Registered Professional Civil Engineer, is married and has two daughters, Charlotte and Rebekah. Joe's wife, Jan, is also an engineer. Joe and Jan have lived in Texas for the past 16 years and are residents of Arlington. The entire family is involved in numerous church activities and also enjoys camping, boating and water skiing.

Joe writes with a style that is easily understood and has extensive experience in teaching introductory Bible study. For 17 years, Joe taught the Bible to both Junior and Senior High students. While working with youth, he developed much of his own curriculum.

During the past seven years Joe has concentrated on introducing the Bible to adults from a "layperson's perspective." He has led studies using nationally known curriculum. He has also led classes that have progressively utilized more and more of his own material. Because of the success of these classes and encouragement from others, Joe decided to formalize his work and share his method of Bible introduction. He likes to refer to *The Baby Boomer Bible Study* as his engineering report on the Bible.

About the Technical Editor

Jerry Chism is currently Senior Minister at St. Luke United Methodist Church in Fort Worth, which has a membership in excess of 1,300 members. Jerry and his wife Liz, a teacher, were both born and raised in the Fort Worth area. They and their son, Danny, age 13, are a close family who love to travel and spend time together, and are actively involved in their church and community.

Jerry received his Bachelor of Science degree in Religion and Philosophy from Texas Wesleyan University, his Master of Theology Degree from Perkins School of Theology, Southern Methodist University, and his Doctor of Ministry Degree from St. Paul School of Theology in Kansas City, Missouri. He has completed additional post-graduate work at Union Theological Seminary in New York, New York.

Joe and Jerry and their families have been friends for nine years. Jerry was founding pastor of St. John the Apostle United Methodist Church. Upon their relocation to Arlington, the Whites joined this church, worked with Jerry in numerous programs and are still active members.

Acknowledgments and Special Thanks

This study is not the product of a large publishing house, seminary or church organization with trained personnel, powerful resources and research capabilities. Rather it is the labor of one layperson who called upon many of his Christian friends to share their talents. As such, many thanks and acknowledgments are in order. Certainly not all of the people who helped me in the development of this study are listed below; however, I am indeed grateful to all who loaned a Christian hand.

Special thanks to my wife, Jan, for her encouragement and work as the study progressed over time. Morning after morning she would arise to find another stack of papers on her dressing table waiting to be proofed and marked.

Special thanks also to my daughters, Charlotte and Rebekah, for being so understanding and helpful. They contributed in many ways, including looking up countless verses and checking many tables.

Many thanks to my close friend Reverend Jeffery A. Smith. He provided technical assistance, advice and, most of all, unmeasured encouragement as the study was formulated.

I am grateful to my parents, Paul and Wanda White, for raising me in a Christian home and instilling in me the discipline of daily Bible reading at a very young age.

Art
Steve Johnson is a heavy equipment maintenance specialist. He is a self-trained artist who specializes in pen & ink and watercolors. Steve drew the Old Testament pictures.

Maps
James N. Finley is a Registered Professional Mechanical Engineer. He is skilled in Computer Automated Drafting. James was responsible for converting my hand drawn maps into camera-ready computer-generated drawings.

Literary Editors
Jeanine P. Smith is a freelance business writer. She was responsible for the literary editing of the study as it was formulated and finalized.

Deborah Reese is an English instructor at the University of Texas at Arlington. She was responsible for the proofreading and literary editing of the completed text.

Printing
Judith Pickering is a sales representative in the commercial printing business. She provided technical expertise pertaining to the printing of the book.

The Idea Committee
For many months these individuals read and commented on ever changing ideas, text, tables, maps and questions:

Ken Adair	Laura Adair	Steve Kole
Leah Smith	Abby Walker	Mark Walker

Explanation of Icons

A unique icon is positioned in the bottom margin of each page to represent that respective chapter or section of the book. One or more of five subject icons may be located in the side margin to indicate subject matter on that particular page.

	Chapter 1		Chapter 11
	Chapter 2		Chapter 12
	Chapter 3		Chapter 13
	Chapter 4		Chapter 14
	Chapter 5	**Glossary** **Answers**	
	Chapter 6		Theologically Speaking
	Chapter 7		Scripture
	Chapter 8		Questions
	Chapter 9		Diagrams
	Chapter 10		Maps

Chapter 1
Introduction to the Bible

THE HOLY BIBLE is the most widely distributed book in the world. The complete Bible has been translated into almost 300 languages and portions have been translated into 1,500 languages and dialects. By far, the Bible leads the all-time best seller list with more than 2.4 billion copies produced since 1816.

The Bible records God's interaction with humanity. Its message is for everyone regardless of age or education level from the youngest child to the greatest theologian. The Bible contains an infinite range of material appropriate for all to study, learn and live by.

There is one characteristic that makes the Bible unique among all the books of the world. The Bible is inspired by God. It is God's own message, written down by people of faith, in God's own Holy Book.

Structure of the Bible

The word "Bible" comes from a Greek word which means "the little books." The Bible is composed of 66 individual books written by approximately 40 authors over a period of about 15 centuries. It is divided into two sections, the Old and the New Testaments.

The Old Testament or Old Covenant records God choosing a person and from that single individual, developing a nation with which to spread His Word. It also shows by the nation's example the power, grace and compassion of God for the entire world.

The New Testament is the fulfillment of the Old Testament. It offers salvation through a New Covenant made between God and the individual. This covenant is not dependent upon birthright or obedience to a set of laws, but is based upon faith and acceptance of Jesus Christ.

The Old Testament contains 39 books and the New Testament contains 27 books. Each book is divided into chapters, in turn the chapters are subdivided into numbered verses. For example, in II Chronicles 15:2, Chronicles is the book in the Bible. A prefix denotes that there is more than one book named Chronicles and II refers to the second book. The 15 references the chapter number and the 2 separated by the colon calls for the second verse in that chapter.

The following table provides information on the breakdown of books, chapters and verses.

Table 1-1   Books, Chapters and Verses

	Entire Bible	Old Testament	New Testament
Books	66	39	27
Chapters	1189	929	260
Total % of Text	100%	78%	22%
Longest Chapter		Psalms 119	
Shortest Chapter		Psalms 117	
Center Chapter		Psalms 117	
Longest Verse		Esther 8:9	
Shortest Verse			John 11:35

Content and Arrangement of the Books

The Bible is not an easy book to read and study. Many people become discouraged when they try to read straight through the Bible page by page, as you would most books. It can be just as discouraging to read individual books without a planned sequence.

The Bible is not arranged in chronological order or by order of subject. Some of the books are simple narratives, others give genealogies and yet others are letters. Some books tell one story or reference a single point in time, while other books chronicle several hundred years of history. Information about the same subject is often found in other places in the Bible, and in a few cases the exact information is duplicated in another book.

It is not necessary to understand the reasons for the arrangement of the Bible; however, it is imperative to be aware of the basic structure. The table on the following page shows the 66 books in order as they appear in the Bible. They are divided into 10 commonly accepted groups.

Table 1-2   A General Grouping of the Books of the Bible

The 39 Books of the Old Testament
(in order as they appear in the Bible)

Pentateuch	Historical	Poetical	Major Prophets	Minor Prophets
Genesis	Joshua	Job	Isaiah	Hosea
Exodus	Judges	Psalms	Jeremiah	Joel
Leviticus	Ruth	Proverbs	Lamentations	Amos
Numbers	I Samuel	Ecclesiastes	Ezekiel	Obadiah
Deuteronomy	II Samuel	Song of Solomon	Daniel	Jonah
	I Kings			Micah
	II Kings			Nahum
	I Chronicles			Habakkuk
	II Chronicles			Zephaniah
	Ezra			Haggai
	Nehemiah			Zechariah
	Esther			Malachi

Table 1-2   (Continued)

The 27 Books of the New Testament
(in order as they appear in the Bible)

Gospels	Church History	Paul's Letters	General Letters	Apocalyptic
Matthew	Acts	Romans	Hebrews	Revelation
Mark		I Corinthians	James	
Luke		II Corinthians	I Peter	
John		Galatians	II Peter	
		Ephesians	I John	
		Philippians	II John	
		Colossians	III John	
		I Thessalonians	Jude	
		II Thessalonians		
		I Timothy		
		II Timothy		
		Titus		
		Philemon		

How We Got Today's Bible

Discussions of the Bible and its makeup naturally lead to the question of how we got our Bible in its present form. It is beyond the scope of this course to provide detailed information in this complicated area. There are countless volumes of information available describing this process which occurred over a period of several hundred years. However, for the purposes of this course, the following simplified information is given:

"Canon" refers to the Biblical books officially accepted by the Church and governing religious body as genuine. The word "canon" is derived from an ancient root word which means "reed." Reeds are very tall straight plants which were used as measuring sticks or rulers. To greatly simplify the overall process, we can list three basic tests that were applied to writings before they were recognized as canon or canonized.

Table 1-3   Basic Tests for Canon

1.	**The Book Itself** The writing must show that it was inspired by God and not just general religious writing.
2.	**Authority of the Writer** What authority did the writer have? Normally, the author of an Old Testament book was a prophet. In the New Testament, the author was usually an apostle or the writing was approved by an apostle.
3.	**Church Acceptance** The early churches had to agree that the writings were of canonical nature. *(There was a clear consensus in the early churches about the books that were accepted.)*

Authority of the Canon

There are two very important points that we must remember regarding the idea of canon and its authority. First is the fact that Jesus read, quoted and taught from the Scriptures that now basically form our Old Testament. This was Jesus' Bible. Second, authority was not assigned to the books by the canon or the canonizing process. The reverse was true; the books became canon or were canonized because they had authority.

Language in the Bible

There are three basic languages of the Bible; Hebrew, Aramaic and Greek. All three are still alive and in use today. These languages, as spoken today, are similar to their ancient forms much as our modern English is similar to eleventh century English.

Hebrew was the primary language of the Old Testament. Hebrew or a similar dialect was commonly spoken around the eastern end of the Mediterranean Sea in early Old Testament times. The greater part of the Old Testament Scriptures were written in Hebrew.

Use of the Aramaic language appeared in the Old Testament as early as Genesis, but was infrequent until the Empire of Assyria strongly implemented its use in the eighth century B.C. Aramaic was commonly spoken in Palestine from post exile times (fifth century B.C.) thru New Testament times. Aramaic was the daily language of Jesus; however, He undoubtedly also had command of Hebrew, which He would have learned in the synagogues and used when reading Scripture.

Although Aramaic was Jesus' language, Greek was the international language and the language of the New Testament. While the official language of the Roman government and its army was Latin, the true language of the Roman Empire remained Greek. Many people, such as the apostle Paul, a Roman citizen, were well-versed in both Greek and Latin. This accounts for the heavy influence of Latin in the New Testament.

Chronology of the Development of the Bible

A simplified chronology of the major steps in the development of the Bible from its early origins to its present day form is given in the following table. The definitions of translation and revision with respect to Biblical usage are necessary while studying this table.

A "translation" goes back to the original ancient texts which are in Hebrew, Greek and Aramaic and actually translates each word or phrase into current language. A "revision" is an update of an existing translation.

Table 1-4   Simplified Chronology of the Development of the Bible

Date	Event
1400 B.C. (approx.)	Six times in the books of Exodus, Numbers and Deuteronomy, God specifically instructed Moses to write down particular information.
450 B.C. (approx.)	Some scholars assert that the Biblical priest and scribe, Ezra, collected all 39 of the books of the Old Testament.
300 B.C. (approx.)	The Hebrew Scripture which is now the Old Testament was translated into Greek. Tradition says that the ruler of Egypt ordered 72 Jewish scholars to make this translation. They completed it in 70 days, hence the name Septuagint, which means 70. The common abbreviation for this translation is simply, LXX. The Septuagint was in common use in New Testament time.
100 A.D. (approx.)	References of the Jewish historian Josephus and other Jewish literature indicate that there were 39 books in the Jewish canon of Scriptures at this time. These are almost the same as our Old Testament.
397 A.D.	The Council of Carthage was the first Church Council to list all 27 books of the New Testament. *(Before this time individual books of the New Testament were separately acknowledged as Scripture.)*
382-404 A.D.	The Vulgate: The standard Latin version of the Bible was prepared by Jerome for the Roman Catholic Church. It was prepared from Old Latin versions and the original language manuscripts. The Vulgate was so named because Latin was the common or "vulgar" language of the people. The Vulgate became the Bible of the West for 1,000 years.
1382	Wyclif's Bible; The first English Bible: This Bible was prepared directly from the Vulgate.
1450's	The printing press was invented by Gutenberg.
1525	Tyndale's Bible: A Bible printed in English which was translated directly from Greek and Hebrew. It was considered more accurate than Wyclif's Bible.

1550's	Paris printer Robert Estienne *or Stephanus* is credited with printing the first Bible to be divided into both chapters and verses. *The actual division of the scriptures into chapters originated in the early thirteenth century and some scholars feel the division into verses predates that of the chapters. However, until the advent of printing, these works were not reproduced and distributed.*
1611	King James' Version: King James I of England commissioned approximately 50 scholars to use Hebrew, Greek and previous Bibles to make a new translation. The King James Version is called the Authorized Version.
1901	American Standard Version: An American revision of the King James Version.
1952	Revised Standard Version: A revision of the American Standard Version. Possibly the most widely accepted English revision of the twentieth century.
to present date	Numerous translations, revisions and paraphrases are available today.

Reliability of Our Present Text

Until modern times the oldest existing copy of the Old Testament dated about 900 A.D. The reason is that the Jews had such respect for their copies of the sacred writing as one became so old it was unusable, they reverently destroyed that copy.

In 1947, ancient scrolls were found in a cave near the Dead Sea. The "Dead Sea Scrolls," as they became known, provided a copy of all the Old Testament books, except Esther, in the Hebrew text. The dates of the scrolls varied from 200 B.C. to 70 A.D. This major discovery and other similar historical checks have proven that we have an extremely accurate text of the Old Testament.

Literally hundreds of manuscripts of the New Testament exist today. Some of these date back to as early as 135 A.D. Most scholars agree that the New Testament is the best attested document of all ancient writings.

Diagram 1-1, Origins of the Bible, is located on the following page. It provides a graphical view of the basic chronology of the development of the Bible.

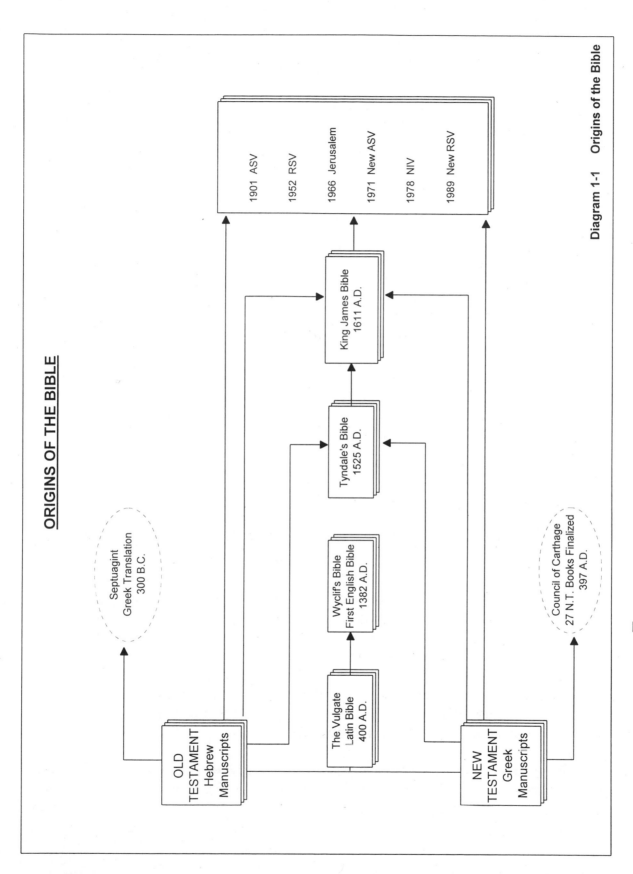

ORIGINS OF THE BIBLE

Septuagint Greek Translation 300 B.C.

OLD TESTAMENT Hebrew Manuscripts

The Vulgate Latin Bible 400 A.D.

Wyclif's Bible First English Bible 1382 A.D.

Tyndale's Bible 1525 A.D.

King James Bible 1611 A.D.

1901 ASV
1952 RSV
1966 Jerusalem
1971 New ASV
1978 NIV
1989 New RSV

NEW TESTAMENT Greek Manuscripts

Council of Carthage 27 N.T. Books Finalized 397 A.D.

Diagram 1-1   Origins of the Bible

Today's Bibles

There are numerous Bibles available on the market today. A few of the well-known versions of the Bible are listed in the next table.

Table 1-5   Popular Versions of the Bible

Bible Name	Abbreviation	Year
King James Version or Authorized Version	KJV	1611
American Standard Version	ASV	1901
Revised Standard Version	RSV	1952
Jerusalem Bible		1966
New American Standard Version	New ASV	1971
The Living Bible (Paraphrased)		1971
Good News Bible		1976
New International Version	NIV	1978
The New King James Version	New KJV	1982
New Revised Standard Version	New RSV	1989

Study Bibles

Many of the modern Bibles listed in the preceding table are available as either ordinary Bibles with only the necessary footnotes and headings or as complete study Bibles.

There are no set criteria for a study Bible; however, the following are typically included: individual book introductions which discuss authors, dates, main characters, chapter outlines, etc.; text pages with headings and subheadings, footnotes at the bottom of the page and cross references normally placed in the side margins of the page. Cross references are used to locate other Scriptures that are relevant to that particular verse. Study Bibles also utilize maps, tables and other study aids. The publisher may offer several different versions (e.g. RSV, KJV, etc.) of the same study Bible using exactly the same notes and aids.

The use of a study Bible is most beneficial to the new Bible student. The selection of a study Bible is strictly a matter of personal taste; however, one should keep in mind, the easier the information is to access, the more readily it will be used while reading and studying.

Study Aids

There are several aids specifically tailored to assist in Bible study. Bible dictionaries list Bible and religious names, terms and places. Bible atlases focus on the maps and information about the lands of the Bible. A Bible concordance is an index of Bible words, normally arranged alphabetically, with book, chapter and verse references. A topical index is used to look up specific topics which may be located throughout the Bible.

Commentaries give background information on specific verses. Commentaries are most useful for in-depth study of particular verses or stories. Commentaries are, as the name implies, additional comments and ideas of that particular Bible scholar or publisher. The student must be aware that commentaries reflect theological viewpoints and can vary greatly.

All of these references come in varying degrees of completeness ranging from a few pages in the back of a study Bible to several volumes of large books. There are concordances available, both in print and on computer disk, that contain every word in the Bible. All of the study aids mentioned and others are readily available at bookstores. These aids make Bible study much simpler and more enjoyable.

Self Evaluation - Bible Reading Background

The following page is a simple self-evaluation to determine how many books of the Bible each student has previously read. This evaluation page may be one of the most important pages in the entire book. The reasons are twofold:

First, the leader needs to know on what level to conduct the study in order to gain and maintain the interest of the majority of the class.

Second, after each student has anonymously filled out the survey and the combined group results are shared, tensions and false apprehensions usually disappear and questions are more freely asked. Past experience has shown that most people attracted to this study have read very few books in the Bible and the entire group is usually near the same level of Biblical knowledge.

Please make copies as needed

BIBLE READING BACKGROUND SURVEY
DO NOT sign your name.

Check the most appropriate blank.

I have read, in entirety, the following:

✓   5 books or less

_____ 10 books or less

_____ 20 books or less

_____ The New Testament   *(27 books)*

_____ The Old Testament   *(39 books)*

_____ The entire Bible   *(66 books)*

Read The Book

1. (T)/ F   The Bible is the most widely distributed book in the world.

2. The name Bible comes from a Greek word which means
    LITTLE   _BOOKS_ .

3. How many individual books make up the Bible? _66_

4. The two major divisions of the Bible are the _OLD & NEW TESTAMENT_
    and the _____ _____ .

5. There are _39_ books in the Old Testament and _27_ books in the
    New Testament.

6. In the following example identify the components: II Timothy 4:7

    II Timothy is the name of the _BOOK_ .
    4 is the number of the _CHAPTER_ .
    7 is the number of the _VERSE_ .

7. Why is the prefix "II" given with "Timothy?"
    TWO BOOKS

8. List the five main divisions in the Old Testament:

    a. _PENTATEUCH_   b. _MAJOR_

    c. _HISTORICAL_   d. _MINOR PROPHETS_

    e. _POETICAL_

9.   List the five main divisions in the New Testament:

a. GOSPELS   b. PAULS
                     LETTERS

c. CHURCH HISTORY   d. GENERAL

e. APOCALYTIC

10.   (T)/ F   Canon refers to the Biblical books officially accepted as genuine by
               the Church and governing religious body.

11.   List the 3 basic tests for canon:

1.   THE BOOK ITSELF

2.   AUTHORITY OF THE WRITER

3.   CHURCH ACCEPTANCE

12.   List the 3 basic languages of the Bible.

GREEK , ARABIC and HEBREW

13.   What was the principle language of the Old Testament? HEBREW

14.   What was the language of the New Testament? GREEK

15.   (T)/ F   Jesus undoubtedly had command of the Hebrew language; however,
               His daily language was Aramaic.

16.   (T)/ F   The 300 B.C. Greek translation of the Old Testament commonly used
               in New Testament time was called the Septuagint.

17.   What is the common abbreviation for the Septuagint? __LXX__

18.   In 1611 A.D., King James did not write, add or change the text of the Bible; he simply authorized scholars to use __HEBREW__ , __GREEK__ and previous __VERSIONS__ to make a new translation of the Bible.

19.   In 1947, ancient scrolls were found in a cave near the __DEAD SEA__ .

20.   The Dead Sea Scrolls contain a copy of every book in the Old Testament except the Book of __ESTHER__ .

21.   If you wish to read additional Scriptures that directly relate to the current passage being read, you should look up the __CROSS REFERENCE__ which is normally located adjacent in the side margin.

22.   (T)/ F   If a study Bible is offered in several versions, (e.g. ASV, RSV, etc.) the footnotes, cross references, maps, etc. are the same in all of the versions. The difference is the exact wording or language of the Scripture itself.

23.   Another name for an alphabetical Biblical index which gives chapter and verse references of specific words is a __CONCORDANCE__ .

Talk The Talk

The canonizing process did not assign authority to the books of the Bible. The books had "authority" therefore they were canonized.

A.   Can you think of other similar occurrences in history?

The president of Harvard University once stated that the necessary books required to provide an excellent education could be placed on a bookshelf five feet in length. He was consequently asked to name those books. This group of authoritative books was selected because of their own merit and became known as the "Harvard Classics."

B.   How was the canonizing process similar to the selection of the "Harvard Classics"?

The three basic languages of the Bible are Hebrew, Aramaic and Greek. During Old Testament times, the Jews spoke Hebrew and likewise the Old Testament was written in Hebrew. Jesus' daily language was Aramaic which was closely related to Hebrew. However, the New Testament was written in the international language of the time, Greek.

C.   *What kind of statement do you think the strict use of Hebrew text made to a Gentile who might have been interested in learning about and possibly worshiping God in Old Testament times?*

D.   *What kind of statement do you think the use of Greek for the text of the New Testament made to the world regarding the openness of the Good News? Why do you think Greek was used?*

Walk The Walk

You have now gained insights concerning the structure of the Bible and how it came into its present form.

E.   *How will this new understanding and information assist you in your personal Bible study and as you hear Scripture taught or preached?*

NOTES

Chapter 2
The Land of the Bible
and
Introduction to the Old Testament

THE LAND OF THE BIBLE

The purpose of the first portion of this chapter is to familiarize the reader with the land of the Bible. If we reflect upon our own nation's history, we have a clear mental image of the east coast being settled by the early colonists and a progressive movement of settlers toward the west. The land of the Bible has a much longer and more complicated history, concentrated in a very compact area; consequently, we may not have a clear mental picture of where particular Bible events occurred.

Becoming somewhat familiar with the geography of the land of the Bible will facilitate our studies of the entire Bible by allowing association between places and events. For instance, we will be able to better understand the familiar New Testament parable of the "Good Samaritan" and his difficult travel from Jerusalem *down to* Jericho when we become aware that this road is crooked, narrow and plunges downward 4,000 feet in 18 miles. This type of familiarity will also be beneficial in connecting Old Testament occurrences with New Testament events that may have happened 2,000 years apart, yet in the same location.

General Location

Most of the events in the Bible are centered in a tiny area on the east end of the Mediterranean Sea, around what is the modern day country of Israel, and parts of the countries immediately adjacent. In the Old Testament, other major areas of importance are what is now Egypt, Saudi Arabia, Iraq, Iran and Turkey. Several of these modern countries and their respective locations can be identified on **Map 2-1, Modern Southwest Asia,** on the following page.

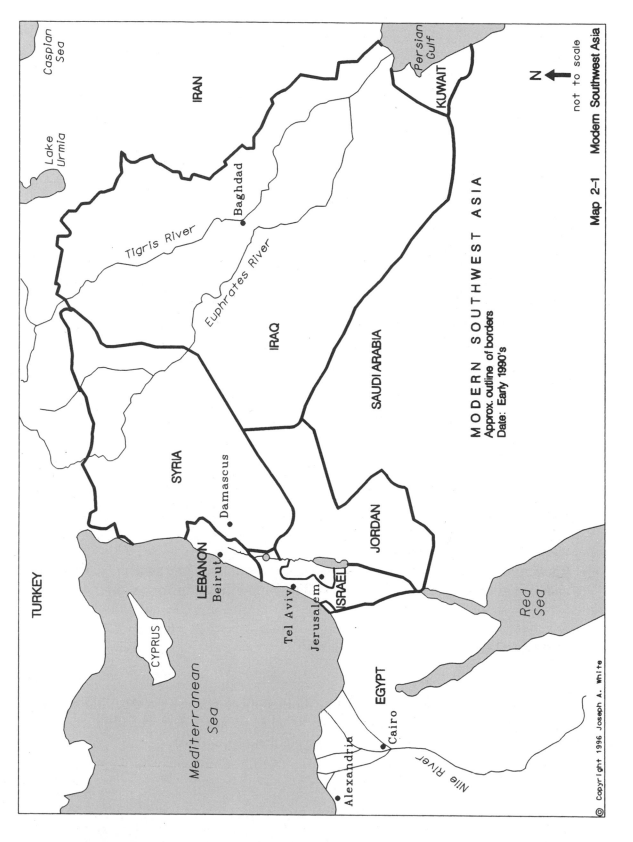

MODERN SOUTHWEST ASIA
Approx. outline of borders
Date: Early 1990's

Map 2-1   Modern Southwest Asia

not to scale

In the New Testament, events were primarily concentrated in Israel until the spread of the gospel. Although news of the gospel was obviously spread all over the world by converted visitors to Jerusalem, the New Testament relates the account of intentional missionary work. This organized effort covered countries of the east end of the Mediterranean Sea, moved up into Turkey, crossed into southern Europe and ultimately to Rome, the capital of the world.

The Holy Land
One Place, Many Names

"The Holy Land" has one of the most complicated histories of any place on earth. In the days of the Patriarchs (Abraham, Isaac, etc.) it was called the land of "Canaan." During the Exodus the Israelites referred to it as the "Promised Land" or the "Land of Milk and Honey." During the reign of the kings it became "Israel" and then split specifically into "Israel," the northern kingdom, and "Judah," the southern kingdom. The kingdom of "Israel" was conquered and the population dispersed. The kingdom of "Judah" was later taken into exile in Babylon. In Babylon, the exiles became known as "Jews." After the return from the exile, the country was called both "Israel" and "Judah." The Greeks and Romans later loosely referred to the area as "Judea." By the time of Christ, the name "Palestine" was commonly used with "Judea" being one of its political districts.

The name "Palestine" is derived from Philistia, an area on the seacoast occupied by the Philistines (people of the sea). The modern dictionary defines "Palestine" as the Biblical land of the "Jews" located on the east coast of the Mediterranean Sea. It also defines "The Holy Land" as the same as "Palestine."

It is important to realize that all of these names refer to the same general location only at different times in history and from writers with different historical perspectives.

The Holy Land
A Mental Sketch

Before you begin to use the maps in this Bible study, it will be helpful to gain a mental picture of the Holy Land, which is always the main point of reference in Biblical maps. The following exercise will place a basic picture in your mind.

1. Place an 8½" by 11" sheet of paper in portrait position. Locate the top left-hand corner of the page. Move right across the top edge to the center of the paper and mark a point. Locate the bottom left corner of the page and mark a point. Connect the points with a slightly wavy line. This line represents the coast of the *Mediterranean Sea*. Shade in and label the area to the left as the sea.

2. Draw an arrow that points to the top of the page and label (up) north.

3. Again starting on the top left corner of the paper, locate the position two thirds of the way to the right on the top edge of the paper. Move one inch straight down the paper and make a point. Use similar steps to locate a like position on the bottom of the page. In order to represent the *Jordan River*, connect the points with a squiggly vertical line. Label the river.

4. One third of the way down the page on your *Jordan River* line draw a circle the size of a dime. Shade the circle and label this the *Sea of Galilee*.

5. On the bottom of the page, where your *Jordan River* line ends, start drawing an oval which is standing upright. The oval is the width of a dime and four times as tall as it is wide. The centerline of the oval should follow your *Jordan River* line. Shade and label the oval as the *Dead Sea*.

6. At the top of the page, approximately one inch to the right of the point that begins your *Jordan River*, draw a small triangle. This represents *Mount Hermon*; its elevation is greater than 9,000 feet. Label the triangle *Mt. Hermon* and write its elevation.

7. Label the elevation of the *Dead Sea* (**- 1,300 feet**). Don't forget the minus sign.

8. The *Jordan Valley* is formed by mountains located on each side of the river that range from 2,000 to 3,000 feet in peak elevation. On the map, the location of the mountains is less than one inch from the river. Shade or sketch mountains in any fashion you wish.

9. On the map, locate and label the following:

    a. The town of *Nazareth*, located one inch to the left of the point where the *Jordan River* exits the *Sea of Galilee*.

    b. The city of *Jerusalem*, located one inch to the left of the point where the *Jordan River* enters the *Dead Sea*.

    c. The town of *Bethlehem*, located one third inch below and slightly to the left of *Jerusalem*.

10. The final step is to understand the distances involved on this map. One inch equals about 18 miles, therefore the width of the entire page is only 144 miles. On a straight line, it is approximately 65 miles between the *Sea of Galilee* and the *Dead Sea*.

Now that you have completed your map, compare it to **Map 2-2, Physical Properties of Palestine,** on the following page.

Always remember that the outline of the Sea of Galilee, the Dead Sea and the Jordan River which connects the two can be distinguished at the eastern end of the Mediterranean Sea on almost any map of reasonable scale.

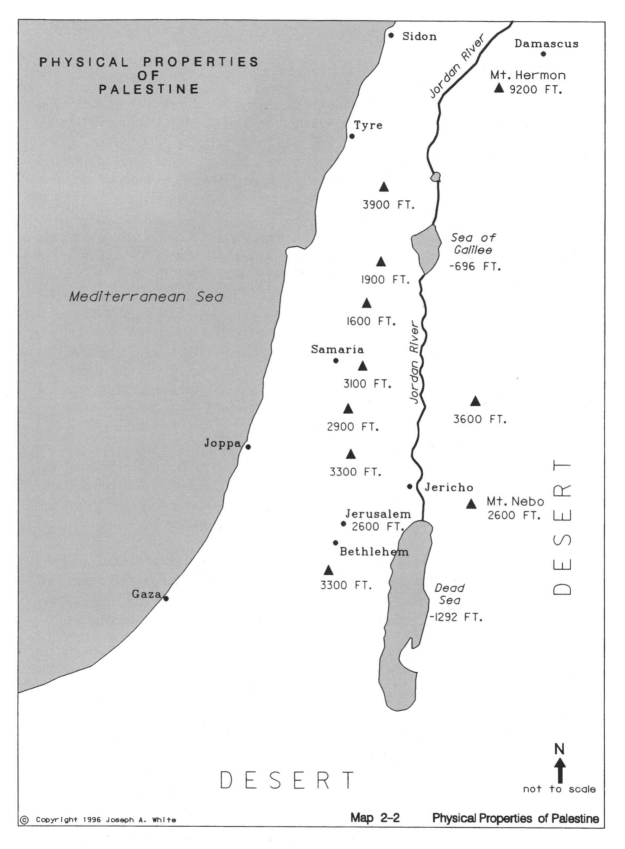

PHYSICAL PROPERTIES
OF
PALESTINE

Sidon

Damascus

Jordan River

Mt. Hermon
▲ 9200 FT.

Tyre

▲
3900 FT.

Sea of
Galilee
-696 FT.

▲
1900 FT.

Mediterranean Sea

▲
1600 FT.

Samaria
▲
3100 FT.

Jordan River

▲
3600 FT.

▲
2900 FT.

Joppa

▲
3300 FT.

Jericho

Mt. Nebo
2600 FT.

Jerusalem
2600 FT.

Bethlehem

D E S E R T

▲
3300 FT.

Dead
Sea
-1292 FT.

Gaza

D E S E R T

N
↑

N
↑
not to scale

Map 2-2   Physical Properties of Palestine

The Holy Land:
The Physical Characteristics

While again referring to Map 2-2, confirm and familiarize yourself with the following information: The Holy Land is approximately 70 miles east to west and 150 miles north to south. It is bordered on the east by desert and on the west by the Mediterranean Sea. The coast of this portion of the Mediterranean offers few natural harbors or inlets. The Jordan River flows through the center of this mountainous area and forms the Jordan Valley.

Mt. Hermon, in the northern region, is the highest mountain in the area with a peak elevation of 9,232 feet. Many of the mountains on each side of the valley in the southern region are in excess of 3000 feet above sea level. These elevations are accentuated by the fact that the Jordan River, located less than 20 miles from several of these peaks, is actually flowing *below* sea level.

The Sea of Galilee, also known in history as Lake Chinnereth, Lake Gennesaret, and the Sea of Tiberias, is located in the Jordan Valley and is actually a fresh water lake approximately eight miles in width and 13 miles in length. Its elevation is also *below* sea level, at a minus 696 feet.

The Jordan River forms the Sea of Galilee, then flows back into its river channel south to the Dead Sea. This 65 miles is the most historic portion of the river. The Jordan is so crooked and winding in this area that the actual channel length is over 200 miles to cover the 65 mile map length. The Jordan River has a total map length of 223 miles from its point of origin at Mt. Hermon to its end at the Dead Sea.

As the Jordan empties into the Dead Sea it reaches the lowest point of land on earth; its shore elevation is 1,292 feet *below* sea level. The Dead Sea has no outlet and depends entirely upon evaporation for control of its water level. The Dead Sea has also been called the Salt Sea, Sea of Arabah, the Eastern Sea and Lake Asphatitis.

Climate and Vegetation

Annual rainfall of the area varies from a few inches to more than 40 inches. The mean temperatures in winter range from the low 40's to the 60's (degrees F). The mean summer temperatures range from the low 70's to the low 90's.

This great diversity in terrain and climate causes an equal diversity in vegetative growth. Rich farm land, forest and desert are located only a few miles apart. This area has at least 11 major classifications of landscape including the following: salt flats, desert, lava beds, wooded hills, snow and ice, shrub and grasslands, grassland and forest, steppe, fertile farm land, Mediterranean vegetation and pasture land.

Modern Day Israel

The Middle East and the country of Israel are constantly in the modern day news. Consequently, most people are familiar with the areas commonly referred to as the West Bank, the Golan Heights and the Gaza Strip. These areas are highlighted on **Map 2-3, Approximate Boundaries of Modern Israel,** on the following page. With the major exception of Tel Aviv-Yafo (ancient Joppa), most of the cities and countries in the immediate area of Israel still have the same names. Also notice the Gaza Strip. Regardless of its varying size, it can almost always be distinguished on most Bible maps as a separate entity throughout history.

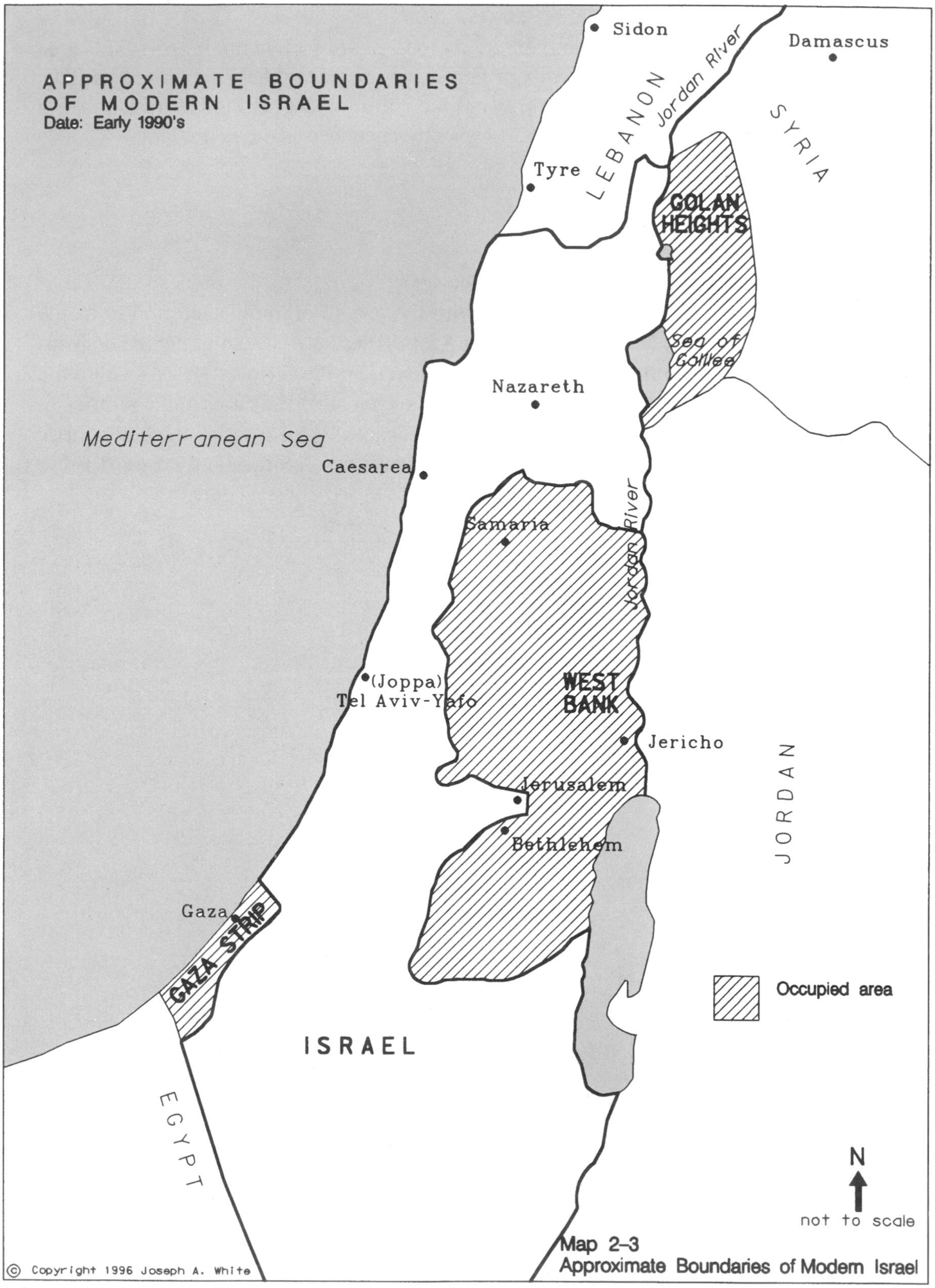
APPROXIMATE BOUNDARIES OF MODERN ISRAEL
Date: Early 1990's
Sidon
Damascus
LEBANON
Jordan River
SYRIA
Tyre
GOLAN HEIGHTS
Sea of Galilee
Nazareth
Mediterranean Sea
Caesarea
Samaria
Jordan River
(Joppa)
Tel Aviv-Yafo
WEST BANK
Jericho
Jerusalem
Bethlehem
JORDAN
Gaza
GAZA STRIP
Occupied area
ISRAEL
EGYPT
N
not to scale
© Copyright 1996 Joseph A. White

Map 2–3
Approximate Boundaries of Modern Israel

General Map Information

You have already used three of the maps in this Bible study. You may have noticed that two of the maps were identical base maps with different information overlaid. That is the concept used throughout the study. There are only three base maps in the entire study. One is the closeup of the Holy Land, one shows the eastern end of the Mediterranean Sea to the Persian Gulf and the third shows the entire Mediterranean Sea west to Italy.

The maps are as *"user friendly"* as possible. The scales do not change, the orientation remains the same and major cities and geographic features remain constant. These maps are not intended to be substitutes for detailed Bible maps. They are elementary maps made specifically to point out areas of interest in this Bible study. **Map 2-4, Base Map Examples,** is on the following page. It exhibits miniatures of the three base maps which compose the 18 maps throughout the study. Once you become familiar with the base maps you will quickly be able to orient yourself on any of the maps.

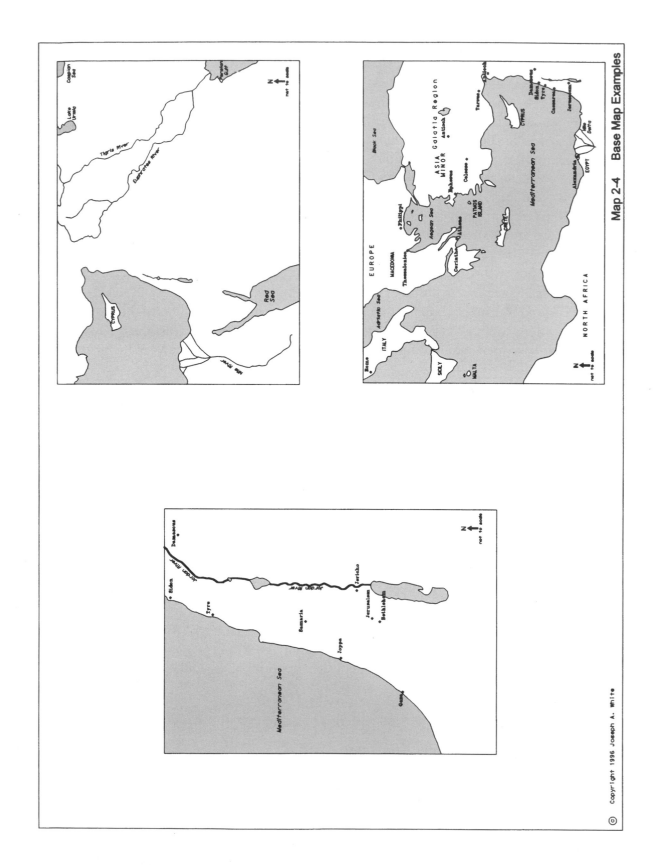

Map 2-4   Base Map Examples

© Copyright 1996 Joseph A. White

INTRODUCTION TO THE OLD TESTAMENT

Testament is another word for covenant. The definition of covenant is a pact, treaty, alliance, or agreement between two parties of equal or unequal authority. The covenant can either be accepted or rejected, but it cannot be changed.

The Old Testament begins with the familiar stories of creation and the great flood. It quickly moves to the selection of a single person with which to begin a nation. God makes a covenant with this believer named Abraham; and generations later, during the time of Moses, God makes a covenant with his descendants, the nation of Israel. Eight centuries later, the Old Testament heralds the news of a future covenant, a New Covenant, which will bring a personal relationship between God and the individual.

You may have heard it said that the Old Testament is only a history of many wars and kings and is not relevant today. If you have heard this, you most likely heard it from someone who has not read and studied all of God's Word. The Old Testament is no less a part of our Christianity than the New Testament. Remember the Old Testament was the Holy Scripture for Jesus.

Christ clearly stated in *Matthew 5:17*: ***"Do not think that I have come to abolish the Law or the Prophets; I have not come to abolish them but to fulfill them."***

This is a scripture that bears repeating and will be used again. The Old Testament is just as alive and important as the New Testament. Including indirect and partial quotations, scholars have counted more than 1,000 Old Testament quotations in the text of the New Testament.

In a simple analogy, you can compare the Old and New Testaments to the steel wheel and rubber tire on your automobile traveling the road of life. The New Testament is the tire that actually makes the contact, brings you home and ultimately saves you on a treacherous road. However, we must recognize that for all its flexibility, the tire must have the steel wheel to support it and to make it function. Likewise the New Testament must have the Old Testament to support it and make it complete.

Books of the Old Testament

The 39 books of the Old Testament span from creation to four centuries before the birth of Christ. They fall into five major groups; the five books of Moses commonly called the Pentateuch, the historical books, the poetical books, the major prophets and the minor prophets.   The exact time of writing of many of the books is open to debate. **Diagram 2-1**, **Approximate Chronology of the Old Testament**, is located on the following page. It presents one possible time scheme.*

The multi-page table following the diagram gives basic information on all of the books of the Old Testament. Both of these references should be used frequently as you progress through the study.

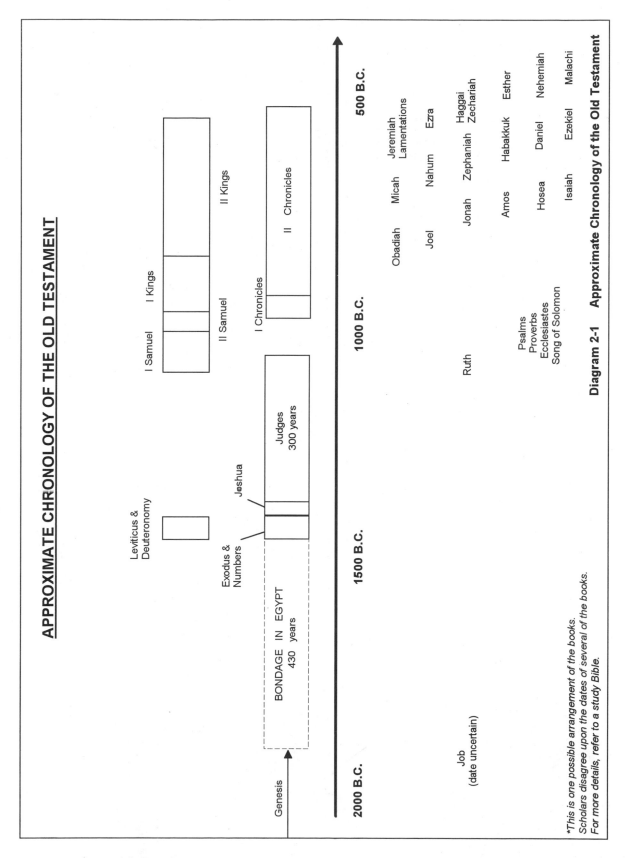

Diagram 2-1   **Approximate Chronology of the Old Testament**

Table 2-1   Basic Information on the Books of the Old Testament

Book	Author	Addresses	Main Subject or Thought
Genesis	Moses	Historical Account Creation to	Genesis is the foundation for all other books of the Bible. "Genesis" means origin. The book begins with the story of creation, moves to the covenant with Abraham and follows the patriarch's family as they progress and eventually move into the land of Egypt in approximately 1850 B.C.
Exodus	Moses	Historical Account	In Exodus, Moses is called by God to lead the Hebrew people out of bondage in Egypt. The book chronicles 81 years and includes the story of Moses, the plagues, the exodus, the covenant, the Ten Commandments, the tabernacle and the ark.
Leviticus	Moses	Historical Account	Leviticus is a guideline for priests who were from the tribe of Levi. It is stated 56 times in Leviticus that, "the Lord gave these words to Moses." The bock shows that even man in his sinfulness has provisions for access to God.
Numbers	Moses	Historical Account	Numbers is so named because of the census figures it contains. The book chronicles 39 years of wandering in the wilderness beginning one year after the exodus. It points out the unfaithfulness of the people and the steadfast faithfulness of God.
Deuteronomy	Moses	Historical Account	"Deuteronomy" means second lawgiving. The book is set up similar to treaties of that time. Moses is now giving the Law and history to a young nation who had not experienced the bondage and exodus from Egypt. This book is actually a form of constitution for the new nation after Moses is gone. Of the 27 books in the New Testament, 17 quote Deuteronomy.

Joshua	Historical Account	Joshua	The Book of Joshua details the conquest and division of the Promised Land. Joshua, Moses' former assistant, a strong military leader as well as spiritual leader, guides the nation against the heathen Canaanites.
Judges	Historical Account	unknown	The Book of Judges presents a young and growing nation which is now without a single primary leader. Approximately 13 individual judges lead the nation through 300 years of turbulent history. Israel was a loose confederacy during this time period. Familiar characters in this book are Gideon and Samson.
Ruth	Historical Account	unknown	Ruth is a narrative of a young Gentile woman who believes in God and remains faithful in a time when many Jews failed to follow God. Ruth is a direct ancestor of King David and is thereby named in the genealogy of Jesus Christ.
I Samuel	Historical Account	Samuel & others	I Samuel begins with the birth of Samuel, the last and most powerful judge, and covers the transition as Israel becomes a monarchy and is governed by its first king, Saul. The book includes the stories of young David as he rises to fame. The conclusion of I Samuel is the death of King Saul.
II Samuel	Historical Account	Samuel & others	II Samuel tells the story of the reign of the second king of the monarchy, David. Included are the stories of David's military victories, making Jerusalem the capital, and personal stories such as David and Bathsheba.
I Kings	Historical Account	unknown	I Kings begins with the death of King David. His son, Solomon, takes over the crown and begins to build the magnificent empire, including the temple. Solomon falls away from God and the kingdom is split into Judah and Israel. The last section of the book contains the stories of the prophet Elijah as he ministers to the northern kingdom of Israel.

Book	Author	Type	Description
II Kings	unknown	Historical Account	I and II Kings were originally one book. II Kings continues to trace the moral and political decline of the divided kingdoms. Assyria conquers the northern kingdom of Israel in 722 B.C. The Babylonian empire rises to world power and conquers the southern kingdom of Judah 135 years later. This begins the 70-year Babylonian Exile. The many miracles and works of the great prophet Elisha are also recorded in this book.
I Chronicles	Ezra (traditional)	Historical Account	I Chronicles provides an account of the history of God's people from creation to King David. Both King Saul and King Solomon are briefly mentioned; however, the bulk of the material is concerned with King David.
II Chronicles	Ezra (traditional)	Historical Account	II Chronicles is actually the second half of I Chronicles. It covers approximately the same time period as I and II Kings; however, it focuses only on the kings of the southern kingdom of Judah. The book concludes with the decree of the Persian King Cyrus which allowed the Jews to return from the Babylonian Exile.
Ezra	Ezra	Historical Account	The Book of Ezra recounts the restoration of the Jewish nation after the return from exile. The Jewish priest and scribe, Ezra, details how three Persian kings helped to accomplish God's plan by allowing the people to return to Judah and the temple to be rebuilt.
Nehemiah	Nehemiah	Historical Account	The Book of Nehemiah appears to have come from Nehemiah's personal diary. Nehemiah was the Jewish cupbearer to a Persian king and held a position of great importance. He was appointed governor, allowed to return to Judah and rebuild the city wall of Jerusalem.

Esther	unknown	Historical Account	Esther tells the story of a young Jewish girl who becomes the queen of the Persian King Xerxes. Esther remains true to her Jewish faith and manages to save the Jewish people from mass destruction.
Job	unknown	Poetry	Job is the story of a very righteous man who is tested and suffers greatly. The age old question of why the righteous suffer is addressed by Job and his friends.
Psalms	various	Poetry	Psalms is composed of 150 songs, laments and praises. This book was assembled to be used as the Jewish hymnal during and after the exile.
Proverbs	Solomon & others	Wisdom	Proverbs is a collection of short wise sayings with very practical meanings and uses. Many of these are comparisons. In fact, the Hebrew term for proverb means comparison. Almost every aspect of spiritual and human life are addressed in this book.
Ecclesiastes	Solomon	Wisdom	Ecclesiastes means the one who speaks or preaches. The author shares his broad life experiences as he studies nature, explores wisdom and searches for the true meaning of life.
Song of Solomon	Solomon	Wisdom	Song of Solomon is a poem in dialogue form that celebrates the love between a woman and a man.

Book	Role	Description
Isaiah	Major Prophet to the kingdom of Judah	Isaiah is often called the Messianic Prophet because no other Old Testament prophet speaks so much of Jesus, the coming Messiah. Isaiah regularly associated with and gave advice to royalty in Jerusalem in spite of the fact that much of his message was unpopular. Isaiah witnessed the downfall of the northern kingdom of Israel and advised the southern kingdom of Judah to hold firm against her foes and to turn to God for protection. In the New Testament, Isaiah is quoted more frequently than all the other prophets combined.
Jeremiah	Major Prophet to the kingdom of Judah	Jeremiah delivered a stern and often unhappy message for over 40 years. For this reason he is referred to as the "weeping prophet." He was often punished harshly for his messages. He warned that Babylon would conquer Judah and that the nation must repent of its sins and rely upon God. Jeremiah preached of restoration after the exile. He also introduced the New Covenant between God and the individual. That would be fulfilled with the coming of Jesus. After the fall of Jerusalem, Jeremiah was taken to Egypt against his wishes.
Lamentations of Jeremiah	Major Prophet to the kingdom of Judah	Lamentations is composed of five poems which describe the fall of the southern kingdom of Judah and the destruction of the capital city, Jerusalem. Jews read the book publicly to commemorate the destruction of Jerusalem in 587 B.C.
Ezekiel	Major Prophet to the kingdom of Judah in exile	Ezekiel, the prophet, was taken from Jerusalem to exile in Babylon where he lived by the river, Chebar. From his rural abode, he prophesied and ministered to the exiles in Babylon. He reminded them of the sins which caused the exile and reassured them of God's future blessings. Ezekiel is often thought of as the rural counterpart to the prophet Daniel.

Daniel	Major Prophet to the kingdom of Judah in exile	Daniel was deported from Judah to Babylon as a youth. He became an important government official in most of eight successive governments for a span of near 75 years. During this entire time, he remained uncompromisingly faithful to God. Portions of the book are straightforward narrative and parts are apocalyptic literature. The New Testament book of Revelation draws from the apocalyptic portions of Daniel.
Hosea	Minor Prophet to the nation of Israel	Hosea began his ministry during a time of great material prosperity in Israel. Despite this fact, he called for reforms and returning to God. He compared God's love for Israel to that of his love for his unfaithful wife. Hosea preached until the fall of Israel.
Joel	Minor Prophet to kingdom of Judah	Joel wrote of a great disaster caused by locusts and God's eventual deliverance. He also preached of the "Day of the Lord," final judgment and blessings.
Amos	Minor Prophet to kingdom of Israel	Amos was an educated sheep breeder who lived in the southern kingdom of Judah. He wrote and preached across the border to the northern kingdom of Israel. Israel was quite prosperous at this time and Amos preached against depending upon power for security. He called for an end to worship of pagans and proclaimed that judgment would come for such sins.
Obadiah	Minor Prophet to the kingdom of Judah	Obadiah is the shortest book in the Old Testament. The time period in which Obadiah was written depends upon which invasion of Jerusalem is being referenced in the writings. The entire book is a denunciation of and prophecy against the rival nation of Edom.

Jonah	Minor prophet to the kingdom of Israel	The Book of Jonah is the familiar narrative of Jonah being sent by God to the evil city of Nineveh. The story shows God's love and interest for Gentile nations and Israel's duty to minister to other countries. In his teachings, Jesus refers to the prophet Jonah.
Micah	Minor Prophet to the kingdom of Judah	Micah prophesied concerning the destruction of both the kingdoms of Judah and Israel. He especially preached against the oppression among the Jews of the poor by the rich upper class. The Book of Micah foretold where the Christ child would be born. Jesus quoted Micah.
Nahum	Minor Prophet to the kingdom of Judah	Nahum prophesied against the nation of Assyria. He predicted and gave details of the fall of Assyria's capital city of Nineveh. Very little is known of the life of this prophet.
Habakkuk	Minor Prophet to the kingdom of Judah	Habakkuk is a dialogue between God and the prophet. Habakkuk asks why the evils of Judah go unpunished and how a nation which is even worse, Babylon, can be used to punish the Jews.
Zephaniah	Minor Prophet to the kingdom of Judah	Zephaniah was of noble birth. He preached about the coming judgment of God. A religious revival took place under King Josiah, and Zephaniah's preaching may have been a major contributing factor.
Haggai	Minor Prophet to the returned exiles	Haggai was the first prophet after Judah's return from exile. He called for the people to complete the construction of the temple, which had been halted for 15 years. Haggai issues a practical call. The book is written in a very straightforward style.

Zechariah	Minor Prophet to the returned exiles	Zechariah was a contemporary of the prophet Haggai. He also urged the people to complete the temple. The book is composed of visions and images. Zechariah also contains a great deal of prophecy about Christ.
Malachi	Minor Prophet to the returned exiles	Malachi was the last prophet before the birth of Jesus. The temple had been rebuilt, the excitement of the return from the exile had subsided and the people had fallen away from the true worship of God . Malachi delivered a strong message of repentance and the true worship of God. Malachi also spoke of John the Baptist being the forerunner of Christ.

Read The Book

Using Map 2-1, Modern Southwest Asia, answer the next question:

1.   Modern Israel is located on the eastern shore of the

      _____ _____ .

2.   Name at least 5 names which have been used to identify the Holy Land.

      A.   B.

      C.   D.

      E.

Using Map 2-2, Physical Properties of Palestine, answer the next 3 questions:

3.   The Jordan River flows south out of the _____ __ _____ and
      empties into the _____ _____ .

4.   The shores of the Dead Sea are the lowest point of land on earth. The
      approximate elevation of its water surface is _____ .   *(Don't forget the
      negative sign.)*

5.   The city of Jerusalem is located on a rocky plateau less than 15 miles from the
      Dead Sea. The elevation of Jerusalem is _____ .

6.   The text states that the Holy Land is approximately _____ miles east to west
      and _____ miles north to south.

7.   The Sea of Galilee has also been known as Lake _____ ,
      Lake _____ , and the Sea of _____ .

8. T / F The Dead Sea empties into the Mediterranean Sea.

9. The Dead Sea has also been called the _____ _____, Sea of _____, the _____ Sea and Lake _____ .

— 10. T / F The Holy Land has such a great diversity in terrain and climate that there are at least 11 major classifications of landscape.

Using Map 2-3, Approximate Boundaries of Modern Israel, answer the next 2 questions:

11. What is the name of the small coastal strip of land that can almost always be identified on a Biblical map regardless of the period in history? _____ _____

12. The area of modern Israel which is commonly referred to as the "West Bank" is actually the west bank of what? _____ _____

13. How many base maps are used throughout the entire book? _____

Using Map 2-4, Base Map Examples, answer the next question:

14. T / F The general reference location of the Sea of Galilee connected to the Dead Sea by the Jordan River can be picked out on all three base maps.

15. What is another word for "covenant?" _____

16. Approximately how many Old Testament quotations are found in the text of the New Testament? _____

17.   What was the Scripture that Jesus used? _____ _____

18.   The 39 books of the Old Testament span from creation to _____ centuries before the birth of Christ.

Using Diagram 2-1, Approximate Chronology of the Old Testament, answer the next — question:

19.   What two historical books cover approximately the same time period, several hundred years, with 750 B.C. being near the midpoint.

__ _____ , __ _____

Using Table 2-1, Basic Information on the Books of the Old Testament, answer the next question.

20.   Who was the author of the Book of Amos and what was his occupation?

_____ , _____ _____

Talk The Talk

The Holy Land is physically a very small area. It has a long history and many countries closely border it.

A.   *How do these geographical and historical factors play a part in today's conflicts in the Middle East?*

B.   *How has land played a significant role in the seemingly neverending struggle between present-day Israel and its neighbors?*

<u>Walk The Walk</u>

We have learned that Jesus used the Old Testament as His Scripture and that there are over 1000 Old Testament quotations in the New Testament.

C.   *How do these facts make the Old Testament more relevant to your belief in the Scriptures?*

D.   *Is the Old Testament as essential to Christian beliefs as the New Testament? Why?*

NOTES

Chapter 3
Creation to Abraham
and
Abraham to Bondage in Egypt

Let us pause and give a brief thought about the time element involved in the first 12 chapters of the Bible. These few pages cover from creation to the time of Abraham, somewhere near 2,000 B.C. These chapters are the beginning of the Pentateuch and are attributed to the prophet Moses as the author or at least the person responsible for having them recorded. The actual recording process started sometime around 1,400 B.C.

These great stories have been preserved and handed down from generation to generation for almost 4,000 years. Some will no doubt ponder: Where do the dinosaurs and cave men fit into the story of creation? How could ancient people build with bricks high enough to reach the heavens? There are also countless more questions which can be asked.

In our modern scientific age, questions such as these have often become stumbling blocks which prevent many people from further studying and accepting the Bible. Are these stories exact accounts of the time and method in which things happened or are they a simplified answer from God for a process too great for mere man to comprehend? Does it really matter? Is the incredible lesson value and usefulness of the stories in any way diminished?

As we strive to study God's sacred Word let us not stumble. But let us pick up these stories, learn from them and claim them as our Christian heritage. Let us make them our stories.

THEOLOGICALLY SPEAKING

One way of approaching a Biblical story or narrative is to read it and then ask three questions:

1. What does the story tell us about God? What kind of God is pictured in this story?

2. What does the story tell us about human nature? What kind of people are the characters in this story? What does it tell us about the human condition?

3. Last, after we have answered the first two questions, we should ask: In what way(s) is this story MY story? Unless it becomes YOUR story, in light

---

nature of God and humanity, it is simply a story. When it becomes YOUR story, then it truly becomes Scripture (God's Word for YOU).[1]

The Stories of Genesis

The Book of Genesis is the foundation for the Bible and bears much information. The precise number of stories contained in Genesis is difficult to determine. There is clearly one long narrative which runs throughout the book; however, it is composed of many shorter stories or episodes. Special attention must be given to many of the characters and events as they set the stage for the other events in the Bible. The stories and events most relevant to this study are outlined in the following table.

THEOLOGICALLY SPEAKING

An etiology is a story which explains why something is "the way it is" when there is no explanation. There are several etiologies in Genesis which will be identified.[2]

Table 3-1   Creation

Genesis Chapter	Event
1	**Creation** God created the universe, the world, and living creatures. In His own image, He created Adam and Eve. God saw that what He had made was good, blessed the seventh day and rested. **Etiology** The earth and nature are entrusted to humanity. People are responsible for caring for and loving each other and taking care of the earth.

2	**Creation Story Repeated** The creation story in chapter 1 is very structured and somewhat poetical showing God's work on each day. The story is repeated in chapter 2 in a form which is more of a narrative. Both clearly show God's power, order and that He created everything.
3	**Temptation and Judgment** Adam and Eve were faced with temptation. They sinned by choosing their own destructive self-interests instead of obeying God. Consequently, they were driven from the Garden of Eden. Etiology This explains why people work so hard to get so little, women suffer in childbirth and snakes crawl on the ground and eat dust.
4	**Cain and Abel and the First Murder** Adam and Eve's children presented offerings to God. Abel's was pure; Cain's was unacceptable. In verse 7, God reached out to Cain, posed a question and gave him an answer. If Cain so chose he could have restored fellowship with God. If not, sin and its effects were waiting for him. Because of his jealously toward his brother, Cain chose sin and killed his brother, thereby committing the first murder.
6-9	**Noah, the Ark and the Great Flood** The world became evil. Noah was commanded to construct the ark and fill it with animals. Noah, his immediate family and seven pairs of each clean animal and one pair of the other animals entered the ark as the flood began. *The ark symbolized God continuing to reach out to humanity and Noah's faith in God.* The rainbow was set in the sky as a promise from God to never destroy the earth again by water. The dove became a symbol of hope and peace. *Jesus referenced Noah and the flood in Luke 17.*

11	**The Tower of Babel** Out of a desire to become superior, the people began to construct a tower to their own glory. God confused their language, and they were forced to disperse throughout the world.

> ### Etiology
>
> This explains the existence of the various languages of the world and the reason for sections of every city where only people considered "powerful and superior" reside.

From Abraham to the Bondage in Egypt

The area between the lower Tigris and Euphrates rivers in modern day Iraq is called Mesopotamia. This region is often referred to as the Cradle of Civilization. It was in this land that God first called his servant Abram who lived in Ur of the Chaldeans. Ur was a thriving pagan city in Chaldea, a land which would later be included in the Babylonian Empire. At God's calling Abram faithfully journeyed hundreds of miles to Canaan, the Promised Land.

Two maps of the of the ancient world are shown on the following pages. The first, **Map 3-1, General Locations in the Ancient World,** shows general locations of the centers of ancient empires of various time periods. The second, **Map 3-2, Journeys of Abraham**, shows the possible route of Abraham as he traveled.

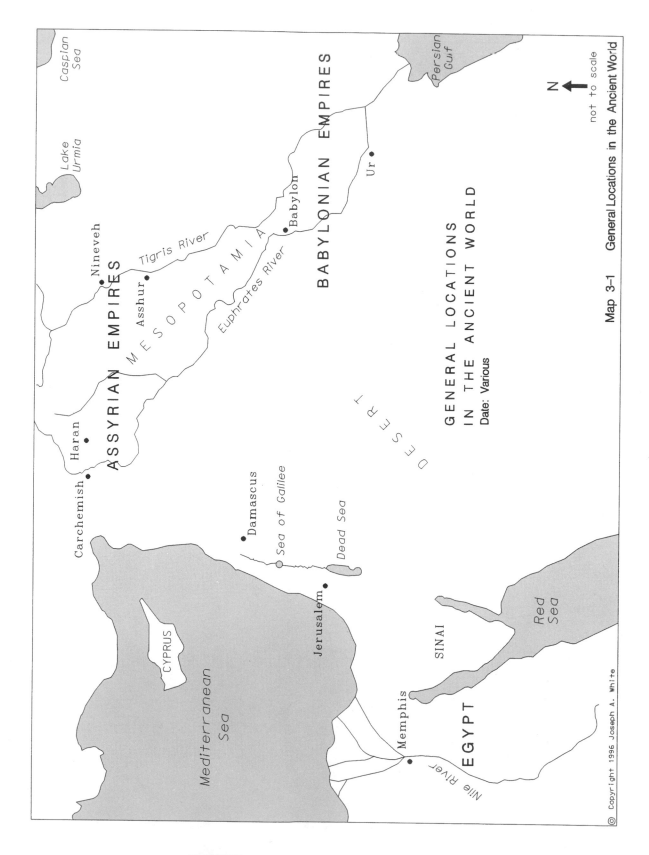

Map 3–1   General Locations in the Ancient World

GENERAL LOCATIONS
IN THE ANCIENT WORLD
Date: Various

N
not to scale

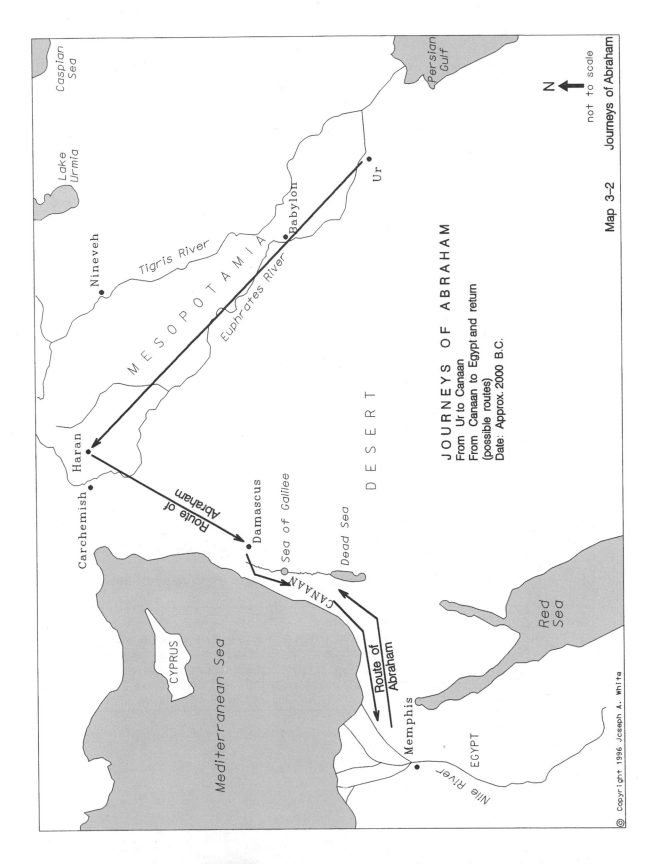

JOURNEYS OF ABRAHAM
From Ur to Canaan
From Canaan to Egypt and return
(possible routes)
Date: Approx. 2000 B.C.

Map 3-2   Journeys of Abraham

Table 3-2   The Call of Abram

Genesis Chapter	Event
12	**God called Abram** God told Abram that the Jewish nation would come from his offspring if he would follow God's direction. Ultimately all of the families of earth would be blessed because of his family. *Galatians 3:6-18 discusses this blessing and connects it with Jesus.* Abram and his wife Sarai followed God's direction and made a journey that passed through the land that they and their descendants would inhabit. This area became known as the Promised Land. Because of a famine in the Promised Land, Abram journeyed on to Egypt, a land not dependent upon rainfall because of the Nile River. *This would be the first of many encounters God's people would have with the Egyptians.*
13-14	**Abram, Lot and the Promised Land** Abram, his nephew Lot and their families moved into the Promised Land. Lot fell victim to a war and Abram and his servants rescued Lot and won a great military victory. Abram was then visited by Melchizedek, the King/Priest of Salem (Jerusalem). Melchizedek was a priest of God and Abram gave him one tenth of everything he owned as an offering to God after the victory. This was the first tithe. *A tithe is one tenth of what one owns offered to God as a gift of love.* *In 14:13, Abram is the first person to be referred to as a Hebrew.*
15	**The Covenant with Abram** God made a covenant with Abram declaring that he would be the father of a great nation. His descendants would be as numerous as the stars in the sky. The 400 year bondage in Egypt and the exodus from slavery in which they would plunder many possessions from their captors was foretold.

16-17	**Abraham, Sarah and Ishmael**
	After Abram lived 10 years in the Promised Land without any children, Sarai gave Abram her Egyptian maid Hagar in order that Abram might have descendants.
	Ishmael was born to Hagar and Abram when Abram was 86 years of age.
	When Abram was 99 years old, God appeared to him. God reassured Abram of the covenant and established the rite of circumcision as the sign of the covenant. God also told Abram that a son named Isaac would be born to Sarai and through Isaac, not Ishmael, the covenant would be established.
	God informed Abram that Ishmael would be the father of 12 princes and that from him would come a great nation also *(the Arab nation)*.
	God then changed Abram's name to Abraham and Sarai's name to Sarah.
	Abraham means "the father of a multitude."

Names in the Bible

The modern Bible student must comprehend that names in ancient times were not just identification. Many names had significant meanings and were meant to be symbolic of actual people and the way they conducted their lives. In the Biblical concept of names, to know the name of a person meant to know their character, to know their actual being. When parents named their children, they many times expressed their hopes and expectations for the future.

The act of renaming exhibited power. This power might be exercised by the person who renames someone or it might stem from a significant event which caused a name change. Many of the places in the Bible also have names which are expressions of the significant events which occurred there.

Table 3-2   (continued)

18-19	**Sodom and Gomorrah**
	God again appeared to Abraham and Sarah. The birth of their son Isaac was again promised.
	Abraham pleaded with God to save his nephew Lot before the cities of Sodom and Gomorrah were destroyed because of their extreme wickedness. God spared Lot and his family.
	Jesus referred to this event in Luke 17.

Abraham Tested

Abraham had been promised a son. He was also told that his descendants would be as numerous as the stars in the sky and an everlasting kingdom would come directly from him and Sarah. Yet, they were already aged and still had no child. This brings us to one of the most well-known and difficult stories of the Bible - the story of Abraham, Isaac and the sacrifice.

After many years God began to fulfill the promise, and a son named Isaac was born. God then asked Abraham to do the unthinkable, to sacrifice Isaac. No attempt will be made to explain why this event occurred; however, there are several pertinent points that must be brought out concerning this event.

God was clearly testing Abraham; however, it was only a test. Child sacrifice was a common practice in many of the surrounding countries. Abraham was undoubtedly acquainted with the practice. God showed that Jews were not to participate in human sacrifice, but that animal sacrifices were appropriate. God asked, but did not require, of his servant exactly what God himself would give 2,000 years later.

Not only is this a parallel in events, it is a parallel in locations. The testing of Abraham occurred near the future location of Solomon's Temple and, consequently, near the location where Jesus would be crucified.

Table 3-3   Abraham's Descendants

Genesis Chapter	Event
21	**The Birth of Isaac** Abraham and Sarah had a son and named him Isaac, which means "laughter," because Sarah had laughed at God's foretelling of Isaac's birth.
22	**Abraham, Isaac and the Sacrifice** God tested Abraham by asking for his son Isaac as a sacrifice. God supplied a ram for the actual sacrifice.

25-27	**Isaac's Sons are Born**
	When Isaac was grown, Abraham sent his servant back to Paddan-aram (Mesopotamia) to find a wife for Isaac. Isaac and Rebekah were married.
	When Isaac was 60, Rebekah conceived, and the twins within her struggled. The Lord told her that two great nations were within her and the older would serve the younger.
	The first born was red and hairy. He was named Esau, meaning "goat" or "hairy." The second twin was born grabbing at the heel of the first. He was named Jacob, meaning "to grab or supplant."
	The names of both sons were double puns.
	Esau thoughtlessly sold his birthright to Jacob. By trickery, Jacob received the blessing from his father, Issac. Afterward Jacob feared Esau.
	Both sons would become fathers of nations; Jacob of Israel and Esau of the Edomites. (Edom means "red.")

Jacob, the Deceiver

The birth of Jacob is detailed in chapter 25 of Genesis. His death is in chapter 49. In these 25 chapters, Jacob is either the central character or his powerful influence can be witnessed as his grown sons come and go at his command. Jacob, the deceiver, struggled with both God and humanity. His name became "Israel."

Table 3-3   (continued)

28-30	**Jacob in Mesopotamia**
	At Rebekah's urging, Isaac sent Jacob to their homeland of Mesopotamia to find a wife. During the journey, at Bethel, Jacob saw a vision of a ladder and vowed to follow God and to give God one tenth of his possessions.
	In Mesopotamia, Jacob was tricked by his uncle, Laban, into marrying Leah.
	Jacob later married Leah's sister, Rachel.
	In Mesopotamia, Jacob had 11 sons by his two wives and their two maids. Rachel was the mother of Joseph, the youngest son. Joseph can mean either "may God add" or "He has taken away."
	Jacob served Laban prosperously for 20 years earning his wives, livestock and many possessions.

31-35	**Jacob Becomes Israel**
	Jacob and his family left Mesopotamia. On the return journey, Jacob was pursued by Laban, confronted by his brother Esau and met God.
	In Jacob's encounter with God, his name was changed from Jacob to Israel, which means "he fights or persists with God" or "strives with God." Jacob limped after this encounter with God.
	Some time later God again appeared to Jacob and renewed the covenant with Jacob that had been made with his grandfather, Abraham. God again called Jacob, Israel. Jacob named the place of this encounter Bethel.
35-36	**The Twelve Tribes of Israel**
	Israel (Jacob) and his family journeyed from Bethel toward Ephrath (Bethlehem). Before they reached Ephrath, Rachel gave birth to the twelfth son of Israel.
	Rachel died as she was giving birth. Rachel named the son Ben-oni, which means "son of my sorrow." But Israel called him Benjamin which means "son of my right hand" (honor or good fortune).
	As the 12 sons grew and raised families, they became the Twelve Tribes of Israel.
37-45	**Joseph and His Brothers**
	Joseph was next to the youngest of the 12 brothers and was Israel's favorite son. He was so unpopular with his brothers that they sold him to Ishmaelite traders as a slave. At 17 years of age, he was then taken to Egypt.
	God favored Joseph, and he prospered in Egypt. Joseph became second in power only to Pharaoh.
	A great famine brought Joseph's brothers to Egypt in search of food for their families. Joseph tested the character of his brothers, forgave them and the family was reunited.
46-50	**Israel and the Twelve Tribes move to Egypt**
	Pharaoh requested that Joseph's father, brothers and their families move to the land of Egypt.
	Seventy family members and all of their servants moved to Egypt as honored guests. They lived in the land of Goshen and prospered keeping their flocks and herds.
	The approximate date of entry was 1850 B.C.

The Twelve Tribes of Israel were complete. Before the death of Israel (Jacob), he assembled his sons and gave each his final blessings. Israel stated that Judah would become the leader among the tribes and that the Messiah would come from the tribe of Judah.

"The scepter will not depart from Judah, nor the ruler's staff from between his feet, until he comes to whom it belongs and the obedience of the nations is his."

Genesis 49:10

Diagram 3-1, From Abraham to the Bondage in Egypt, is located on the following page. It provides a flow chart of the major characters and events in the Book of Genesis after the creation stories.

FROM ABRAHAM TO THE BONDAGE IN EGYPT

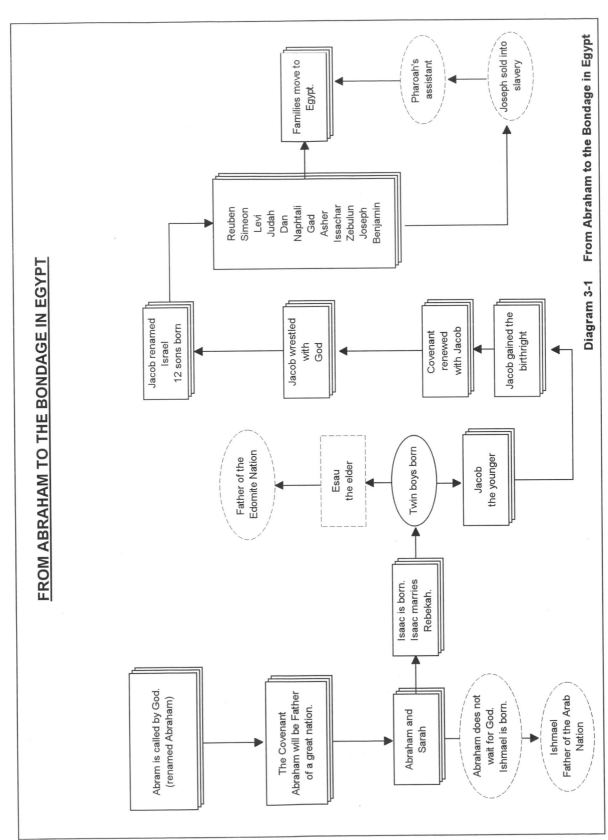

Diagram 3-1   From Abraham to the Bondage in Egypt

The People of Genesis

Genesis tells us who God's people are and where they came from. It also tells us what kind of people they were. We often think of Bible characters as heroes with strength, courage and unyielding faith in God.

As we look more closely, we find that most Bible characters were no different from people of any other generation. They were human, and as such, were faced with problems and choices. Often their reactions were neither courageous nor faithful. They had weaknesses and failures, but God accepted them and used them in spite of their faults.

The stories listed in the following table *(some are in addition to the main lesson sequence)* provide a unique glimpse into the nature of the people in Genesis. Many of these stories serve as examples for humanity and can be summed up by paraphrasing Genesis 50:20. This verse is Joseph's statement of reassurance to his brothers after their father Israel died. "You meant it for evil, but God meant it for good."

Table 3-4   Selected People and Events in Genesis

People	Event	Chapter
Adam & Eve	In the garden, Adam and Eve attempted to deceive God.	3
God & Cain	After Cain killed Abel, he denied to God what he had done.	4
Abram & Pharaoh	In Egypt, Abram misrepresented that Sarai was his wife.	12
God & Sarah	Sarah laughed when God said she would have a child. When God questioned her she denied she laughed.	18
Abraham & Abimelech	Abraham again misrepresented that Sarai was his wife.	20
Isaac &Abimelech	Just as his father Abraham had done, Isaac misrepresented that Rebekah was his wife.	26
Jacob & Rebekah	Rebekah helped her son, Jacob, trick Isaac, her own husband, into a blessing.	27

Jacob & Laban	Laban tricked his nephew, Jacob, into marrying Leah.	29
Rachel & Laban	Rachel stole from her father, Laban, and then deceived him.	31
Jacob's sons and daughter	Jacob's sons tricked the neighboring town and gained revenge. Jacob was consequently also deceived and shamed.	34
Joseph & brothers	Joseph's brothers sold him as a slave and deceived their father, Israel (Jacob).	37
Judah & Tamar	Judah failed to follow the law and deceived Tamar. Tamar enforced the law by more deception.	38
Joseph & brothers	Joseph deceived his brothers when they visited him in Egypt.	44

The Nations of Genesis

Chapter 10 in Genesis can be called the chapter of nations. It lists the descendants of the sons of Noah; Shem, Ham, and Japheth. However, there are several other nations which originate much later in Genesis that also play major roles in Biblical history. Most of these nations were formed as a direct result of inappropriate actions by individuals in the Bible.

Table 3-5   Selected Nations of Genesis

Nation	Origin and History	Genesis
Arabs (Ishmaelites)	Ishmael was born to Abraham and the Egyptian servant Hagar. His birth was the result of the unwillingness of Abraham and Sarah to wait on God to fulfill His promise of a son from Sarah.	16:16
	The Arabs have been at odds with the Israelites throughout history. Joseph was sold to Ishmaelite traders.	

Moabites	Moab was born to Lot and his older daughter as a result of an incestuous relationship.	19:37
	Reference to this nation is made in approximately 22 books in the Old Testament. The majority of interaction between the Israelites and the Moabites was very unfriendly. Ruth was a Moabite.	
Ammonites	Ben-ammi was born to Lot and his younger daughter as a result of an incestuous relationship.	19:38
	Reference to this nation is made in approximately 20 books of the Old Testament. The Ammonites were a fierce nation that was hostile to the Israelites.	
Midianites	Midian was born to Abraham and Keturah, his second wife or concubine.	25:2
	Midianite traders were involved with Joseph being sold into slavery. Moses fled to the land of Midian. In the book of Judges, Midianites oppressed the Israelites. Midianites are referenced in 10 books of the Old Testament.	
Edomites	Esau was the older twin born to Isaac and Rebekah. He was deceived by his brother, Jacob, with the aid of their mother.	25:26
	Edomites are referenced in 20 books of the Old Testament. The Edomites caused many wars and problems for the Israelites. They aided in the destruction of Jerusalem. Several prophets specifically prophesied against the Edomite nation.	

Read The Book

1.   The first 12 chapters of the Bible cover from the _____ ____
        _____ to approximately _____ B.C.

2.   The Book of Genesis is the _____ for the Bible.

3.   When Adam and Eve were tempted, they _____ by choosing their
        own destructive self-interest instead of obeying God.

4.   God reached out to Cain, posed a question and gave him the answer. This
        question regarded _____ with God versus _____ and its effects.

5.   T / F   The rainbow was set in the sky as a warning from God.

Using the text and Map 3-2, Journeys of Abraham, answer the next 2 questions:

6.   God called Abram out of ____ .   This city was located in
        _____, the region often referred to as the Cradle of
        Civilization.

7.   T / F   Abram's first journey was from Ur to the land of Canaan.

8.   After Abram moved into the Promised Land and won a military victory, he
        gave an offering of one tenth of everything he owned to God. This offering
        was the first _____ .

9.   God made a covenant with Abram and promised that he would be the
        _____ of a great nation and his descendants would be as numerous
        as the _____ in the sky.

10. God told Abram that his descendants would be in bondage in Egypt for _____ years.

11. God then changed Abram's name to _____ and Sarai's name to _____.

12. The sign of the covenant was the rite of _____ .

13. T / F   In many cases, the meanings of names in the Bible are much more significant than just identification of a person or place.

14. Abraham pleaded with God to save his nephew _____ before the wicked cities of Sodom and Gomorrah were destroyed.

15. In their old age, Abraham and Sarah had a son named _____ , which means "laughter."

16. Isaac and Rebekah had twin sons named _____ and _____ .

17. The younger brother, _____ , bought the older twin's birthright and by trickery received the _____ from his father.

18. Jacob had 12 sons. God renewed the covenant he had made with Jacob's grandfather, Abraham, and changed Jacob's name to _____ .

19. T / F   Jacob's new name, "Israel," means "one who fights, strives or persists with God."

20. Jacob eventually had 12 sons who became known as the Twelve Tribes of _____ .

21.   Of the 12 brothers, _____ was next to the youngest. He was sold as a _____ by his brothers and taken to Egypt.

22.   Joseph prospered in Egypt and became assistant to Pharaoh. Because of a great _____ Joseph was reunited with his family.

23.   When the tribes of Israel left the Promised Land and moved to Egypt, there were _____ family members as well as a large number of servants.

24.   The approximate date of entry into Egypt was _____ B.C.

25.   Before Israel's (Jacob's) death he blessed each of the 12 sons. He stated that _____ would become the leader among the tribes and the _____ would come from that tribe.

Using Diagram 3-1, From Abraham to the Bondage in Egypt, answer the next question:

26.   Because Abraham did not wait for God, Ishmael was born. Ishmael is the father of what nation? _____

27.   List 5 nations, other than Israel, whose origin is described in Genesis after chapter 10.

_____   _____
_____   _____
_____

Talk The Talk

The stories in Genesis illustrate that God allows humanity free will; yet there will be consequences for one's inappropriate actions. In the following stories identify the free will, the actions, and the consequences:

A.　　*The creation story.*

B.　　*The flood.*

C.　　*The Tower of Babel.*

D.　　*Can you identify an event in your life in which you exercised free will inappropriately and suffered consequences for your actions?*

We learned that names are very significant in the Old Testament, significant enough that God actually interacted in the naming process.

E.   *Do you think the significance of names continues into the New Testament? In the glossary or a dictionary look up the words Christ and Messiah. What do they mean?*

F.   *Read Matthew 16:17-18. What does Peter mean?*
          (Hint: the Greek word for Peter is "Petros.")

Read Proverbs 22:1 and Ecclesiastes 7:1. Both of these verses concern the importance of a good name.

G.   *In what ways are names important in our present-day culture?*

H.   *If a person's name is "tainted" or "defamed," does it still present the same problem as it did:*

20 years ago?

50 years ago?

in Old Testament times?

Walk The Walk

In the beginning of the chapter, item number 3 in the "Theologically Speaking" section discusses how a Bible story must become your story. The end of the chapter contains an entire section on the people of Genesis and how they reacted to various situations.

I.   *We soon recognize the true nature of many of the people of Genesis and the way God used them despite their shortcomings and weaknesses. How are the people of Genesis and the people of today alike?*

J.   *God calls us all. As you attempt to answer God's call, how will you redirect your life to overcome some of your past failures and present weaknesses?*

NOTES

Chapter 4
Exodus to the Promised Land

The book of Exodus tells the story of a family who originally went to a foreign country as guests, but overstayed their welcome. Through the generations, the family grew into such a large population that they were eventually enslaved by the natives of the land. Exodus goes on to tell how the slaves cried out to God, who raised up a deliverer. Through the deliverer, Moses, God made a nation from what was once a family with 12 sons.

There are several factors that may have influenced the change from being guest in the land to being slaves. The first chapter of Exodus states that a new king, who did not know Joseph, arose in Egypt and made the people of Israel slaves. Genesis 46:34 clearly points out that from the beginning, the people of Egypt did not like shepherds. Also, the Egyptians worshiped many gods as opposed to the Israelites who worshiped only the one true God. In addition, Egypt was in a constant state of war with other countries; therefore, it was quite normal that the Egyptians would be somewhat fearful of their rapidly multiplying disgruntled captives.

In four centuries of captivity, a family of 12 households grew into a nation. After the actual departure from Egypt, Moses took a census at Mount Sinai which revealed a population of 603,000 males twenty years and older. An annual growth rate of less than five percent would easily produce this population during the bondage period.

Chapter 15 in Genesis records God's covenant with Abram. The events in Exodus fulfilled several of the promises in this covenant. An entire nation had developed; they had been in bondage for the predicted length of time. They would leave to journey to the Promised Land with great wealth and possessions given them by their captors.

Table 4-1   The Bondage and Moses

Exodus Chapter	Event
1	**Background Information** Following the death of Joseph, a new Pharaoh came to power who began to oppress the people of Israel and eventually made them into slaves. After four centuries of bondage, the people of Israel had a great population and the Egyptians began to fear the Hebrews. Pharaoh commanded that all of the newborn sons of the Hebrew people be killed. *Note that a similar situation occurred in the New Testament when Jesus was an infant. This time instead of fleeing from Egypt, Joseph and Mary fled to Egypt to save the baby Jesus.*
2	**Moses, the Baby** Shortly after Moses was born, he was placed in a tiny floating basket and set among the reeds in the Nile River in order to save his life. Pharaoh's daughter found the infant and raised him as her own. *The name Moses means "one who draws out."* *The Hebrew word for "basket" and "ark" are the same. This is an interesting point considering Noah's ark saved humanity and the tiny basket saved the Hebrew nation. Paul, the apostle to the Gentiles, was also saved by being lowered down the city wall in a basket.*
2	**Moses, the Young Man** The New Testament Book of Acts, chapter 7, tells us that Moses was raised in Pharaoh's house and was well-educated. When Moses was grown, he saw an Egyptian beating a Hebrew slave. Moses killed the Egyptian. In turn, Pharaoh wanted to kill Moses for siding with the Hebrews. Moses then fled to the Land of Midian. The Book of Acts also states Moses was 40 years old when this event occurred.
2	**Moses, the Shepherd** Moses found a new home in the Land of Midian, married and became a shepherd. He spent 40 years living and working in the wilderness for his father-in-law, Jethro. *Jethro was also called Reuel.*

3-4	**Called by God** **Moses, the Leader** On Mount Sinai, Moses saw a burning bush which was not consumed. Moses drew near and was called by God to be the leader of the people of Israel. God promised Moses that he would strike Egypt with miracles (plagues), plunder the land and the people of Israel would go to the Promised Land, a land flowing with milk and honey. Moses was reluctant to answer the call and offered objections. God responded by showing Moses signs. God used leprosy and a serpent to reassure Moses. God also allowed Moses to have the help of his brother Aaron. Moses answered the call and returned to Egypt where he was welcomed by his brother Aaron.

The Pharaoh, who sought to kill Moses, had died; but the plight of the Hebrew nation had not improved. Upon his return to Egypt, Moses and his brother Aaron assembled the elders of the Hebrew people and spoke the words of the Lord to them. The people believed and worshiped. Moses and Aaron then went before the new Pharaoh and asked that God's people be released from bondage. The Pharaoh responded by being even harsher to the people. Consequently, the plagues were brought upon the land of Egypt.

Table 4-2   The Ten Plagues of Egypt

Number	Exodus Chapter & Verse	Description of Plague
First	7:14	Water of the Nile River turned to blood.
Second	8:1	Frogs covered the entire land.
Third	8:16	Gnats or lice were on both man and beast throughout Egypt.
Fourth	8:20	Great swarms of flies came upon the Egyptians; however, no flies were in the land of Goshen where the Israelites lived.
Fifth	9:1	Death by disease came upon the Egyptian livestock only.
Sixth	9:8	Boils broke out on both man and beast among the Egyptians.

Seventh	9:13	A plague of hail and lightning struck the Egyptians; there was no hail in the land of Goshen. However, the Egyptians that heeded Moses' warning were allowed to avoid this plague.
Eighth	10:1	Locusts covered the surface of the entire land of Egypt and devoured every living plant that survived the hail.
Ninth	10:21	A heavy darkness fell upon the entire land for three days, a darkness so heavy that it could be felt. Only the Israelites had light in their dwellings.
Tenth	11:1	The plague of death came to the first born, both human and cattle.

Egyptian history indicates that the people, especially the royalty, worshiped many gods that were directly related to at least eight of the 10 plagues. For example, the plague of darkness was a direct defeat of their highly worshiped sun god, Ra which was their national god.

The Tenth Plague and the Passover

The tenth plague would bring death to all of the first born. This included male, female, young, old and even extended to the cattle, a prize possession of the Egyptians. The Passover was instituted to prevent the Israelites from being affected by the plague of death. The Israelites avoided the plague by killing an unblemished lamb, cooking the lamb, serving the meal in a particular fashion and sprinkling the blood of the lamb on the doorpost and lintel of the home. The plague of death passed over the protected home, and all who were in the house were spared.

The idea of killing a lamb and sprinkling blood seems foreign to our modern society; however, we must remember that only a few generations ago, our ancestors killed or at least prepared much of their own meat. Therefore, a ritual such as this would not necessarily seem strange to ancient people and would, in fact, be convenient to accomplish.

A modern day parallel of the Passover ritual might be similar to the following: Each household on the street is told to gather inside, order fast food (e.g. pizza) and place the empty boxes at an exact location near the front door at midnight as a secret sign to denote that household chooses to participate.

The celebration of the Passover became one of the most important yearly events for the Jewish people. It is no coincidence that 1,400 years later the last meal that Jesus shared with His 12 apostles was the Passover Feast. During that meal (often called The Last Supper), Jesus transformed the Jewish Passover into Holy Communion for Christians. He told the apostles that the wine and the bread represented his blood and body and to drink the wine and eat the bread in remembrance of Him.

Notice the parallels of the Passover lamb and of Christ. The offering was to be without blemish; it must be killed; no bones were to be broken and the blood, which was the symbol of life, was to be shed. Jesus would now be the sacrifice for the sins of the entire world.

The Exodus

Map 4-1, The Exodus and the Wandering, is located on the following page. It shows Egypt, the Promised Land and a general route which the Israelites might have followed during the Exodus.

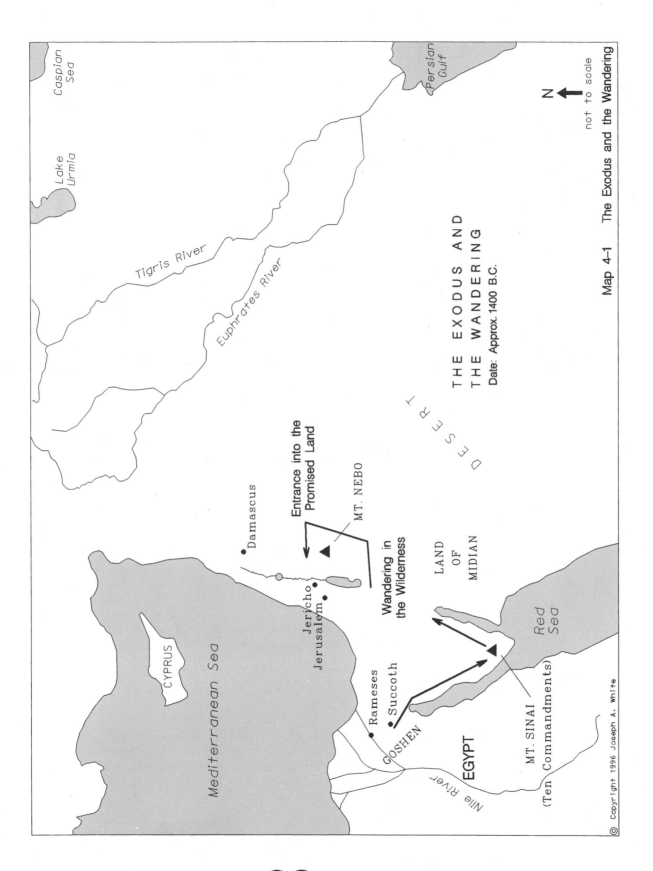

THE EXODUS AND
THE WANDERING
Date: Approx. 1400 B.C.

Map 4-1   The Exodus and the Wandering

not to scale

N

> ### THEOLOGICALLY SPEAKING
>
> Throughout the ages, Rabbis have pointed out an ironic twist to the story of Moses. Egyptians not only revered their Pharaohs, but considered them divine. Yet, as the story progresses, we find this "god" (Pharaoh) is so ignorant and weak, when compared to the God of Israel, that he rears and educates the very person (Moses) who would one day conquer his empire. The story of Exodus is a testament to the superior nature of God in relation to all other gods and countries, even in comparison to a superpower like Egypt.[1]

Table 4-3   The Exodus

Exodus Chapter	Event
12-14	**The Departure** After the tenth plague, the Egyptian nation urged the Israelites to leave. The Egyptians gave them great amounts of silver and gold as they left to journey to the Promised Land, thus the Israelites plundered Egypt. Their time in Egypt had been 430 years. There were 600,000 men in the exodus besides the women and children. God led the people with a pillar of fire by night and with a pillar of cloud during the day. The Egyptian army was destroyed as the soldiers attempted to overtake the Israelites during the crossing of the Red Sea.
16-18	**Caring for the Masses** Quail and a fine bread from heaven called manna were supplied by God for the people to eat. When water was in short supply, God made a stream flow from a rock. A great military victory was won by God's direct intervention. When Moses' hands were held up, the battle turned in favor of the Israelites, but when his hands were lowered the enemy prevailed. The responsibility of leading the people was systematically assigned into divisions. *These Scriptures demonstrate that when the people obeyed God's instructions given through Moses, God's direct response was to provide for all of their needs. On many more occasions in the Old Testament people's needs were directly cared for by God. In the New Testament, Jesus twice fed the masses in a similar fashion.*

19-32	**The Ten Commandments and the Golden Calf** In the third month after the exodus, God called Moses to the top of Mount Sinai (or Horeb) and He gave him the Ten Commandments (Ex. 20) written on two stone tablets, front and back, by the finger of God. While Moses was gone, the people, fearing Moses' demise, built and worshiped a golden calf. When Moses' returned, he destroyed the Ten Commandments and God punished the people.
33-34	**The Ten Commandments Repeated** Moses again ascended to the top of the mountain, this time God instructed Moses to cut out and bring with him two blank stone tablets that the Ten Commandments might be written once more. *The first four commandments concern the individual's responsibility to God. The last six concern the individual's responsibility to other people. The last commandment deals with thought and not action.*

The Law

The term "law" can be used loosely to refer to the Ten Commandments, the first five books of the Old Testament or even the Old Testament or God's will. Whatever term is applied, God gave Moses much more than just the Ten Commandments in his two 40-day sojourns on Mount Sinai. Moses received a multitude of specific instructions which included how to build a place of worship and make necessary worship accessories. God also told Moses how to establish an order of worship.

The giving of the Law started a new era for God's chosen people. They would now construct an elaborate tabernacle or tent to be used as a sanctuary for worship. Contained in the tabernacle was to be fine furniture and utensils for the specific purpose of worship. The most important object would be the ark of the covenant. The ark, a small golden trunk, would hold Aaron's rod, a golden vessel that contained manna, and the two stone tablets on which were written the Ten Commandments.

The Ten Commandments

I. You shall have no other gods before me.

II. You shall not make for yourself a graven image.

III. You shall not take the name of the Lord your God in vain.

IV. Remember the Sabbath day to keep it holy.

V. Honor your father and mother.

VI. You shall not kill.

VII. You shall not commit adultery.

VIII. You shall not steal.

IX. You shall not bear false witness against your neighbor.

X. You shall not covet.

Reduced to the simplest form from Exodus chapter 20.

Table 4-4   Implements of Worship

Exodus Chapter	Item
various	**Implements of Worship** God gave Moses a complete list of items to be built and detailed instructions to ensure that the Israelites would be able to accomplish the construction. Included in the list was the tabernacle, the ark of the covenant, a table covered with gold, a lampstand, trays, dishes, jars and bowls - all made of gold. The patterns to make the intricate garments and accessories for the priests were also provided. God even blessed certain people with the necessary skills to make these masterpieces. *The gold and silver required for construction were plundered from the Egyptians during the exodus.*
25-34	**The Tabernacle** The tabernacle was the largest item. *This structure is so important that 50 chapters in the Bible contain instructions relating to the tabernacle.* The tabernacle was a portable tent approximately 18 feet in width by 44 feet in length. It was constructed of an excellent wooden frame with a covering composed of four defined layers of materials; linen, goat hair, ram skin and goat skin. The entire structure was colorful, very ornate, and trimmed in precious material, including a great deal of gold and silver. The tabernacle was located inside a courtyard which was approximately 75 feet in width by 150 feet in length. The walls were over seven foot in height. They were constructed from wooden frames with fine linen curtains secured on them. The tabernacle was always positioned to face the east and in the center of the camp. *Dimensions are derived from using the Egyptian cubit which equals 52 centimeters.*
25	**The Ark of the Covenant** The ark of the covenant was a small wooden box approximately 51 inches long, 31 inches high and 31 inches wide. The ark was overlaid with pure gold both inside and out. It stood upon four legs or pedestals and had rings of gold which two long poles were drawn through to make a litter type arrangement for carrying the ark. The poles were also overlaid with gold and were left permanently in place. The ark was covered with a lid called the mercy seat which was also very ornate. The ark contained the tablets on which the Ten Commandments were written, a jar of manna* and Aaron's rod* or staff which had budded. *Hebrews 9:4

The Ark of the Covenant

The Tabernacle

26	**The Holy of Holies**
	The tabernacle was divided into two rooms. The large front room was the holy place, the small room in the rear was the Holy of Holies. It was in the Holy of Holies that the ark was placed.
	A large curtain or veil divided the two rooms. No one other than the high priest could enter the Holy of Holies and this entrance was limited to only certain times.
	This curtain, then, effectively excluded the people from the immediate presence of God. God could only be approached through the priests. It was this type of curtain (a replacement for the original) which was ripped in two pieces when Jesus died on the cross, symbolically proving that all believers now have direct access to the Father. (Mark 15)

This portable sanctuary would travel with the Israelites and serve as their center of worship for the next four centuries until King Solomon constructed a permanent temple. Even after the temple was dedicated, the priesthood, ceremonies, religious feasts and methods of worship remained unchanged.

Table 4-5   Worship

Leviticus Chapter	Event
various	**The Priesthood** God instituted the priesthood in order to provide consecrated individuals for the specific function of acting as a mediator between God and the people. The priesthood was designated to be within the tribe of Levi.
various	**Rules for the Priests** The Book of Leviticus is basically the handbook for the priests, the Levites. It provides the specific requirements of worship. These requirements fall into two very broad divisions.
	The first portion of Leviticus deals with "The Way to God." This is the animal blood sacrifice system.
	The second portion is "The Walk With God." This is sanctification of the people through ceremonies and holiness.
	The New Testament refers to Leviticus about 90 times.

These celebrations were much more than just periodic festivals for the Israelites; they were a way of life. The celebrations combined the sacrifices or offerings (normally blood sacrifices, symbolizing life) and the rigid ceremonies demonstrating the holiness of the process. The following table outlines selected Jewish celebrations and relates how some are significant to Christianity.

Table 4-6   Selected Jewish Celebrations

Name	Description	Date Observed in Jewish month	Selected Scripture	Christian Significance
Passover and/or **Feast of Unleavened Bread**	Prescribed by the Law. Established before the exodus to allow the plague of death to pass over the Israelites. A lamb was sacrificed and unleavened bread was prepared to symbolize the haste of departure. In ancient Israel, 2 separate celebrations.	14th day of first month *(approx. April)*	Ex. 23 Lev. 23 Num. 28 Deut. 16	Jesus' journeys to Jerusalem. Jesus' last meal. As such, He transformed that meal into Holy Communion for Christians.
Pentecost **Feast of Weeks** **Feast of Harvest** **Day of First Fruit**	Prescribed by the Law. Celebrated the end of the grain harvest. Later tradition associated Pentecost with the giving of the Law at Sinai.	50 Days after Passover *(approx. June)*	Ex. 23, 34 Lev. 23 Num. 28 Deut. 16	Holy Spirit descended upon the apostles on Pentecost. Birthday of the Church
Feast of Trumpets **New Moon** *Rosh Hashanah*	Prescribed by the Law. Marked the beginning of the civil year calender.	1st day of seventh month *(approx. Oct.)*	Lev. 23 Num. 28	

Feast	Description	Date	Reference	New Testament
Day of Atonement *Yom Kippur*	Prescribed by the Law. (only fast required) Day of penitence and mourning. High Priest confessed the sins of the community and entered the Holy of Holies in the temple. A scapegoat was also released during this ceremony of great detail.	10 days after the Feast of Trumpets *(approx. Oct.)*	Lev. 16, 23	
Feast of Tabernacles **Feast of Ingathering** **Feast of Booths**	Prescribed by the Law. The people lived in booths to commemorate the wandering and the entrance into the Promised Land. In New Testament times, water was carried from the Pool of Siloam as part of the observance.	5 days after the Day of Atonement *(approx. Oct.)*	Ex. 23, 34 Lev. 23	In John 7, Jesus referred to himself as "living water" at this feast.
Feast of Lights *Hanukkah*	Commemorates the cleansing of the temple by Judas Maccabeus during the Intertestamental Period.	25th day of ninth month *(approx. Dec.)*		In John 10, Jesus described himself as the Messiah during this celebration.
Feast of Purim	Memorial to the event in which Queen Esther saved the Jews in Persia from death.	14th day of twelfth month *(Mar./Apr.)*	Esther 9	

This single generation of Israelites had experienced immense changes and had personally witnessed incredible miracles performed by God on their behalf. These people had ascended from the depths of complete slavery to be a free nation - led, cared for and protected by God himself. All that God asked in return was faithfulness and obedience to the Law which He had given them.

In spite of all that the people of Israel had observed and experienced, they still lost faith and rebelled against God when adversity appeared.

Table 4-7   Wandering in the Wilderness

Numbers Chapter	Event
13-15	**40 Years for 40 Days** After the first year in the wilderness, the people were led to the border of the Promised Land. Spies were sent to explore the land and report their findings. The majority of the spies reported negatively. Even after this eventful first year, the people still lacked faith and rejected God's offer of entry into the Promised Land. The people were punished and sentenced to wander in the wilderness for 40 years, one year for each day the spies were gone. This time period was sufficient to ensure that all of the adults who witnessed the great miracles in both Egypt and the wilderness, yet still lacked faith in God, would die a natural death before the next appointed time to enter the Promised Land.
20	**The Sin of Moses** During the 40 years in the wilderness, Moses became proud and disobeyed God's direct instruction. Because of his disobedience Moses was not allowed to enter the Promised Land.
22	**Other Information** Numbers, Chapter 22 contains an interesting account which gives insight into the perspective of other nations viewing the Israelites. This event also includes the occurrence of the donkey talking to its master. Aaron's Prayer, given in Numbers 6:24-26 is well known, yet few people recognize its origin.

Deuteronomy (general)	**The New Generation** After completion of the 40 years of wandering in the wilderness, Moses assembled all the people and told the complete story of Israel. He read the Law to this generation who had not witnessed the great miracles in Egypt or the giving of the Law at Mt. Sinai. This new and younger generation would be led into the Promised Land by a new and inexperienced leader, Joshua. *Deuteronomy means second lawgiving. The book repeats many of the events during the exodus and wandering. It can be viewed as a historical summation and a type of constitution or treaty for the young nation about to enter a foreign land.* *Seventeen of the 27 books of the New Testament quote from Deuteronomy.*
34	**The Death of Moses** God took His faithful servant, Moses, to the top of Mount Nebo, a mountain east of the Jordan River. From that summit, God showed Moses the Promised Land. Moses died, and the Lord buried him in the valley of the land of Moab. No one knows where.

"Moses was a hundred and twenty years old when he died, yet his eyes were not weak nor his strength gone." Deuteronomy 34:7

"Since then, no prophet has risen in Israel like Moses, whom the Lord knew face to face." Deuteronomy 34:10

Diagram 4-1, The Exodus and the Wandering, is located on the following page. It provides a graphical view of the major events during the exodus and the 40 years in the wilderness.

THE EXODUS AND THE WANDERING

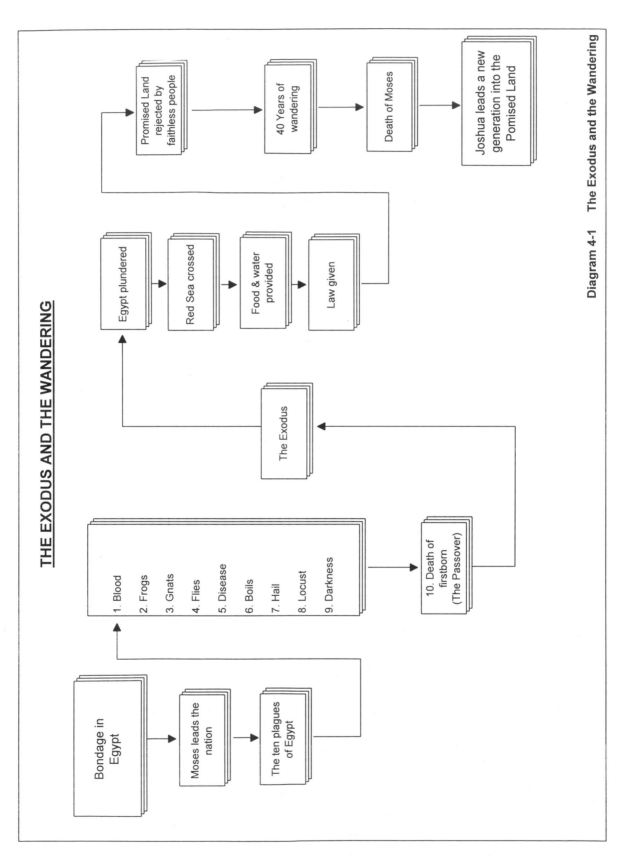

Bondage in Egypt

Moses leads the nation

The ten plagues of Egypt

1. Blood
2. Frogs
3. Gnats
4. Flies
5. Disease
6. Boils
7. Hail
8. Locust
9. Darkness

10. Death of firstborn (The Passover)

The Exodus

Egypt plundered

Red Sea crossed

Food & water provided

Law given

Promised Land rejected by faithless people

40 Years of wandering

Death of Moses

Joshua leads a new generation into the Pomised Land

Diagram 4-1   The Exodus and the Wandering

Read The Book

1. After the death of Joseph, the people of Israel became _____ under the new Pharaoh.

2. List three of the major differences and fears between the Israelites and Egyptians that possibly caused Pharaoh to take this action.
    Hint: One is social, one is religious and one is political.

    a._____

    b._____

    c._____

3. T / F   After four centuries of bondage, Pharaoh commanded that the newborn sons of the Hebrews be killed.

4. The baby Moses was found and raised by
    _____ _____.

5. Moses spent how many years in the house of Pharaoh? _____

    Moses spent how many years in the wilderness as a shepherd?_____

6. On _____ _____ , God called Moses by using a _____ bush.

7. Moses returned to _____ and there he was welcomed by _____, his brother.

8.   Because Pharaoh would not allow the Israelites to leave, God brought 10 different plagues upon Egypt. List the 10 plagues:

_____   _____   _____

_____   _____   _____

_____   _____   _____

_____

9.   T / F   Egyptian history reveals that the people worshiped many gods that were directly related to the types of plagues.

10.   The tenth and final plague brought death to the _____ _____ .

11.   The _____ was instituted in order that the plague of death would literally pass over the protected houses.

12.   Fourteen hundred years after the exodus, Jesus shared His last Passover celebration with the apostles and gave specific instructions which transformed that final meal into what celebration that Christians observe today?

_____

13.   After the tenth plague, the Egyptians were so fearful that they gave the Israelites great amounts of _____ and _____ as they departed.

14.   Pharaoh's heart was once again hardened and he sent his army after the Israelites. The Egyptian army was destroyed attempting to cross the _____ _____ .

15. What three things did God directly provide to ensure the physical needs of the multitude were met during the exodus?

    a. _____

    b. _____

    c. _____

16. T / F   God gave Moses the Ten Commandments on the top of Mount Sinai.

17. As Moses received the Ten Commandments, the people below made and worshiped a _____ _____.

18. The Ten Commandments are broken into two divisions; those that concern God and those that concern other people. How many fall into each division?

    _____ responsibility to God

    _____ responsibility to other people

19. During Moses' two trips to the mountain, he received numerous instructions which included how to build a _____ of worship, worship accessories and establish an _____ of worship.

20. T / F   The tabernacle was a permanent structure in which to worship.

21. What three items did the ark of the covenant contain?

    _____

    _____

    _____

22.   The tribe of _____ was designated to provide the personnel for the priesthood.

23.   T / F   The book of Leviticus is basically a handbook for the priests.

24.   One year after the exodus the people rejected the opportunity to enter the Promised Land. Because of their lack of faith they wandered in the wilderness one _____ for each _____ the spies were gone.

25.   After _____ _____ of wandering a new generation was ready to enter the Promised Land.

26.   Deuteronomy means second lawgiving and can be viewed as a summation and type of _____ for a young nation.

27.   Deuteronomy closes with the death of _____ at 120 years of age.

Talk The Talk

In the section covering Exodus chapter 2, it is pointed out that Noah, Moses and the Apostle Paul were all saved by the use of a basket or ark. Respectively, humanity, the Hebrew people and the Gentiles were also consequently saved. As the study progresses we will see many such parallels in the Bible.

A.   *Are such striking parallels merely coincidences that we notice or are they the signature of God's work molded in the Scripture for a particular purpose?*

B.   *Does the way in which we interpret such occurrences necessarily reflect our faith and belief in Scripture?*

The Book of Numbers states that after the first year in the wilderness the people rejected God's offer of entry into the Promised Land. This was due to lack of faith, fear of abandonment and their selfish desires.

C.   *How is it possible that the same nation that witnessed the hand of God working countless miracles in a one-year period could now doubt and reject God?*

D.   *Could such an unthinkable rejection of God occur in modern times? If so,
name an example.*

Walk The Walk

The importance of the Passover as a Jewish religious celebration cannot be overemphasized. Neither can we overemphasize the fact that Jesus selected this event as His last meal and transformed it into Holy Communion.

E.   *When did you become aware of this connection?*

F.   *Does (or will) the knowledge of this connection make Holy Communion more serious or more meaningful for you personally in the future?*

The tenth commandment (*You shall not covet.*) deals with thought and not action; however, we all recognize that thoughts generally lead to deeds.

G.   *After careful consideration of the broad scope of this commandment, will you try to change or curb any of your present thoughts?*

Chapter 5
From the Entry into the Promised Land
to
King Solomon's Reign

After 40 years of waiting and wandering, Moses led the nation to the border of the Promised Land. From the top of Mount Nebo, God gave Moses a marvelous view of the new land before he died. Moses' faithful assistant, Joshua, became the new leader and remained so for the rest of his life.

After Joshua's death, the nation was governed by a series of leaders called judges. The people were constantly influenced by the surrounding non-Jewish nations. Because these nations were ruled by monarchs, the Israelites began to demand a king. God strongly warned the people of the many problems of being ruled by a king before He allowed Saul to be anointed as the first king. After the reign of King Saul, David the former servant of Saul became king. King David was succeeded by his son, Solomon.

The major events of this great transformation of leadership from a single leader directly under God's command to a judge system and finally to a kingdom are presented in this chapter.

THEOLOGICALLY SPEAKING

It was commonplace throughout the Canaanite provinces surrounding Israel for the central place of leadership to reside with one person (usually referred to as a king). At this time in Israel's history, their form of government was best described as a "Theocracy" (God was their king). Yet, most of the people resented this approach to being ruled and began to plead for a "Monarchy."

As unsatisfactory and ineffective as it seemed, Theocracy worked quite well, and soon after they got their Monarchy, the Hebrews began to realize that having a king is not as wonderful and satisfactory as they thought it would be. Their first king would go mad; their second king would take another man's wife and then command that her husband be killed in battle and their third king would use the people to build his empire, marry foreign wives and eventually worship their pagan gods.

Table 5-1   Entry into the Promised Land

Joshua Chapter	Event
1	**The New Leader** Upon the death of Moses, Joshua became the nation's leader. Although Joshua was chosen by God to be Moses' successor and he was trained by Moses himself, Joshua was a more powerful military leader than a spiritual leader. Joshua did not enjoy the privilege of direct communication with God as did Moses. Joshua often required the help of priests in seeking the will of God.
2-5	**Entry Into the Promised Land** The first act of the new leader was to send spies to the city of Jericho and prepare for the crossing of the Jordan River. As the nation prepared to cross the river, the waters stopped flowing and the riverbed dried up. This event not only paralleled the crossing of the Red Sea 40 years earlier, it demonstrated to the Israelites and to the native people that the power of God was still with the nation and its new leader. Once in the Promised Land, Joshua reinforced the original covenant with Abraham by a nationwide ceremony of circumcision. Next, the Passover was celebrated. Immediately afterward the manna ceased to appear as it had for the last 40 years. The people then ate from the bounty of the Land of Milk and Honey instead of the food God directly supplied.
6-24	**Division of the Land** The city of Jericho was conquered with a great victory because of the direct intervention of God. Joshua continued to lead the nation in numerous military victories. These victories were due to faith in God, not military superiority. The very name "Joshua" (which means "Lord is Salvation") shows the true character of the new leader. Before the death of Joshua, almost all the Canaanites were driven out of the Promised Land. After a relatively peaceful existence was secured, the Promised Land was officially divided among the individual tribes of Israel.

The book of Joshua and the leadership of the man himself again demonstrated that if the leaders and the people sought the will of God and were obedient to the Law, their efforts would be blessed by God and they would be successful.

The Period of Judges

After the death of Joshua, the nation became a loose confederacy of 12 tribes bonded together only by their God. This new independence still required faithfulness to God and it also required a great deal of self-discipline. Under Joshua's leadership, the non-Jewish nations had been driven out of the land; but it was now up to the individual tribes of Israel to complete the conquest and ensure that the Canaanites did not return to spread the influence of their foreign religions.

Unfortunately, on more occasions than not, the people ceased to follow God and were consequently oppressed by the surrounding nations. Just as Joshua had shown that faithfulness and obedience to God brought prosperity and peace, disobedience and idolatry brought oppression and death.

"Then the Lord raised up judges, who saved them out of the hands of these raiders."
Judges 2:16

These judges were a series of spiritual, military and civil leaders. They were called upon to lead the people out of their oppression. Individual judges did not necessarily rule the entire land, and many judges ruled concurrently. Depending upon the exact definition of "judge," approximately 13 judges ruled for a period of around 300 years. Three of the most significant and interesting judges are listed in the following table.

Table 5-2   Selected Judges of Israel

Judges Chapter	Name
4	**Deborah** God used Deborah, a prophetess and a judge, to give direct commands to the Israelite army of over 10,000 soldiers. A great battle was won, and the honor went to a woman, not the commanding general. Both the outcome of the battle and the placement of honor were precisely as Deborah had prophesied.

6-9	**Gideon** God called a young man named Gideon to tear down the altar of the pagan God, Baal, and to lead the Israelite people against the Midianites who were oppressing them to the point of starvation. God's call to Gideon, His signs to Gideon using a wet and dry fleece and the way that Gideon's soldiers were selected by God are all exciting stories. Gideon became a popular and powerful military leader. He won a major victory with an army of only 300 select warriors because of his great faith and obedience to God.
13-17	**Samson** Samson, the strong man, is by far the best known and most colorful judge. An angel of the Lord appeared to Samson's mother before his birth and announced that Samson would deliver the Israelites from the hands of the Philistines. *This divine pre-birth announcement is similar to that experienced by the mothers of Isaac and Samuel, the father of John the Baptist, and Mary, the mother of Jesus.* Some of Samson's most exciting exploits included the use of foxes to burn the wheat harvest, a riddle and a lion, stealing the gates of a city, and winning a great victory with the jawbone of a donkey. The final story of Samson involved being betrayed by the beautiful Delilah. In the resulting capture, Samson eventually lost his life, but also won his greatest battle for God.

THEOLOGICALLY SPEAKING

It is not unusual to have Christian ministers and teachers present Samson as the great Old Testament Hero, simply because he was strong and is listed as one of the early judges of Israel. Yet, this concept has seldom been upheld within the Jewish community. The Rabbis have traditionally used him as an example of "how not to be."

Following the Exodus, there developed a special classification of people with the Hebrew community known as "Nazarities." These persons were believed to be highly religious and "set apart" from the general population for a life of extreme commitment to God and a lifestyle dominated by a strict code of behavior.   Biblical characters such as Daniel and John the Baptist are examples of Nazarites. A Nazarite would be immediately distinguishable in a crowd because of their strange dress (usually made from skins of wild animals), unusual diet, and unkept, uncut hair.   Their appearance and lifestyle was radical and might have appeared strange to us, but they were highly respected within their community and considered to have a unique, divinely directed purpose within the history of God's people.

Like Daniel and John the Baptist, Samson was raised as a Nazarite. Daniel served as a moral and religious standard for his people during a time when they were in exile in Babylon. John the Baptist was the prophet who was to precede and proclaim Jesus as the Messiah. Samson had miraculous strength and physical ability to single-handedly conquer the enemies of Israel.

Unfortunately, Samson did not focus on the needs of his people and seldom exhibited faith in God. He spent most of his time with his Philistine friends and girlfriends. At the time, Israel had no greater enemy than the Philistines. Most of his story is comprised of his being taken in and duped by the Philistines, and his vengeful retaliation against them. His battles against the enemy are not for the betterment of God's people, but are simply ways of getting back at those who have made a fool out of him. His final demise comes at the hands of a Philistine woman named Delilah, when he gives away the secret of his great strength (his hair) and, while he sleeps, she clips off his hair. The Philistines blind him and cruelly force him to serve as a slave and occasional displays of pathetic entertainment. In the end, God grants him his strength one last time, as he brings down a building, killing himself and many Philistines.

Samson serves as an example of "what could have been," had he lived a life focused on faithfulness and commitment to God and his people.[1]

The era of the judges ended with the final judge being what many consider to be the most powerful judge of all time. This judge is Samuel. His many years of leadership closed the period of judges, began the period of kings and extended through anointing the second king of the monarchy, David. Two books in the Old Testament bear his name, and he is a key character in the early chapters of the book of First Samuel.

The Transition

The Israelite people cried out to be governed by a king like the people of the neighboring countries. God warned that they would be oppressed by a king and that they would be unhappy, but God finally granted their plea. Samuel was the person designated by God to anoint the first king and coordinate the transition from the judge system to a monarchy.

The major events which lead up to and constitute this transition are presented in the table below:

Table 5-3   Transition from Judges to Kings

I Samuel Chapter	Event
1-3	**Samuel, the Last Judge** Samuel's mother, Hannah, prayed for a son and promised to dedicate him to the Lord if her prayers were answered. A son, Samuel, was born and was raised by a priest named Eli. The boy ministered to the Lord before the priest. One night the boy, Samuel, was called by God four times before he recognized it was God speaking to him. *"In those days the word of the Lord was rare; there were not many visions."* I Samuel 3:1b
4-8	**The Ark Taken by the Philistines** One of the most unusual occurrences during Samuel's leadership was when the ark of the Lord was misused and consequently captured during a battle with the Philistines. God cursed the Philistines for taking the ark: Their god, Dagon, was destroyed: the people were plagued with tumors and mice overran the land. After seven months, the Philistines returned the ark and were so frightened they made mice and tumors of gold and presented them as a guilt offering in an attempt to appease the God of the Israelites. Samuel grew old, and the people cried out for a king to be appointed. God then designated Samuel to anoint the first king of Israel.

9-15	**Saul, the First King** God chose a young man named Saul to be the first king and sent him to Samuel. Samuel anointed Saul. The Spirit of the Lord came mightily upon Saul, transformed him and gave him the power to perform as king. *There are two very important concepts in this event; anointment and the Spirit of the Lord coming upon someone.* *1. Anointment will be carried through the line of kings and into the New Testament. "Messiah" is Hebrew for "anointed one"' and "Christ" is Greek for the same term.* *2. The Spirit of the Lord coming upon someone will be demonstrated many times in the Old Testament and will become the permanent indwelling of the Holy Spirit in the New Testament.*

The Decline of King Saul
and the Rise of David

King Saul soon became disobedient to God, acted foolishly and then refused to confess his sins. God withdrew his blessings from Saul and also withdrew the future kingdom from Saul and his heirs. After Samuel delivered to Saul this message from God, he refused to visit or even acknowledge King Saul from that day forth.

God then chose a new person for king and once again God's faithful servant, Samuel, carried out the process.

Table 5-4   David is Chosen to be King

I Samuel Chapter	Event
16	**Chosen by God** God instructed Samuel to visit the home of Jesse where he would anoint one of Jesse's sons as the future king. God advised Samuel not to consider the physical appearance of the sons. *"The Lord does not look at the things man looks at. Man looks at the outward appearance, but the Lord looks at the heart."* *I Samuel 16:7b* God indicated his choice, and Samuel anointed Jesse's youngest son, David, to be the next king. *(This is the first of the three times David was anointed.)*

17-18	**The Rise of David**
	The young man, David, continued to keep his father's sheep for a period of time.
	"Now the spirit of the Lord had departed from Saul." *I Samuel 16:14a*
	David was selected to play the harp for King Saul in an effort to calm his fits of anger and evil spirit. During this time period, David also fought the Philistine giant, Goliath, and won favor with King Saul.
	David became like a brother to King Saul's son Jonathan. David became a commander in Saul's army and was highly esteemed.
	David next became Saul's son-in-law and won even more battles. Saul grew afraid of David and became his enemy.
19 - 30	**David the Fugitive**
	David's popularity with the people became so great that Saul plotted to kill David. First, Jonathan warned David of his father's plan and next, David 's wife saved him from her father, King Saul.
	In self-defense, David fled, organized his own army and fought a guerrilla war against King Saul. David became the national hero, and was protected by Samuel, Jonathan and many other people.
	Although constantly fleeing from and fighting Saul and his army, David still respected God's anointed king and spared Saul's life during battle. Once David was so close to Saul that he cut off the edge of Saul's robe without his knowledge. On another occasion David took Saul's spear and water jug from beside Saul while he was asleep.
31	**The Death of King Saul**
	During a battle with the Philistines, King Saul was mortally wounded and fell upon his own sword before the Philistines could capture him. Jonathan was also killed in the same battle.

After the death of King Saul, David called upon the Lord for guidance concerning where he should go next. The Lord sent him to Judah.

"Then the men of Judah came to Hebron and there they anointed David king over the house of Judah." *II Samuel 2:4*

(This was the second time David was anointed.)

One of Saul's sons became a king over some portion of the northern tribes of Israel; however, the Philistines had control over other portions of Israel at the same time.

"The war between the house of Saul and the house of David lasted a long time. David grew stronger and stronger, while the house of Saul grew weaker and weaker." II Samuel 3:1

Table 5-5   David Becomes King

Chapter	Event
II Samuel I Chron.	**The City of David** David was king of Judah for over seven years before he united the country and was made king over all the tribes of Israel. *(This was the third time David was anointed.)* David conquered the city of Jerusalem and established it as his capital city. Jerusalem was an excellent military location as well as a good political choice because it was considered a neutral area between Judah and Israel.
II Samuel 6-7 I Chron. 15-17	**The Ark, the Temple and the Messiah** God continued to bless David and his kingdom. David prepared a place for the ark of the covenant and pitched a tent for it in the city of Jerusalem. The tabernacle was left in its previous location at Gibeon. The ark was transported by the Levites in a great ceremony. David then requested that God allow him to build a temple in which to place the ark of the covenant. God refused his request to build the temple; instead, God made a covenant with David that his son would be allowed to build the temple and, far more importantly, that the Messiah would ultimately come from David's family. *This promise of the Messiah refers to the genealogy of Christ traced through his legal father, Joseph. This genealogy is located in the first chapter of Matthew.*

Psalms	**King David's Worship** David wrote all types of psalms to worship God. These included psalms of sadness, grief, fear, repentance, thanksgiving and joy. David is noted in the title of 73 of the 150 psalms in the Book of Psalms. These psalms were both songs and poetry which were used in worship. David also demonstrated an important principle in sacrificial giving when he insisted on paying full price for an offering that he could have obtained at no cost to him. ***"No, I insist on paying you for it. I will not sacrifice to the Lord my God burnt offerings what cost me nothing."*** *II Samuel 24:24*
II Samuel 11-12 **I Chron. 21**	**King David's Sins** Even David, a person that the Lord said was "a man after His own heart," fell short and sinned. David committed adultery with Bathsheba and had her husband murdered in an attempt to cover up his wrongdoing. David was confronted with his sins and punished by the death of his and Bathsheba's first child. David recognized his sins, repented and was forgiven for his transgressions. David again sinned by conducting a census and relying upon the sheer numbers of his military for power instead of relying upon the power of God. David was again confronted with his sin, was punished, repented and was forgiven. David was a warrior his entire life. His early years were filled with military and political victories due to his obedience to God. His later years were troubled with family problems and rebellion in the kingdom due to lack of obedience to God.

The Peaceful Kingdom

David was king for a total of 40 years; seven years in Judah and 33 years over the united kingdom in the City of David, Jerusalem. Even though David's reign was one of war, it also firmly established the united kingdom and prepared the way for a peaceful time when the new king, Solomon (his son), could turn to building, commerce and formal worship of the Lord.

Diagram 5-1, Joshua to King Solomon, is located on the following page. This diagram provides a graphical view of the main events in this time period.

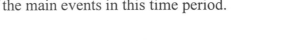

JOSHUA TO KING SOLOMON

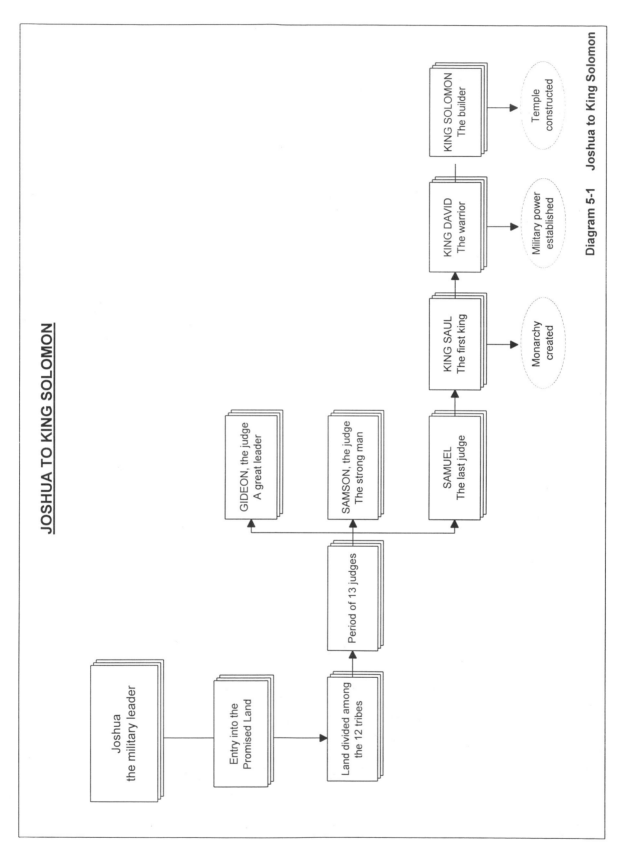

Joshua
the military leader

Entry into the
Promised Land

Land divided among
the 12 tribes

Period of 13 judges

GIDEON, the judge
A great leader

SAMSON, the judge
The strong man

SAMUEL
The last judge

KING SAUL
The first king

Monarchy
created

KING DAVID
The warrior

Military power
established

KING SOLOMON
The builder

Temple
constructed

Diagram 5-1 **Joshua to King Solomon**

Table 5-6   King Solomon

Book Chapter	Event
I Kings 1 I Chron. 29	**Solomon Becomes King** Solomon was the second son of King David and Bathsheba. God instructed David that Solomon would be the next king and that he would be the one to build His holy temple. In his last days, King David gave Solomon specific instructions for building and furnishing the temple. He then crowned Solomon as successor to the throne before his death. During these ceremonies, David and the leaders of the country gave over 300 tons of gold to be used for the temple construction and operation. They gave even larger amounts of silver, brass and iron. *Much of this wealth had been given to the Israelites as they left bondage in Egypt generations earlier.*
I Kings 2--10 II Chron. 1-9	**Solomon's Wisdom** In a dream, God appeared to Solomon and asked him what he desired. Solomon asked for wisdom to lead his people. God granted his request for wisdom and also granted him great riches and honor. Solomon wrote and assembled great volumes of wisdom literature. Part of this material is now found in Psalms, Proverbs, Ecclesiastes and Song of Solomon. Solomon was also interested in the study of nature and science. His wisdom and knowledge was known and respected throughout the world.
I Kings 5-10 II Chron. 2-9	**Solomon's Temple** Just as God had promised to David; Solomon's kingdom was peaceful and prosperous. This allowed Solomon to concentrate on the construction of the temple. The temple was considered the most magnificent building in the world. A large percentage of the entire building was overlaid in gold and silver. One room alone, the Holy of Holies, was overlaid with 45,000 pounds of gold. At the dedication of the temple 22,000 oxen and 120,000 sheep were sacrificed. The temple was not the only extensive building project completed by Solomon. He build a palace, stables, complete cities and a great navy. Solomon was the richest king on earth.

Solomon's Temple

I Kings 11	**Solomon's Downfall**
	In Solomon's later years, he married wives from many of the foreign countries with which he did commerce. God had forbidden the Israelites to have any contact with a significant number of these countries. Not only did Solomon marry 700 wives, he allowed them to worship their own respective foreign gods. In his old age, he actually participated in the worship himself.

Solomon turned his heart away from God. The Lord told him that the greater portion of the kingdom would be taken away from his family. Only for the sake of the promise to King David would God wait until after Solomon's death to divide the kingdom. |

Although God chose Solomon to replace David as king, his kingship was not without personal responsibility.

"I will establish his kingdom forever if he is unswerving in carrying out my commands and laws, as is being done at this time." *I Chronicles 28:7*

By being faithful and dedicated to God, Solomon ensured his success in his early years and built an extraordinary kingdom. Likewise, by being disobedient and turning away from God, Solomon ensured the destruction of his kingdom.

Although Solomon's kingdom was immediately divided after his death, he did accomplish many things that endured for generations to come. The temple was the greatest of these accomplishments. This structure and its two successive replacements would serve the Jews for 1,000 years.

The temple was far more meaningful to the Jews than just a building. The temple replaced their beloved tabernacle and as such became the center of worship for the Jews. When the people followed God, their lives revolved around the Law. A great deal of the Law revolved around ceremonies and sacrifices, which were now centered in the temple.

The temple was so important that Jesus made this statement about himself:

"I tell you that one greater than the temple is here."   *Matthew 12:6*

Read The Book

1. _____ was the leader of the nation after Moses. He was a more powerful _____ leader than a _____ leader.

2. As the people entered into the Promised Land, what physical event that occurred during the exodus 40 years earlier was paralleled?

   _____

3. Immediately after the Israelites entered the Promised Land, they held what nationwide ceremony which reinforced the original covenant with Abraham?

   _____

4. T / F   The Passover was celebrated immediately after the ceremony of circumcision.

5. After 40 years what now ceased to appear? _____

6. T / F   Jerusalem was soon conquered because of direct intervention by God.

7. T / F   Joshua led the people in many military victories. These victories were due primarily to the military superiority of the Israelites.

8. Before the death of Joshua, what was divided among the tribes of Israel?

   _____

9. List the 3 general areas of leadership provided by the judges.

   _____ _____ _____

10. In broad terms, a total of _____ judges ruled for about _____ years.

11. T / F   Deborah was not only a judge, she was also a prophetess.

12. The best-known and certainly the most colorful judge was _____,
    the _____ man.

13. God warned the people they would be _____ by a king, yet
    they persisted in asking.

14. Samuel is considered to be the last judge or the first prophet of Israel. In his
    old age, he was designated by God to _____ the first king of Israel.

15. What is the Greek word for "anointed one?" _____

    What is the Hebrew word for "anointed one?" _____

16. Soon after becoming king, Saul became _____ to God and
    refused to confess his _____.

17. Because of King Saul's actions and refusal, God's _____ were
    withdrawn from him.

18. While Saul was still king, Samuel was sent to _____ the young man
    David to be the successor to the throne.

19. T / F   As a young man, David is best known for killing the giant, Goliath,
            and playing the harp.

20. T / F   David was King Saul's son-in-law.

21.   T / F   David eventually was forced to kill King Saul. Because of this action David became king in his place.

22.   How many times was David anointed? _____

23.   What city did David conquer and establish as the capital city? _____

24.   In lieu of God granting David's request to build a temple, God made a covenant with David that promised two very important things. What are they?

_____

_____

25.   T / F   Just as obedience to God brought success to David's early years, disobedience brought rebellion in the kingdom and family problems in his later years.

26.   King _____ succeeded King David; he was the _____ son of David and Bathesheba.

27.   T / F   Before King David died, he gave specific instructions to Solomon concerning the temple and its furnishings.

28.   David and the leaders of the country gave how many tons of gold to be used in the construction and operation of the temple? _____

29.   Solomon's greatest construction accomplishment was the temple. How long did that building and the two replacements serve as the center of worship for the Jewish nation? _____

30. T / F In Solomon's later years, he turned his heart away from God. Consequently the kingdom was later split.

Talk The Talk

During the period of judges, an angel delivered a divine prebirth announcement to Samson's mother. Samson was clearly set apart by God.

A.   *Considering the divine announcement and the enlightening information given in the "Theologically Speaking" section, does it appear that Samson fulfilled his role to his fullest potential?*

B.   *Do you consider the Biblical character Samson a "Bible Hero?" In what ways is he good? In what ways is he bad?*

David was a king of war and military power.   Solomon was a king of peace, commerce and education.

C.   *How did their personal relationships with God mirror each other during their youth?*

D.   *How did their personal relationships with God mirror each other during their later years?*

Walk The Walk

When God sent his servant Samuel to find and anoint young David as the future king, he gave Samuel very specific advice concerning the way God views people as opposed to the way humanity views people.

E.   *According to the statement found in I Samuel 16:7b, how does God view people?*

F.   p *Will reflecting upon this story and, specifically, this statement enable you to feel more secure and proceed more confidently in certain areas of your life?*

G.   *God looks at the heart and not the outward appearance. Is it the same to apply this concept and say that God looks at the heart (intentions, motives, desires) and not necessarily just the resulting outward physical actions?*

Do these concepts bring you comfort or uneasiness?

NOTES

Chapter 6
The Kingdom Splits, Struggles and Goes Into Exile

The history of God's people now becomes much more difficult to follow. Until this point, with the exception of the period of judges and early in David's reign, a single leader specifically chosen by God had primary responsibility for the leadership of a unified people.

The splitting of Solomon's kingdom immediately brought about a dual history. This is further complicated by the number of kings who rule, the length of their reigns and the nature of their leadership, good or evil. The next complication comes from the method by which God chose to deliver His messages; seldom did he communicate directly with the rulers during this period. Instead he used prophets to bring written and oral messages to both the royalty and the common people. These messages from God, delivered through the prophets, dealt with both the present and the future. The final factor that enters into the history is the account of numerous enemies that rise to fight and sometimes conquer God's chosen people.

How Will We Follow This Intricate Plot?

As one might expect, the documentation and details that comprise such a diverse history are themselves complex. We must also understand that the primary purpose of the Bible is not to be a history. Even the "Historical Books" of the Old Testament have a greater purpose. They present the historical facts needed for documentation and preservation, but the writings are religious, and, as such, are meant to inspire, educate, encourage and sometimes warn fellow believers in both present and future generations.

When an Old Testament book was written, the events described, whether current or past history, were very much a part of the lives of the authors as well as of the intended readers. Therefore, it was neither customary nor necessary to record and describe every detail.

Seldom is all the information concerning a significant Old Testament historical event found in one location. In fact, it is typical to read about a major event in Kings or Chronicles and find additional illuminating details in one or more of the books of the major or minor prophets, which may be located several hundred pages away.

In order to gain a clear view of the actual events without becoming bogged down in innumerable details, we will now focus primarily on the events, dates and characters, dispensing with the exact Scriptural locations in this and the following chapter.

Solomon's Death Brings Two Successors

After Solomon's death, his son, Rehoboam, became king. Because Solomon's great commerce and many building programs had oppressed the common people, they gathered to officially ask the new king if the hard service and heavy yoke of Solomon could be lightened. This assembly was lead by Jeroboam, a powerful leader and former servant of Solomon. Jeroboam had fled to Egypt to escape death from King Solomon because a prophecy had foretold that 10 tribes would be taken from Solomon and given to Jeroboam.

The new king, Rehoboam, not only refused to lighten the burdens of the people, he promised to be even harsher than his father. Because of this verdict all of the tribes, except Judah and Benjamin, refused to be ruled by Rehoboam and chose Jeroboam to be their king. Thus the prophecy of the divided kingdom was fulfilled, and God's chosen people officially became the nations of Judah and Israel.

Fate of the Two Nations

During the two centuries that both nations existed separately, the Bible makes little, if any, distinction between the two. The text moves back and forth covering the history and events of both nations with few comments indicating which nation is the subject, other than an occasional reference to the current king.

Although the nations became rivals and actually fought battles against each other, both countries were still regarded as God's chosen people. When they followed God's law they prospered; when they disobeyed they did not prosper.

Israel survived for two turbulent centuries before being completely conquered by Assyria and having large numbers of its population deported to other countries. These exiles never returned to their homeland, and are sometimes referred to as the "lost tribes of Israel." The Assyrians also brought in foreigners to repopulate the country. The intermarriages of the remaining Israelites with these foreigners began the new mixed race known as the Samaritans.

Judah continued to struggle as an independent nation for another one and one half centuries after the fall of Israel. Judah was eventually conquered by Babylon. The capital city, Jerusalem, was destroyed; the temple was demolished and the educated and skilled people deported to Babylon. This was the predicted 70-year Babylonian exile.

Table 6-1   Comparison of the Two Nations

	Judah	Israel
Tribes	2	10
Location	South	North
Capital City	Jerusalem	Samaria
First King	Rehoboam	Jeroboam
Total Number of Rulers	19 Kings 1 Ruling Queen	19 Kings
Length of Independence	345 years	209 years
Conquered by	Babylon King Nebuchadnezzar (587 B.C.)	Assyria King Shalmaneser V started the siege and Sargon II completed it. (722 B.C.)
Exile	Three major deportations to Babylon. Many Jews also fled to Egypt.	Population was scattered to various other countries. Israel was repopulated with foreigners who intermarried and started the Samaritan race.
Post Exile	Three major returns from exile. The temple and the city were rebuilt.	The exiles never returned.

Map 6-1, The Divided Kingdom, is located on the follow page. It shows one representation of the boundaries of Judah and Israel. Due to constant conflicts and wars, the exact boundaries often varied.

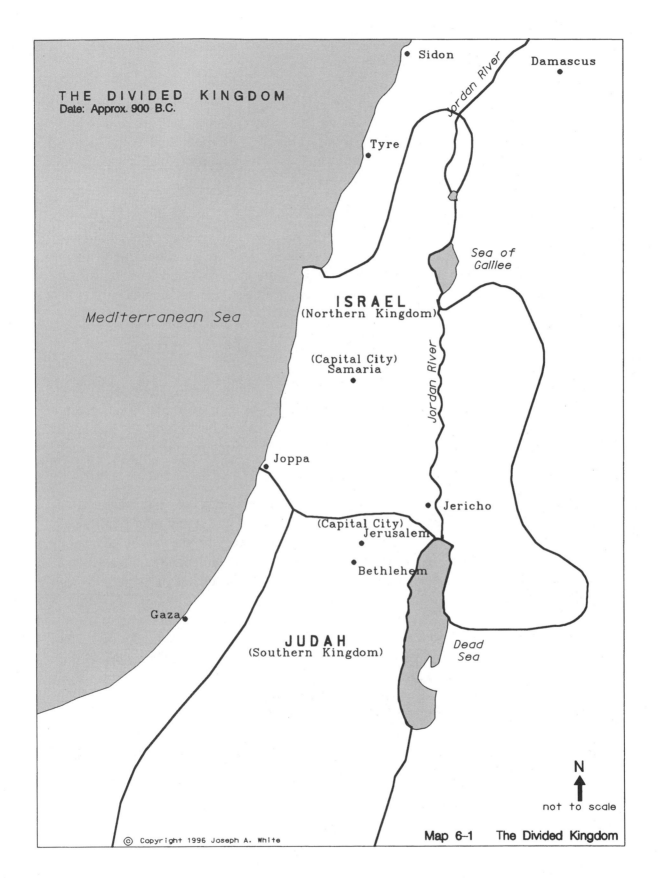

THE DIVIDED KINGDOM
Date: Approx. 900 B.C.

Sidon

Damascus

Tyre

Jordan River

Mediterranean Sea

Sea of Galilee

ISRAEL
(Northern Kingdom)

(Capital City)
Samaria

Jordan River

Joppa

Jericho

(Capital City)
Jerusalem

Bethlehem

Gaza

JUDAH
(Southern Kingdom)

Dead Sea

N

N

not to scale

Map 6-1   The Divided Kingdom

Delivery of the Word of God

The leadership of the nation was not the only element of God's people undergoing great changes. The method in which the Word of God was delivered was also drastically changing. From the time of the patriarchs until the period of the judges, God's recorded communication concerning matters of the nation as a whole was almost exclusively directed to the leader.

During the reign of the first two kings a transition began. Samuel, the judge and prophet, and Nathan, the prophet, were heavily involved in receiving God's word and then delivering it to Saul and David. After the split of the kingdom, the primary method of delivering God's message to both common people and leaders was by prophets. Unfortunately, for the most part, their messages went unheeded.

The Prophets

The term "prophet" is found at least 240 times throughout the Bible. There are several prophets that appear in the Old Testament who are seldom, if ever, mentioned again. However, the prophets on which we now wish to focus are the 16 prophets that have Old Testament books bearing their names and two non-writing prophets that were very active in the time of the kings.

It is important to understand that prophets spoke as directed by God. The messages of the prophets were delivered by spoken word, written word and sometimes by physical demonstration. The majority of the time these messages were directed at the people of that time, for that time. In most cases, these prophecies challenged conditions and behaviors and were not received favorably. Only a small percentage of the prophecies dealt with the future.

There are three major periods into which the work of the prophets can be divided. The first period (the longest, 345 years) was during the divided kingdom. The work of the prophets during this period can be seen as almost equally dispersed between the two kingdoms and their respective peoples. The second period was during the 70-year exile in Babylon. The final period was during the return from the exile.

The following table groups the four major prophets and the 12 minor prophets according to their time periods and the people to whom they prophesied.

Table 6-2   Major and Minor Prophets

To Whom They Prophesied	During the Divided Kingdom	During the Exile in Babylon	After the Return from the Exile
Nation of Edom	Obadiah		
City of Nineveh (Assyria)	Jonah Nahum		
Nation of Israel	Amos Hosea		
Nation of Judah	Joel Isaiah Micah Zephaniah Jeremiah Habakkuk Lamentations (of Jeremiah)		
Jews in Babylon		Daniel Ezekiel	
Jews that had Returned			Haggai Zechariah Malachi

The Kings of Two Nations

The main chronology of the kings of Judah and Israel after the division of the kingdom is found in the books of First and Second Kings and Second Chronicles. Other information concerning their reigns is contained in several of the books of the major and minor prophets. The details of the combined 39 reigning monarchs spanning three and one half centuries is a history within itself. The following table lists the monarchs and the prophets and provides an approximate time frame.

Table 6-3   Kings and Prophets of the Divided Kingdom

Date	The Southern Kingdom of Judah		The Northern Kingdom of Israel	
	King	Prophet	King	Prophet
931 B.C.	Rehoboam		Jeroboam	
	Abijam		Nadab	
	Asa		Baasha Elah	
			Zimri Omri	
	Jehoshaphat		Ahab	ELIJAH**
	Jehoram		Ahaziah	
	Ahaziah		Joram	
	Queen Athaliah	OBADIAH*	Jehu	ELISHA**
	Joash	JOEL		
			Jehoahaz	
	Amaziah	JONAH*	Jehoash	
	Uzziah		Jeroboam II	AMOS
	Jotham		Zechariah Shallum Menahem Pekahiah	
		MICAH ISAIAH	Pekah	HOSEA
	Ahaz			
722 B.C.			Hoshea	*Dispersion by Assyria*
	Hezekiah			
	Manasseh			
	Amon	ZEPHANIAH NAHUM*		
	Josiah			
	Jehoahaz	HABAKKUK		
	Jehoiakim			
	Jehoiachin	JEREMIAH		
587 B.C.	Zedekiah		*Babylonian Exile*	

* *Prophesied to other countries*   ** *Non-writing prophet*

This table is not to scale with respect to time or length of reign. This is one of several possible placements of the prophets. Judah and Israel used a different system to record lengths of reigns. Reigns overlap due to fathers crowning their sons during their own lifetime and allowing dual reigns.

Similarities of the Two Kingdoms

The histories of Judah and Israel during the divided kingdom were very similar. Even though they sometimes fought against each other, the two countries shared many things other than the same God. Some of their kings and queens were closely related and several of the prophets monitored the religious and political activities of both countries and gave warnings using the other country as an example. Both nations experienced periods of revival and decline in their spirituality. The periods of decline were more pronounced and longer than the periods of revival.

Evils of the Two Kingdoms

Just as the kings of Israel were condemned by the Scriptures for "doing what was evil in the sight of the Lord," so were all but two of the kings of Judah, Hezekiah and Josiah. Even though they were praised in the Scripture for doing right, it is also pointed out that they failed to eliminate the worship of foreign gods.

It is difficult to comprehend exactly how evil some of the rulers, people and their practices actually were. Some of the atrocities committed by the monarchs are listed in the following two tables. Keep in mind that many of these practices filtered down to the common people from the monarchy as well as from the neighboring non-Jewish nations.

Chronology of the Divided Kingdom

Some of the major events, important characters and most interesting happenings in the history of the divided kingdom are listed in the following table. The majority of the Scripture references for the table are located in First and Second Kings and Second Chronicles. Events concerning Judah will be shaded in the left column; those concerning Israel will not be shaded.

Table 6-4   Selected Chronological Events During the Divided Kingdom

Date & Kingdom	Event
931 B.C. *Israel*	**Jeroboam, the First King of Israel in the Divided Kingdom** Jeroboam was an able leader and rapidly organized the 10 northern tribes into a new country. These tribes retained the name *Israel.* Samaria was purchased to become the capital and major city of Israel. Solomon's Temple, the center of religion, was now located in a foreign country, Judah. Therefore, Jeroboam constructed two shrines to compete with worship at Solomon's Temple. He also allowed people other than Levites to become priests. Jeroboam led the people away from God and is blamed for much of the future sin of Israel's kings.
931 B.C. *Judah*	**Rehoboam, the First King of Judah in the Divided Kingdom** Solomon's son, Rehoboam, became king and declined the counsel of his father's trusted advisors. He refused to improve the conditions of the common people, thus causing a rebellion. Only the tribes of Judah and Benjamin followed Rehoboam. They were referred to as *Judah,* the southern kingdom. This split fulfilled the prophecy from God which proclaimed that, because Solomon had worshiped other gods, the kingdom would be torn apart. Still the two smaller tribes remained a separate country under David's grandson, thus maintaining God's promise to David of a continuing kingdom of his lineage.
874 B.C. *Israel*	**King Ahab** Ahab was the seventh king of Israel. Ahab is considered by scholars to be the most wicked king in Israel's history. His wife, Queen Jezebel, was equally corrupt and also very powerful. She openly promoted the worship of Baal.
Israel	**Elijah the Prophet** For 20 years the prophet Elijah battled both King Ahab and Queen Jezebel. Although Elijah was not a writing prophet and has no book that bears his name, he had a major influence on the history of God's people. Elijah is referred to by name at least 28 times in the New Testament. This includes the return of Elijah as John the Baptist and Elijah's appearance with Jesus on the Mount of Transfiguration. *(Matthew 17:3,12-13)*

Israel	**Works of Elijah** Listed below are the topics of some of the greatest stories of this colorful and powerful prophet. 1. Elijah called for a famine over the entire land. 2. God provided directly for Elijah by using ravens to bring him food. 3. God sent a perpetual supply of food to a widow because she shared the last of her food with Elijah. 4. By the power of God, Elijah raised a child from the dead. 5. Elijah won a deadly contest with Queen Jezebel's priest of Baal by calling down fire from heaven. 6. God spoke to Elijah in a still, small voice. 7. Elijah never died. He was taken directly to heaven by a chariot of fire in a whirlwind.
842 B.C. *Israel*	**Oppression Begins and Tribute is Paid** The first indication of a problem maintaining political sovereignty could be seen over 100 years before the fall of Israel. At that time King Jehu paid tribute to Shalmaneser III, king of Assyria. Political conditions continued to deteriorate over the next century.
841 B.C. *Judah*	**Queen Athaliah** Athaliah, the daughter of Ahab and Jezebel *(king and queen of neighboring Israel)*, was the seventh ruler of Judah and the only ruling queen of Judah. She gained this position by killing her own grandchildren, the rightful heirs to the throne.
Judah	**King Joash** One of Queen Athaliah's infant grandsons, Joash, was rescued and hidden by his aunt and several priests for six years. When Joash was seven years old, the Queen was overthrown and Joash was made king. He reigned successfully for 28 years under the guidance of his uncle, the high priest. Unfortunately, upon the death of his uncle, Joash fell away from the Lord and began to worship idols.
Israel	**Elisha the Prophet** Near the end of Elijah's ministry, the Lord chose Elisha to be the great prophet's successor. Elisha was anointed to carry on Elijah's work. He requested twice the prophetic powers of his teacher. God granted the request; consequently, in the next 50 years Elisha worked more recorded miracles than anyone in the Bible except Jesus himself.

Israel	**Works of Elisha** Listed below is a sample of Elisha's works. 1. Salt was used to purify a stew that was accidentally poisoned. 2. An ax head was made to float in the river. 3. A poor widow and her sons were saved because of her faith in God when she asked Elisha for help. 4. A foreign general was healed of leprosy because of the faith of a little Israelite slave girl. 5. A young boy was raised from the dead. 6. The Syrian army was blinded and captured.
Israel	**Writing Prophets - Amos and Hosea** Approximately 50 years after Elisha completed his ministry, the prophets Amos and Hosea called for Israel to repent and return to the Lord. Their combined ministries spanned the last years of the independence of Israel.
Israel	**Amos** Amos lived in the southern kingdom of Judah. He was called by God to travel north to Israel and deliver a message to repent or face judgment. At this time, Israel was in a state of material prosperity and spiritual poverty. His oral message faced so much opposition in Israel that Amos returned to Judah and placed it in writing.
Israel	**Hosea** Hosea proclaimed the steadfast love of God for the nation of Israel despite their continued unfaithfulness. He used his own unfaithful wife and his continued love for her as a vivid analogy.
740 B.C. *Judah*	**Isaiah the Prophet** Isaiah is often called the Messianic Prophet because he spoke more of Christ than any other prophet. Isaiah is also quoted more in the New Testament than all of the other prophets combined. Isaiah was most likely born into a influential upper class family and *"was called to be a prophet in the year King Uzziah died."* He lived in Jerusalem where he associated with and gave advice to royalty. For approximately one half century, he ministered to the southern kingdom of Judah. Isaiah was very aware of the political situation to the north, in Israel. As Israel was slowly falling to Assyria, Isaiah prophesied that Babylon, not Assyria, would conquer his own country of Judah in the future and that Judah must look to God for help and not to foreign countries. The fall of Israel did occur during Isaiah's ministry, and he spoke much about Israel as an example for Judah. Isaiah warned against depending on foreign countries for protection instead of relying upon God. He also assured the people that after the predicted exile the nation would eventually be restored. Isaiah is one of the four major prophets in the Old Testament.

735 B.C. *Judah*	**King Ahaz** Ahaz became the twelfth ruler of Judah. He was such a wicked king that he actually burned some of his own children in child sacrifice. Ahaz's 20-year reign was during the first portion of the ministry of Isaiah.
Israel	**The Evils of Israel** The Scripture condemns all of the kings of Israel for " having done what was evil in the sight of the Lord."
725 B.C. *Israel*	**Israel Revolts** Hoshea was the 19th and final king in the 209-year history of Israel during the divided kingdom. In 725 B.C., Israel revolted and refused to pay tribute to Assyria. *Samaria, the capital city, was placed under siege by Shalmaneser V. After three years of war, the Assyrians were victorious under the leadership of Sargon II.*
722 B.C. *Israel*	**Israel is Conquered by Assyria** During the third year of the siege, the city of Samaria fell. The educated and skilled people were deported to various countries held by Assyria. Sargon II recorded that 27,290 Israelites were deported. This action by Assyria was more nearly a dispersion of the population than a deportation, because these exiles would never return and foreigners were brought in to repopulate the country. *This repopulation resulted in a new religion which combined Judaism and the Canaanite religion. The far-reaching effects of this mixture can be seen in the days of Jesus's ministry, when Samaritans were looked down upon for not being pure in either race or religion.*
Israel	**The Words of the Prophets** Hosea and Amos had prophesied the fall of Israel. Both stated the fall was due to the spiritual and moral decay of the people. Isaiah, in neighboring Judah, referred to Assyria as " the rod of God's anger." ***"Woe to Assyria, the rod of my anger, in whose hand is the club of my wrath! I send him against a godless nation, and dispatch him against a people who anger me, to seize loot and snatch plunder, and to trample them down like mud in the streets."*** <div align="right">*Isaiah 10:5-6*</div>

"So the people of Israel were taken from their homeland into exile in Assyria, and they are still there."

II Kings 17:23b

Map 6-2, Exile of Israel to Assyria, is located on the following page. It shows the northern kingdom of Israel, a possible exile route and a graphical representation of the center of the Assyrian Empire. Over the years, the borders of the Assyrian empire changed drastically and included many countries.

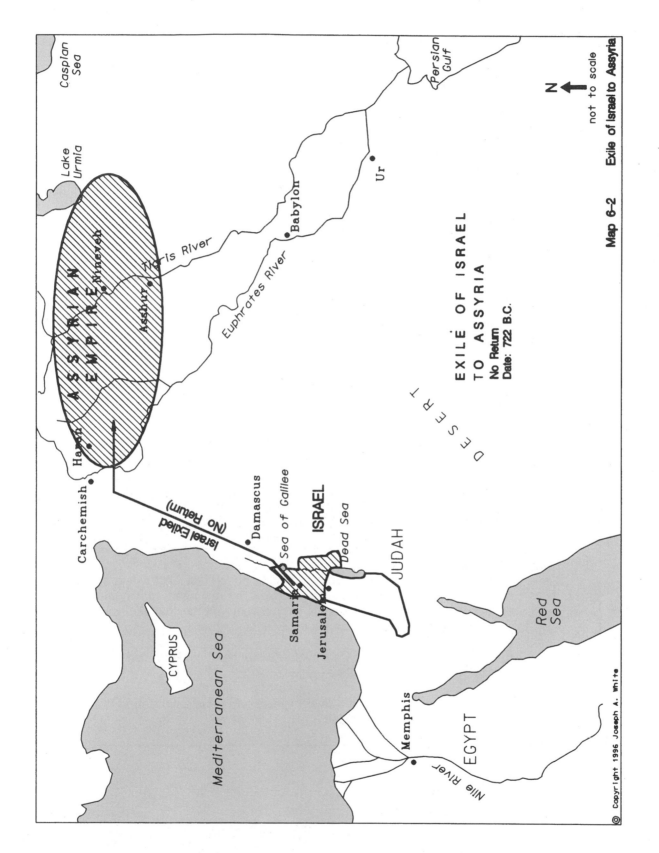

Map 6-2   Exile of Israel to Assyria

not to scale

EXILE OF ISRAEL TO ASSYRIA

No Return
Date: 722 B.C.

Table 6-5   Selected Chronological Events in the Remaining Kingdom of Judah

Date	Event
715 B.C.	**King Hezekiah** Ahaz's son, Hezekiah, was quite the opposite of his immoral father. He remodeled the temple and held the greatest Passover celebration since Solomon's reign. The Scripture refers to him as "Good King Hezekiah." He reigned during the last portion of Isaiah's ministry and was heavily influenced by the powerful prophet. During Hezekiah's reign, the mighty Assyrian army, led by King Sennacherib, invaded Judah and besieged Jerusalem. During this seemingly hopeless situation, King Hezekiah called upon God and followed the instructions of the prophet Isaiah. The Lord miraculously defeated the Assyrian army and saved Judah from destruction. When King Hezekiah was once at the point of death, he again called upon the Lord. Through the prophet, Isaiah, the Lord gave him a sign and assured him he would recover from his illness and live an additional 15 years. *Both of these events are so significant that they are found in II Kings, II Chronicles and Isaiah.*
695 B.C.	**Manasseh, the Most Evil King** Manasseh, the son of Hezekiah, succeeded him on the throne. However, Manasseh's reign had no similarity to that of his father. Manasseh was considered the most evil king in the history of Judah. He nullified the reforms made by his father and promoted the worship of pagan gods. He sacrificed his own son and actually built foreign altars in Solomon's Temple.
640 B.C.	**King Josiah** Josiah, the sixteenth ruler of Judah, maintained the last lengthy reign of the monarchs, 31 years. The Scriptures state that "his reign was right in the eyes of the Lord." He made repairs to the temple, renewed the covenant with God and made major religious changes throughout the nation. King Josiah celebrated the Passover in a manner in which it had not been carried out since the days of the judges. Josiah became king when he was eight years old. He is also referred to in the Scriptures as "Good King Josiah."

627 B.C.	**Jeremiah the Prophet** *"Before I formed you in the womb I knew you, before you were born I set you apart; I appointed you as a prophet to the nations."* *Jeremiah 1:5* Jeremiah is often called the "Weeping Prophet." Jeremiah was called by God to be a prophet in the last years of "Good King Josiah," and he enjoyed a good relationship with the king. Jeremiah continued to minister for 40 years; however, his relationships with the next four kings were not always cordial. Although Jeremiah was recognized as a prophet of God and his advice and counsel was often sought by the kings, his life was more than once in danger because his messages were stern, unaltered by politics and required radical change. He constantly advised that Babylon would conquer Judah and that Judah must turn away from its wickedness. Jeremiah recommended national surrender to Babylon. He called Nebuchadnezzar a "servant of God," predicted the 70 years of captivity and preached of restoration of the nation after the return from Babylon. During the fall of Jerusalem, Jeremiah was taken to Egypt against his wishes. Despite the turbulent and dark times in which Jeremiah ministered, he announced the good news of the coming new covenant: *"The time is coming," declares the Lord, "when I will make a new covenant with the house of Israel and with the house of Judah."* *Jeremiah 31:31* Jeremiah is one of the four major prophets.
605 B.C.	**The Battle of Carchemish** Carchemish was a major historic battle that marked the end of the Assyrian period and the beginning of Babylon's authority over all of western Asia. Egypt was defeated in this battle by the Babylonians as they tried to aid Assyria. Egypt's interest was to keep Assyria as a buffer state between their country and the aggressive Babylonians.
605 B.C.	**First Invasion of Jerusalem by Nebuchadnezzar** After the victory at Carchemish, King Nebuchadnezzar quickly invaded Jerusalem and set up an overlord system of government. He captured a selective group of Jews to take back to Babylon and also raided Solomon's Temple and took some of the vessels. This event marked the beginning of the 70-year Babylonian captivity.

"This whole country will become a desolate wasteland, and these nations will serve the king of Babylon seventy years."   Jeremiah 25:11

Map 6-3, Exile of Judah to Babylon, is located on the following page. It shows the southern kingdom of Judah, a possible exile route and a graphical representation of the center of the Babylonian Empire. Just as with Assyria, the borders of Babylon changed drastically over the long life of the empire.

Diagram 6-1, The Divided Kingdom, is located immediately after Map 6-3. This diagram provides a very basic graphical view of the divided kingdom.

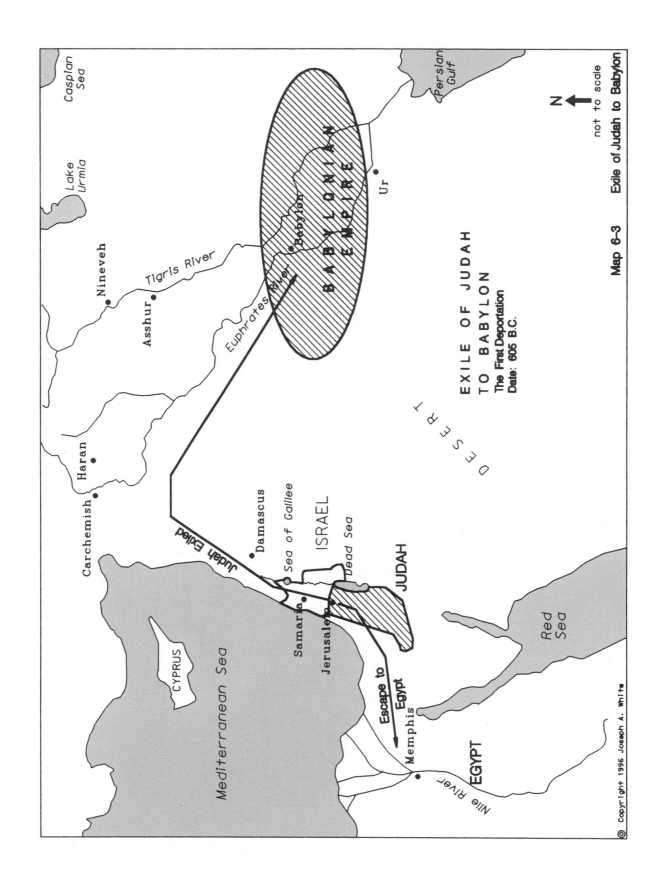

EXILE OF JUDAH
TO BABYLON
The First Deportation
Date: 605 B.C.

Map 6-3   Exile of Judah to Babylon

THE DIVIDED KINGDOM

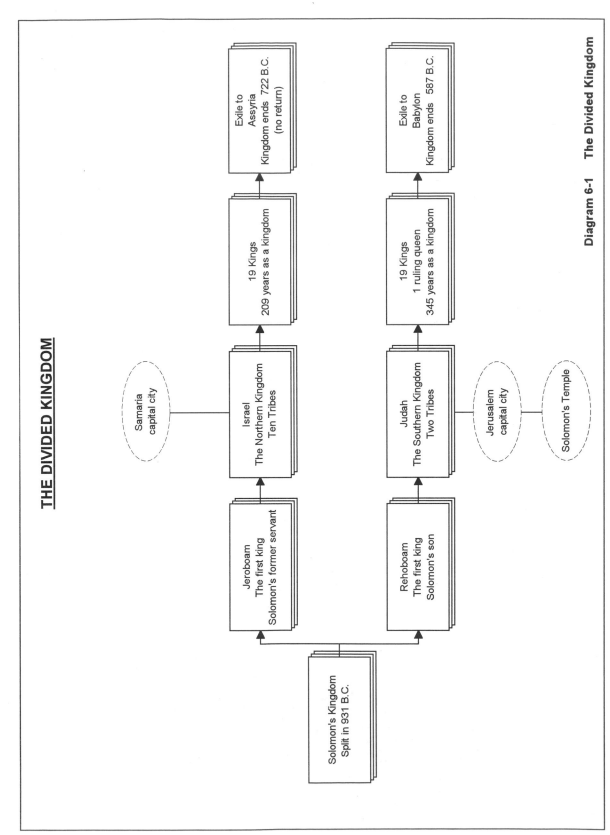

Solomon's Kingdom
Split in 931 B.C.

Jeroboam
The first king
Solomon's former servant

Israel
The Northern Kingdom
Ten Tribes

Samaria
capital city

19 Kings
209 years as a kingdom

Exile to
Assyria
Kingdom ends 722 B.C.
(no return)

Rehoboam
The first king
Solomon's son

Judah
The Southern Kingdom
Two Tribes

Jerusalem
capital city

Solomon's Temple

19 Kings
1 ruling queen
345 years as a kingdom

Exile to
Babylon
Kingdom ends 587 B.C.

Diagram 6-1   The Divided Kingdom

REVIEW EXERCISE
Chapter 6
LEADERSHIP OF ISRAEL

This is a simplified time block diagram of the leadership of Israel.

1. Place one name or phrase in each block.
2. Use each name or phrase only once.
3. Begin on the left and work to the right.
   (Genesis would be on the left)
4. Blocks are not to "actual" scale with respect to time.

King Saul
Kingdom of Israel
Exile in Babylon
Abraham
King David

King Solomon
Slavery in Egypt
Moses
Judah Restored
Jacob / (Israel)

Kingdom of Judah
Isaac
Joshua
Population Dispersed
Judges

Read The Book

1.   T / F   The primary purpose of the "Historical Books" of the Old Testament is to record exact chronological detail.

2.   After King Solomon's death, the kingdom was split between _____, the king's son and _____, an exiled servant of Solomon.

3.   The tribes of Judah and Benjamin followed the king's son and became known as the kingdom of _____ .

4.   The other 10 tribes were known as the kingdom of _____ .

5.   T / F   For approximately a 200-year period there is a simultaneous history of two nations contained in the pages of the Old Testament.

Using Table 6-1, Comparison of the Two Nations and Map 6-1, The Divided Kingdom, answer the next 4 questions:

6.   The capital of the southern kingdom of _____ was the city of _____ .
Hint - The two J's go together.

7.   The capital of the northern kingdom of _____ was the city of _____ .
Hint - I and S go together, the first letters in Israel.

8.   How long was Israel a separate independent nation? _____

9.   How long was Judah a separate independent nation? _____

10.   Prophets spoke, wrote and sometimes acted as directed by _____ .

11.   Prophets dealt more with the _____ time than they did with the future.

Using Table 6-2, Major and Minor Prophets, answer the next 2 questions:

12.   Name the three periods into which the work of the prophets can be divided:

_____   _____

_____

13.   T / F   The subject of the prophets or to whom they prophesied was strictly limited to Israel and Judah.

Using Table 6-3, Kings and Prophets of the Divided Kingdom, answer the next question:

14.   How many ruling queens are listed during the divided kingdom? _____

15.   Ahab is considered by scholars to be the most _____ king in Israel's history. His wife, Queen _____ , promoted the worship of Baal.

16.   Which prophet battled King Ahab and Queen Jezebel? _____

17.   T / F   Elijah was a writing prophet.

18.   Elijah is referred to a minimum of how many times in the New Testament?

_____

19.   T / F   Problems with political sovereignty could be seen over 100 years before the fall of Israel.

20.   _____ was chosen by God to be Elijah's successor. In the next 50 years he worked more recorded miracles than anyone in the Bible except _____.

21.   The people of Israel did not want to believe the message of the prophet Amos, which called for repentance or judgment, because the nation was in a state of material _____ .

22.   T / F   The prophet Hosea used the example of his wife to make an analogy about God and the people of Israel.

23.   Isaiah is often referred to as the "_____ Prophet."

24.   Which prophet is quoted more in the New Testament than all of the other prophets combined. _____

25.   In 722 B.C., the _____ nation conquered the kingdom of Israel.

26.   T / F   "Good King Hezekiah" was influenced by the prophet Isaiah.

27.   Jeremiah is often called the "_____ Prophet."

28.   Because Judah refused to turn away from its_____, Jeremiah warned that Babylon would conquer the nation.

29.   Jeremiah predicted the _____ years of _____ and preached of the restoration of the nation afterward.

30.   Whom did Jeremiah call a "servant of God"? _____

31.   In 605 B.C., Babylon gained power over all of western Asia and implemented what type of system in Judah? _____

Talk The Talk

When Solomon's kingdom was divided there was only one temple. This temple, the exclusive place of worship and sacrifice, was now part of the southern kingdom of Judah. Jeroboam, the new king of Israel, constructed two shrines to compete with Solomon's Temple and allowed people other than Levites to act as priests.

A.   *Under the given circumstances, were these actions proper?*

B.   *What type of precedents did these actions set for the future kings and the people?*

After the fall of the northern kingdom of Israel and its capital city, Samaria, the population was dispersed. Only the poor and uneducated of Israel were allowed to remain, and foreigners were brought in to repopulate the area. The result was a mixed culture and religion.

C.   *For decades the prophets had warned of the consequences of continued spiritual and moral decay. Who was primarily responsible for the deterioration of the nation of Israel?*

Judah's King Ahaz was so wicked that he burned some of his own children in child sacrifice. Ahaz' son, King Hezekiah, was such a religious king and excellent leader that he is called "Good King Hezekiah" in the Scripture. Hezekiah's son, King Manasseh, promoted pagan worship, nullified his father's reforms, sacrificed his own son and is considered the most evil king in Judah's history.

D.   *How can such an incredible contrast in father, son and grandson be possible?*

E.   *Isaiah's ministry spanned portions of the reigns of both Ahaz and Hezekiah. In what ways could Isaiah's influence have affected Ahaz and Hezekiah?*

Chapter 1 verse 5 of Jeremiah states that he was called to be a prophet before he was even born.

F.   *Does God still call people today? Can you share an example of someone being called by God?*

The prophet Amos pointed out that the country of Israel was in a state of material prosperity and yet moral poverty. The Jews believed strongly in the idea that if the nation as a whole obeyed and followed God, the nation as a whole would prosper.

G.   *How and for how long could such a state as Amos described exist?*

I.   *List examples of present-day material prosperity being accompanied by moral decay.*

H.   *Why was Amos' message rejected?*

Walk The Walk

We have learned that prophets spoke, wrote and sometimes physically demonstrated the messages that God directed them to convey. We have also learned that the vast majority of these messages dealt with the present spiritual situation, not the future.

I.   *After considering this new image of prophets, can you think of modern-day examples of prophets?*

J.   *Could a message from God come from someone or something else and be directed at you? If so how should you listen for it, identify it and respond to it?*

K.   *Have you had an experience in your life when you believe God was communicating a message to you? If so, did it involve someone or something other than yourself?*

Chapter 7
*Exile, Return, Rebuilding the Temple,
and Waiting for the Messiah*

During the exile and the post-exile periods there were many important occurrences with far-reaching effects on the future of Judaism. It is intuitive to speculate that these events were precipitated by the capture and exile itself.

Since the exodus some seven centuries earlier, the nation had experienced prosperity as well as oppression under a variety of leaders; however, they had managed to remain sovereign and, most importantly, their structure and method of worshiping God was always intact and available if they chose to use it.

The exiles now found themselves scattered in a foreign land, without a country, without a leader, without a temple, without a functioning priesthood and without a structured order of worship. Yet, there was an encouraging side to their situation. The Babylonians allowed the Jews a reasonable amount of freedom to live, work and worship. Babylon was known for its high degree of civilization and well-developed writing, which included libraries of law, science and math.

Considering these conditions, it is no wonder that the changes listed in the following table occurred during and immediately after the exile.

Table 7-1   Major Changes in Judaism During and After the Exile

Cause or Reason	Effect or Event
There was no homeland and little sense of social community	The people of Judah were first referred to as Jews while in Babylon. The name, Jew, was a common identifying bond.
There was a lack of a central religious community. There was no temple in which to worship or sacrifice.	Synagogues were first built and used as schools to teach theology and Scripture. They developed into centers for worship. *Synagogues could not be used for sacrificial worship.*

The oral tradition began to breakdown.	Prior to the exile, Scripture was seldom written down, but during the exile it was recorded in an effort to save the Hebrew stories, culture and holy teachings. The Torah was placed in its final form.
The written word took a greater place of importance.	The major importance of the Torah was established and the "Jews" became known as, "the People of the Book." The final editing of the "Historical Books" was completed and the "Wisdom Literature" was assembled.

Location of the People

The geographic trail of God's Chosen People started in the land of Ur (Mesopotamia), where God called Abraham to travel to the Promised Land. The patriarchal family later moved to Egypt to survive a famine. Four centuries later, they left Egypt and returned to the Promised Land where they remained until the exile. Due to the exile, the additional locations of Assyria, Babylon and Egypt became important.

The following table provides the geographic locations after the exile.

Table 7-2   Geographic Locations after the Deportations

Israel	After the deportation by the Assyrians, the remaining population of Israel was primarily poor uneducated farm people. The Assyrians then imported their own people and religious leaders. This was the beginning of a mixed population which eventually produced the Samaritan community.
Assyria	The exiles of Israel were transported to various countries held by the kingdom of Assyria. These exiles never returned. Very little is known of their location or life. They are sometimes referred to as "the lost tribes of Israel."
Judah	The country of Judah was not completely destroyed when it was captured. Jews that had fled before the actual deportations later returned. Rural farmers were left to work the land. Limited worship was sporadically carried on in the ruins of the temple.

Egypt	Many Jews fled to Egypt to escape the Babylonian siege despite the warning from Jeremiah not to make that choice. Jewish influence in Egypt was considerable. A strong Jewish community was established. Egypt is where the Septuagint was later produced.
Babylon	This country became the center of the Jewish life. The people farmed, became merchants and enjoyed a reasonable amount of religious and social freedom.

Chronology of the Events

The easiest way to understand the events of the exile and the return is to develop a simplified chronology. Many of the major events are established dates in history; however, some dates are attached to the reign of particular monarchs, some Jewish and some foreign. Also many of these rulers had more than one name and some of their children and grandchildren later reigned with the same name. There are also other reasons scholars debate over the exact time and physical location of some characters of this era.

Scriptural Location of the Information

The actual Scriptural location of information regarding the exile and post-exile periods is very scattered. This lesson is composed of information located in the following books of the Old Testament:

II Kings	Esther	Daniel	Zechariah
II Chronicles	Isaiah	Hosea	Malachi
Ezra	Jeremiah	Amos	
Nehemiah	Ezekiel	Haggai	

To avoid confusion, only a few actual Scriptural references will be given. Several of the dates and a small amount of the non-Biblical information comes from other accepted historical sources. An approximate time line of the major events composing the period of the exile and the return is presented in the following table.

Table 7-3   Time Line of the Exile and Return

Date	Event
605 B.C.	Babylon became the world power at the battle of Carchemish and immediately afterwards entered Jerusalem. Nebuchadnezzar set up an overlord system of government which forced Jewish King Jehoiakim to pay him tribute. Nebuchadnezzar also deported a small select group of Jews and removed a token amount of treasure from Solomon's Temple. This event marked the beginning of the 70-year Babylonian exile. *(For several years previous, Judah had been paying tribute to Egypt.)*
605 B.C.	**Daniel the Prophet in Babylon** Daniel was among the group taken to Babylon in Nebuchadnezzar's first invasion of Jerusalem. He was a youth at this time. Daniel was selected to live and continue his education in Nebuchadnezzar's palace. Daniel rose to high political positions and steadfastly demonstrated his faith in God while serving for approximately 70 years in most of the successive governments which ruled the area referred to as Babylon. Daniel is one of the four major prophets.
	The Book of Daniel The Book of Daniel contains both history of the exiled Jews during the Babylonian and Persian Empires and apocalyptic writings. Some of the best-known stories in the entire Bible are found in Daniel: 1. Daniel and the lion's den. 2. Daniel's three friends and the fiery furnace. 3. Daniel interprets God's handwriting on the wall.
597 B.C.	**The Second Invasion** Jewish King Jehoiakim rebelled against the overlord system. He died before Nebuchadnezzar arrived in Jerusalem. Jehoiakim's young son, Jehoichin, was king by the time Nebuchadnezzar invaded the city to put down the rebellion. Jerusalem was captured. The temple was severely plundered, but not destroyed. Nebuchadnezzar placed Zedekiah as a new king and deported the young king, the skilled laborers and the educated people to Babylon. II Kings states that 10,000 Jews were deported to Babylon at this time. This was the first major deportation. ** II Chronicles gives slightly different information regarding King Jehoiakim.*

Ezekiel the Prophet in Babylon

Ezekiel was a priest who was called by God to be a prophet. Most scholars feel he was taken from Jerusalem to Babylon in the deportation of 597 B.C. He settled in the country by the river Chebar.

For at least 20 years, he ministered to the exiles in Babylon and maintained correspondence with people remaining in Judah. He brought a message to the people that God was present with them in Babylon and that He was not confined to Jerusalem.

Ezekiel is considered by some scholars to be the country counterpart to Daniel, who was in the city. Many of Ezekiel's prophecies were in the form of visions. He worked to remind the exiles of the sins that had caused their present situation and reassured them of God's future blessings.

Ezekiel is one of the four major prophets.

The Book of Ezekiel

The Book of Ezekiel is broken into sections about the destruction, the enemies and the future of Judah. Unlike other Old Testament books, many sections begin with a date. The book contains prophecies, vivid visions, parables and actions which are symbolic.

Some of the notable happenings in the Book of Ezekiel are listed below.
1. Ezekiel uses the term "son of man" about 90 times. This was later one of Jesus' favorite terms for Himself.
2. Ezekiel was required to cook, drink, shave and prophesy in a specific posture in order to be symbolic about his messages.
3. The vision of the "valley of dry bones coming to life" is one of the most vivid in the Bible.

587 B.C.

The Kingdom of Judah Ends

In the ninth year of his reign, King Zedekiah rebelled against King Nebuchadnezzar. This led to the ultimate fall of the capital city of Jerusalem and the nation of Judah.

Nebuchadnezzar and his army returned for the third time and placed the city under siege. After 18 months the city fell, primarily due to starvation. Jerusalem was burned, the city walls were torn down and the temple was totally destroyed. King Zedekiah was blinded and he and the remainder of the educated and skilled people were led away into exile in the land of Babylon.

This was the second major deportation to Babylon. The kingdom of Judah finally ended after 345 years with 19 kings and one ruling queen.

"So Judah went into captivity, away from her land."
                                                        II Kings 25:21b

582 B.C.	**The Final Deportation to Babylon** A third small deportation was conducted, possibly as punishment for assassinating the puppet governor in Jerusalem placed there by the Babylonians.
538 B.C.	**Babylon Falls to Persia** The Book of Daniel provides a narrative account of the end of the Babylonian empire. Babylon was in danger of attack by Persia. In the king's extended absence, his reigning son, Belshazzar, gave a great feast. As the feast progressed, the royalty became very bold and drank from the holy cups taken from Solomon's temple. A strange hand appeared and wrote a message on the wall which no one could understand. Daniel was called to interpret the writing, which revealed that the kingdom would be taken over by the Persians. That night the Persian army captured the city; Belshazzar was killed and Babylon fell. Both Jeremiah and Isaiah had also prophesied the fall of Babylon. ** There is some disagreement among scholars concerning the exact names of the Babylonian and Persian rulers in this account. The word "father" in chapter 5 may have the broader meaning of "ancestor."*
538 B.C.	**The Decree of King Cyrus** Soon after coming to power in Babylon, the Persian king, Cyrus, gave a decree that the Jews could return home and rebuild God's temple. This decree fulfilled two major prophecies: 1. Jeremiah's prediction of the exile and its 70-year length is found in Jeremiah 25:11-12. 2. Isaiah's prediction specifically naming King Cyrus as God's shepherd who would cause Jerusalem to be rebuilt and the temple foundation to be laid is located in Isaiah chapters 44 & 45.
	The First Return From Exile Sheshbazzar, a prince of Judah, was chosen by Cyrus to lead the return. He was instructed to immediately start work on rebuilding the temple. Ezra recorded that 42,360 Jews and an additional 7,337 servants returned to Jerusalem. With them they brought approximately 17,300 pounds of gold and 6,250 pounds of silver. The gold and silver were comprised of donations given by the Gentiles in Babylon plus original temple articles, plundered by Nebuchadnezzar, and returned by King Cyrus.

Map 7-1, Return of Judah from Babylon, is located on the following page. The map shows a possible route of the return of the exiles. Also notice that the center of the Persia Empire is graphically represented around three of its major cities.

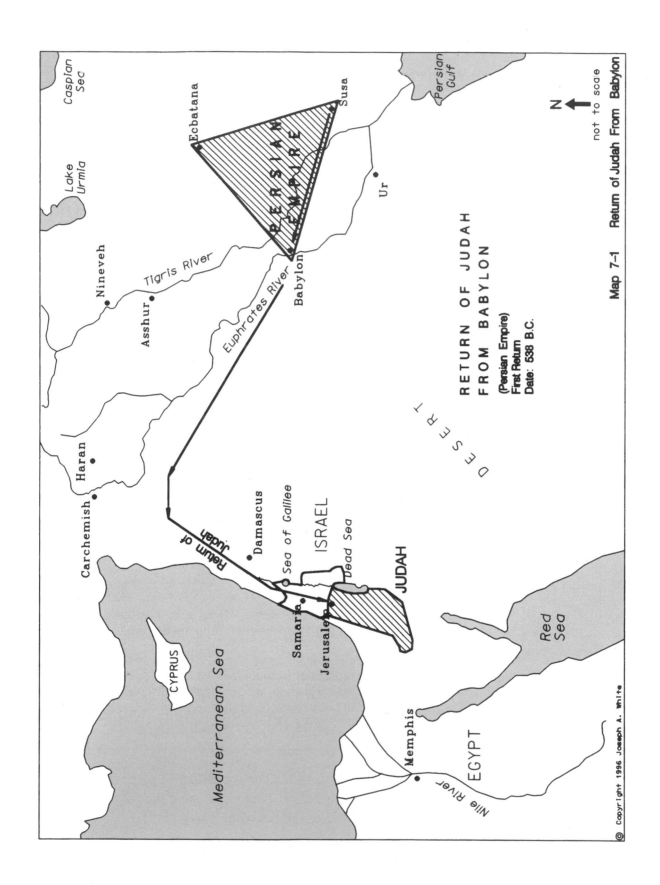

RETURN OF JUDAH FROM BABYLON

(Persian Empire)
First Return
Date: 538 B.C.

Map 7-1   Return of Judah From Babylon

© Copyright 1996 Joseph A. White

Travel to and from Babylon

The straight line distance from Jerusalem to Babylon can be measured on a map as about 550 miles. However, it is clear that the journey would be much longer if one traveled north around the desert. According to the exact route, estimates are around 900 miles.

We have no way of knowing what kind of traveling conditions the captives faced during the deportations or how long the journeys lasted. It is evident that most of the people were forced to walk and carry what few possessions they were allowed to take. This is a significant point because it is clear that the Jews took many of their writings and Scriptures with them. These would be in the form of scrolls which were large and heavy and would most likely be carried in place of their personal belongings.

During the returns, however, we do have more information regarding the travel. Chapter 7 of Ezra gives a length of four months for the journey from Babylon to Jerusalem during the return that he led. Unlike the deportations, this was a journey of choice under favorable conditions:

"For the gracious hand of his God was on him."   *Ezra 7:9b*

Table 7-3   (continued)

535 B.C.	**The Foundation of the Temple is Laid**
	The placement of the temple foundation in 535 B.C. marked the end of the 70-year captivity by Babylon. Nebuchadnezzar gained power in 605 B.C. He immediately deported small numbers of Jews, although the major deportations and the fall of Jerusalem was several years later.
	Ezra 3:8 names Zerubbabel as the leader of the work on the foundation of the temple, hence the common name, Zerubbabel's Temple. *(Sheshbazzar may have been a Babylonian name for Zerubbabel.)*
	The local people, many of whom were Samaritans, objected to the return of the exiles and the reconstruction of the temple. Due to their constant interference, very little work was completed after the foundation was laid.
522 B.C.	**Zerubbabel is appointed Governor of Judah**
	A new Persian king, Darius I, appointed Zerubbabel governor.* Two years later, Darius further aided the Jews by giving encouragement, political support and financial support for the completion of the temple.
	Haggai 1:1

520 B.C.	**Haggai and Zechariah** The two minor prophets, Haggai and Zechariah, encouraged the new governor of Judah and the people to resume construction on the temple. Later, Zerubbabel mysteriously disappeared. Writings in the Book of Haggai concerning the Messiah could have made the Persians think that Zerubbabel was the expected Messiah. *(Haggai 2:20-23)*
515 B.C.	**The Temple is Completed** In 515 B.C., under the reign of Persian King Darius I, the reconstruction of the temple was completed. This structure could in no way compare with the magnificent Solomon's Temple which it replaced; however, the Jews again had a central point of worship and a place in which to sacrifice. The temple was dedicated and the Passover celebrated.
	About the Temple This second temple was later profaned by the Greeks and rededicated by Judas Maccabeus in 164 B.C. *(Hanukkah honors this event.)* The same structure remained unchanged until Herod the Great came to power in 37 B.C. In order to please his Jewish subjects and improve the Roman image, Herod the Great expanded and remodeled the temple. This was the temple during Jesus' ministry and was sometimes referred to as Herod's Temple. This third structure was destroyed by the Romans in 70 A.D.

Diagram 7-1, The Exiles, is located on the following page. This diagram provides a graphical presentation of the major events during the exiles.

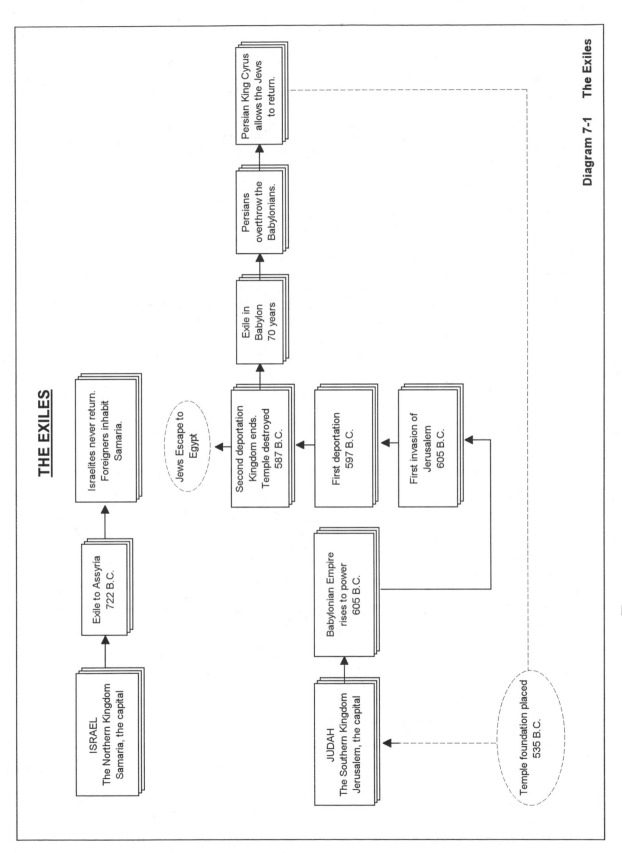

Diagram 7-1   The Exiles

Table 7-3   **(continued)**

475 B.C. (Approx.)	**Esther** Esther lived during the reign of the Persian king, Ahasuerus (Xerxes I, 486-464 B.C.). Esther, a Jewish orphan, became queen of a foreign nation and yet remained faithful to God. At the risk of her own life she saved the Jewish people from mass destruction. (The word God is not found in the Book of Esther.) *The Festival of Purim is observed to celebrate this event.*
458 B.C.	**Ezra** **(The Second Return From Exile)** Ezra was a Jewish priest and scribe who served under the Persian king, Artaxerxes. Ezra returned from Babylon, then under Persian rule, with 200 priests, an additional 1,500 men, a large amount of gold and silver and a letter from the Persian king which gave him great power and authority. He established "the Book of the Law of the Lord" and brought about great reforms and a revival in the Jewish community. One of the major problems that Ezra faced was that of Jews marrying foreign wives.
445 B.C.	**Nehemiah** **(The Third Return From Exile)** Nehemiah was a Jew who held the trusted position of cupbearer to the Persian king, Artaxerxes. The King obviously knew Nehemiah well and liked him. Nehemiah was unhappy because Jerusalem was in great disrepair and there were no plans to improve its condition. Nehemiah petitioned the king for help. He was appointed governor of Judah and allowed to return to Jerusalem for the purpose of rebuilding the city walls. With God's help and excellent planning, the city walls were rebuilt in 52 days despite strong local opposition. With Nehemiah as governor and Ezra as priest a great revival occurred. Ezra stood in a pulpit , publicly read the law and preached to the people. The people responded by making confessions and worshiping the Lord. Nehemiah returned to Artaxerxes' court after 12 years as governor in Judah.

After 432 B.C.	**Nehemiah's Second Trip to Jerusalem** Nehemiah made a second trip of undetermined length to Jerusalem and brought about major reforms. He cleansed the temple, restored the practice of tithing, corrected Sabbath wrongs and dealt with those who continued to marry foreigners.
	Malachi, the Last Prophet Malachi prophesied near the time of Nehemiah's second return. Much of the initial enthusiasm created by the rebuilding of the temple and the city walls was gone. Malachi was concerned with tithing, divorce and mixed marriages. Malachi rebuked the people for their failure to truly worship God and called them to repentance. Malachi plainly announced that Elijah the prophet (John the Baptist) would return before the coming of Christ.

"Behold, I am going to send you Elijah the prophet before the coming of the great and terrible day of the Lord."   Malachi 4:5

Read The Book

1.   For the first time in seven centuries, the people of Judah, exiled in Babylon, found themselves without five major things.   List these things.

_____   _____

_____   _____

_____

2.   Because the exiles were from the country of _____ , the people in Babylon referred to them as _____ .

3.   In Babylon, because there was no temple, _____ were first built and used as places of education and worship.

4.   T / F   During the exile, the Jews placed less importance on actually writing down Scripture.

5.   To what country did many Jews escape during the Babylonian siege of Judah?

_____

6.   The stories of the exile and post-exile periods are found in _____ books in the Old Testament. Are these books located consecutively in the Bible? _____

7.   After the Babylonians gained power, King Nebuchadnezzar soon invaded Jerusalem. This marked the _____ of the Babylonian Exile.

8.   Nebuchadnezzar deported a small select group of Jews to Babylon. A youth by the name of _____ was taken in this group.

9.   T / F   Daniel rose to high political positions in Babylon while remaining a
                 faithful Jew.

10.   Due to a rebellion in Jerusalem against the overlord system, Nebuchadnezzar
        severely _____ but did not destroy the temple.

11.   _____ , the prophet, lived in Babylon by the river Chebar.

12.   T / F   Some scholars consider Ezekiel to be the country counterpart to
                 Daniel, the prophet in the city.

13.   After another rebellion in Jerusalem, Nebuchadnezzar _____ the city,
        tore down the _____ and totally destroyed the _____ .

14.   As Babylon was about to fall to Persia, who was called to interpret a strange
        handwriting on the wall? _____

15.   Which Persian king gave the decree allowing the Jews to return to Judah and
        rebuild the temple? _____

16.   How many Jews, not including servants, returned from Babylon to Judah in
        the first return from the exile?_____

17.   The returning party brought with them several tons of gold and silver with
        which to finance the rebuilding of the temple. From what two sources did
        these items come?_____
        _____

Using Map 7-1, Return of Judah from Babylon, answer the next question:

18.   Ancient travelers journeying from Babylon to Judah would most likely go north around what major geographic obstacle? _____

19.   Approximately how far is the straight line distance between Babylon and Judah? _____

20.   Chapter 7 of Ezra states that one of the journeys from Babylon to Jerusalem was completed in _____ months.

21.   The beginning and the end of the 70-year exile was marked by two events. What were they and what were their respective dates?

Beginning: _____ B.C. _____

Ending : _____ B.C. _____

22.   Due to local opposition, construction on the temple soon ceased. A new Persian king named _____ further aided the Jews and encouraged construction efforts on the temple.

23.   During the same time period, the minor prophets _____ and _____ were also encouraging that construction resume.

24.   How many years elapsed between the foundation of the temple being laid and the completion of the temple? _____

25.   _____ was a young Jewish orphan girl who married the Persian King Ahasuerus (Xerxes I).

26.   As queen, she remained a faithful Jew and saved the Jewish people from mass
_____ .

27.   Both _____ and _____ were Jews in Babylon under the
reign of Persian King Artaxerxes.

28.   Ezra was a Jewish _____ and a _____ .

29.   Nehemiah was _____ to the Persian king.

30.   Nehemiah was appointed _____ of Judah. His initial objective
was to rebuild the city _____ .

31.   The final prophet of the Old Testament was _____ .

32.   In a time when much of the newly restored nation's enthusiasm was gone,
Malachi announced that _____ would precede the coming
of Christ.

Talk The Talk

It is evident that the exiles were allowed some degree of freedom after being settled in Babylon. However, it is also evident that their initial capture in Judah and the ensuing 900 mile trip was an act of war with little or no regard for human life.

A.   *How would you envision the exiles traveling and how many possessions would they be allowed to bring?*

B.   *The sacred writings and copies of the Law that existed at this time were on heavy scrolls. What kind of sacrifice do you suppose was made to bring these items along on the journey?*

For 700 years the Jewish nation had experienced God in very physical and tangible ways. A tabernacle, a temple, an ark, and a visible and active priesthood are just a few of the examples. Now, exiled far away in Babylon, the people surely felt all was lost. Everything tangible was gone.

C.   *List ways that you feel establishing synagogues and increasing religious writing would help reassure and comfort the exiles.*

At the end of the 70-year exile, the Hebrew people returned home. When they arrived at the city of Jerusalem they found the temple destroyed. The temple was the center of their spiritual and national identity.

D.   *Have you ever experienced the death of someone or destruction of something that helped mold or define your identity?*

Walk The Walk

The majority of the exiles were skilled and educated people. Once relocated in Babylon, they apparently were allowed to carry on with their occupations and seemed to adapt well to their new environment. The fact that Ezra reported over 7,000 servants accompanying the Jews in the first return substantiates this concept.

E.   *After almost 70 years in Babylon, what would the exiles now have to give up in order to return to Judah?*

F.   *Have you ever found yourself having to adapt to a new difficult existence? (i.e. moved to a residence which involved a different culture, country or language) Discuss ways in which you did or did not adapt to this "strange new world."*

G.   *Have you in the past or are you now being called by God to make significant changes in your life? How will you respond?*

NOTES

Chapter 8
Hebrew Poetry and Other Selected Books

HEBREW POETRY

Poetry has been called a song of the soul. The Hebrew poetry of the Old Testament certainly holds true to form. It is very deliberate and purposeful. The authors are expressing the innermost feelings of human relationships. Those relationships are with God, with other people, and with inner-self.

The message of Hebrew poetry is universal; however, the mechanics of the poetry is unique and very different from that of Western culture. Hebrew poetry does not have balanced patterns of lines, accented syllables or rhyme. Instead it is primarily rhymed in thought. If there is a rhythm to a particular piece, it is rhymed by accent and tonal stress on significant words.

In this type of poetry, there are two main techniques for conveying thought; parallelism and figures of speech. Parallelism is the act of stating an idea in the first line and then reinforcing it in the succeeding lines. This process creates two, four, six and sometimes up to eight lines echoing the same thought. However, the complementing lines can be used in a number of ways to reinforce the first; for example, they can complete the first thought, present similar ideas, contrast, or illustrate the initial thought.

The figure of speech technique is very straightforward. The Hebrew poets were masters at the use of the familiar metaphors, similes, rhetorical questions, and other literary devices which they used to create vivid visual images.

Poetical Books

The Poetical Books of the Bible are Job, Psalms, Proverbs, Ecclesiastes and Song of Solomon. Of the five books, only Job and Ecclesiastes contain a small amount of prose. The remainder are all poetry, although some portions of the poetry may not be readily apparent due to translation.

Psalms and Song of Solomon may be considered lyric or song-like poetry. Job, Proverbs and Ecclesiastes may be considered didactic or teaching poetry. The didactic poetry can be further grouped into poetry for instruction, such as Proverbs and Ecclesiastes, which are composed of short sayings or maxims, and Job, which tells a story in narrative form.

The Book of Psalms

The Book of Psalms is one of the best known and most widely used books in the Bible. It is comprised of 150 different psalms which were originally individual poems. King David is credited as author of 73 of these psalms, 50 have unknown authors, and the remaining are attributed to six additional authors.

The earliest known psalm was written by Moses. At least one psalm was written in Babylon during the exile. The majority were written during the time of David and Solomon. The actual Book of Psalms was assembled during and after the exile for use as a prayer and hymn book in the second temple.

The familiarity and use of the psalms is witnessed by the fact that there are 116 New Testament quotations from the psalms. The psalms can be broken into groups such as thanksgiving, lament, praise and many more; however, some of the best known are the Messianic psalms. Ten psalms are specifically considered in the Messianic group and over 20 passages from this group and other psalms make specific statements that refer to Christ. Several of these passages are listed in the table below.

Table 8-1   Selected Messianic Passages Found in Psalms

Partial Quotation or Subject	Psalms	New Testament*
"Even my close friend, in whom I trusted, Who ate my bread, Has lifted up his heel against me."	41:9	Luke 22:47
"They also gave me gall for my food, And for my thirst they gave me vinegar to drink."	69:21	Matthew 27:34, 48
"They divide my garments among them, And for my clothing they cast lots."	22:18	John 19:24
"They pierced my hands and my feet."	22:16b	John 19:34 John 20:27
"He keeps all of his bones; Not one of them is broken."	34:20	John 19:32-33
"For Thou wilt not abandon my soul to Sheol; Neither wilt Thou allow Thy Holy One to undergo decay."	16:10	Mark 16:6

Note: There are several additional New Testament verses that also fulfill these passages.

Table 8-2   General Themes of the Psalms

Theme	Psalm
Worship	15, 24, 50, 68, 81, 82, 115, 134
Personal Struggle and Conflict	3, 4, 5, 6, 7, 9, 10, 13, 14, 17, 22, 25, 26, 27, 28, 31, 35, 38, 39, 40, 41 , 42, 43, 51, 52, 53, 54, 55, 56, 57, 59, 61, 64, 69, 70, 71, 77, 86, 88, 89, 102, 109, 120, 130, 139, 141, 142, 143
Community Struggle and Conflict	12, 44, 58, 60, 74, 79, 80, 83, 85, 90, 94, 123, 126, 129, 137
Giving Thanks and Praise to God	8, 18, 19, 30, 32, 33, 34, 40, 65, 66, 67, 75, 92, 100, 103, 104, 107, 111, 113, 114, 116, 117, 118, 124, 136, 138, 145, 146, 147, 148, 149, 150
Wisdom	1, 19, 36, 37, 49, 73, 78, 112, 119, 127, 128
Trust	11, 16, 23, 27, 62, 63, 91, 121, 125, 131
Homeland	46, 48, 76, 84, 87, 122
Kingship of Israel	2, 18, 20, 21, 29, 45, 47, 72, 78, 89, 93, 95, 96, 97, 98, 99, 101, 110, 132, 144
*Psalms classified twice	18, 19, 27, 40, 78, 89
*Psalms not classified	105, 106, 108, 133, 135, 140

Some psalms are familiar enough to be mentioned by number. An example is the 23rd Psalm with its comforting words. Portions of other psalms that may be unrecognized by number are often quoted in songs and responsive readings used in church. One such example is frequently used to begin sermons:

"Let the words of my mouth and the meditation of my heart
Be acceptable in Thy Sight, O Lord, my rock and my Redeemer."

Psalms 19:14

The Song of Solomon

The Hebrew title taken from the first verse of the Song of Solomon is "Song of Songs," meaning the best or greatest of songs. Verse one also names Solomon as the author, although this phrase in Hebrew can also mean "for or about Solomon." The entire book is a detailed love story about King Solomon as he courts and eventually marries a young girl.

There are a number of ways to interpret the meaning of this beautiful story. Some scholars feel it is an historical record of the actual courtship and marriage of King Solomon. The Jewish tradition states that the story is an allegory which demonstrates God's love for his chosen people by using Solomon and the young lady as characters. Finally, the story can be viewed as a ideal love and marriage relationship and is simply a fitting example for all of God's people to follow.

Wisdom Literature

A portion of the Hebrew poetry can be further classified into what is commonly referred to as "wisdom literature." Job, Proverbs and Ecclesiastes are in this category. Wisdom and its pursuit are fundamental concerns of all humans regardless of culture, nation or race. However, for the ancient Jew and certainly for today's Christian, wisdom can be called the proper and godly application of knowledge.

One of the most notable differences between wisdom literature and the other books of the Old Testament is the absence of references to and constant reminders of Israel's unique history with God, the covenant relationship and the Law. Another obvious feature of wisdom literature is its focus on the individual instead of on the nation.

Wisdom literature can be placed into two distinct groups. The first group is concerned with searching for and reflecting upon the true meaning of life. The books of Job and Ecclesiastes are prime examples. The second group extends advice on how to live a godly and successful day-to-day life. The Book of Proverbs is clearly a work of art for this purpose.

The Book of Job

The Book of Job is the first book of wisdom literature. It has often been called a literary masterpiece. Job deals with the age old question of why the righteous suffer. The author and date of the events are unknown; however, the relevancy of the book is as fresh today as it was at the time of its writing.

Job was a very righteous and prosperous person who was most pleasing to God. He later lost his possessions, family and health. He ended up sitting on an ash heap at the edge of town. As one calamity after another fell upon Job, his learned friends gathered to submit their reasons for these misfortunes. None of their explanations for his suffering were adequate.

In the final chapters of the book, Job was awed when God entered the dialogue with question after question that mere man could not answer. Consequently, Job realized that the ways of God are above our understanding. Due to God's concern and generosity, Job was restored to health and happiness.

The Book of Ecclesiastes

The word "ecclesiastes" means teacher, preacher or one who convenes over or leads an assembly. The first and twelfth verses of the book state that King Solomon is the author. The book combines both poetry and narrative to deal with meaning and satisfaction in life.

The word "vanity" is used throughout the text and has a slightly different meaning than normal. The Hebrew word from which vanity is derived is either *"hevel,"* meaning breath or breeze, or "hebel," meaning vapor. In either case, the word "vanity" means temporary, to pass away, or not lasting. The wise author constantly shows that all of man's endeavors and accomplishments will indeed pass away and that one must fear God and keep God's commandments in order to enjoy life.

Table 8-3   Selected Verses from Ecclesiastes

Chapter & Verse	Scripture
1:2	"'Vanity of vanities,' says the Preacher, 'Vanity of vanities! All is vanity.'"

2:24	"There is nothing better for a man than to eat and drink and tell himself that his labor is good. This also I have seen, that it is from the hand of God."

3:1-8	"There is an appointed time for everything. And there is a time for every event under heaven-
	    A time to give birth, and
	    a time to die;... "
	(There are 13 more "a time to" couplets in this sequence.)

3:12-13	"I know that there is nothing better for them than to rejoice and to do good in one's lifetime; moreover, that every man who eats and drinks sees good in all his labor - it is the gift of God."
4:9,12	"Two are better than one because they have a good return for their labor." "And if one can overpower him who is alone, two can resist him. A cord of three strands is not quickly torn apart."
4:13	"A poor, yet wise lad is better than an old and foolish king who no longer knows how to receive instruction."
7:1a	"A good name is better than a good ointment."
10:1	"Dead flies make a perfumer's oil stink, so a little foolishness is weightier than wisdom and honor."
10:10a	"If the ax is dull and he does not sharpen its edge, then he must exert strength."
10:20	"Furthermore, in your bed-chamber do not curse a king, and in your sleeping rooms do not curse a rich man, for a bird of the heavens will carry the sound, and the winged creature will make the matter known."
11:1-2	"Cast your bread on the surface of the waters, for you will find it after many days. Divide your portion to seven, or even to eight, for you do not know what misfortune may occur on the earth."
12:1	"Remember also your Creator in the days of your youth, before the evil days come and the years draw near when you will say, 'I have no delight in them.'"
12:13-14	"The conclusion, when all has been heard, is: fear God and keep His commandments, because this applies to every person. For God will bring every act to judgment, everything which is hidden, whether it is good or evil."

The Book of Proverbs

The Book of Proverbs is comprised of several collections of wise sayings and general instructions for life. King Solomon, the wisest person who ever lived *(I Kings 3:12)*, is the author of the largest group of proverbs. In the first chapter, the purpose of the Book of Proverbs is clearly pointed out, namely, that the readers might know wisdom and use that wisdom to guide them in a godly life.

Verse seven of the first chapter is sometimes considered the theme or the perspective for understanding all of the proverbs. The verse states plainly, ***"The fear of the Lord is the beginning of knowledge."*** The "fear of the Lord" is a reverence and respect for God and an understanding that we must be obedient to His will. The proverbs explain that wisdom is obtained from God through a right relationship with Him and that, without wisdom, knowledge will not be properly used.

The proverbs deal with every aspect of living. A few of the best known proverbs are listed below.

Table 8-4   Selected Proverbs

Chapter and Verse	Key Portion of the Proverb
1:7	"The fear of the Lord is the beginning of knowledge; Fools despise wisdom and instruction."
2:6	"For the Lord gives wisdom; From His mouth comes knowledge and understanding."
3:5	"Trust in the Lord with all of your heart, And do not lean on your own understanding."
3:9	"Honor the Lord from your wealth, And from the first of all you produce."
5:18b	"Rejoice in the wife of your youth."
6:16	"There are six things which the Lord hates, Yes, seven which are an abomination to Him: ... " *(Verses 17-19 list these items.)*

6:20	"My son, observe the commandment of your father, And do not forsake the teaching of your mother."
10:2	"Ill-gotten gains do not profit, But righteousness delivers from death."
11:1	"A false balance is an abomination to the Lord, But a just weight is His delight."
14:1	"The wise woman builds her house, But the foolish tears it down with her own hands."
15:1	"A gentle answer turns away wrath, But a harsh word stirs up anger."
15:16	"Better is a little with the fear of the Lord, Than great treasure and turmoil with it."
16:3	"Commit your works to the Lord, And your plans will be established."
18:24b	"But there is a friend who sticks closer than a brother."
19:14	"House and wealth are an inheritance from fathers, But a prudent wife is from the Lord."
20:1	"Wine is a mocker, strong drink a brawler, And whoever is intoxicated by it is not wise."
22:6	"Train up a child in the way he should go, Even when he is old he will not depart from it."
23:7a	"For as he thinks within himself, so he is."
23:13a	"Do not hold back discipline from the child."
24:3	"By wisdom a house is built, And by understanding it is established."

24:33-34	"'A little sleep, a little slumber, a little folding of the hands to rest,' Then your poverty will come as a robber, And your want like an armed man."
25:11	"Like apples of gold in settings of silver Is a word spoken in right circumstances."
25:17	"Let your foot rarely be in your neighbor's house, Lest he become weary of you and hate you."
26:17	"Like one who takes a dog by the ears Is he who passes by and meddles with strife not belonging to him."
26:27a	"He who digs a pit will fall into it."
27:1	"Do not boast about tomorrow, For you do not know what a day may bring forth."
27:2	"Let another praise you, and not your own mouth; A stranger, and not your own lips."
27:17	"Iron sharpens iron, so one man sharpens another."

OTHER SELECTED BOOKS

The Book of Jonah

Jonah, one of the 12 minor prophets, is one of the most recognized names in the Bible because of the children's story of Jonah and the whale. Jonah is actually swallowed by a great fish, and this incident is only a small fraction of this powerful and lesson-filled book. Unlike many of the prophetic books, Jonah is a simple narrative in chronological order which is sheer reading and studying pleasure.

The main theme of Jonah is that God cares for the people of the entire world and reaches out to all. This was clearly demonstrated when God called the prophet Jonah to preach to the city of Nineveh, the capital of the feared Assyrian nation. God's concern is further evidenced throughout the story by a number of miracles and events.

There are also additional themes and lessons in the book. When one closely examines Jonah, it can be seen that extreme righteousness can lead to prejudice. Other characters in the book sometimes demonstrate more compassion than God's chosen, and foreigners sometimes repent and do God's will more freely than Jonah.

The Book of Ruth

Ruth is classified as one of the Historical Books of the Old Testament. The book is very short in length and tells a complete story in itself without requiring information from other books of the Bible. The time period is during the turbulent years of the judges when many of God's people had fallen away and become unfaithful.

Ruth is an inspiring story of a foreign girl who married into a Jewish family and, after the death of her husband, continued to stay with her mother-in-law Naomi and worship God. The story demonstrates that God cares for everyone.

Ruth's faithfulness was rewarded. The genealogy of Christ found in Matthew lists Ruth as the grandmother of King David and consequently as a direct ancestor of Christ. Certainly, the best known verse in the Book of Ruth is when she addresses Naomi and makes her choice to worship God.

But Ruth said, "Do not urge me to leave you or turn back from following you; for where you go, I will go, and where you lodge, I will lodge. Your people shall be my people, and your God, my God."

Ruth 1:16

Read The Book

1.   Hebrew Poetry is very different from the poetry to which most Westerners are accustomed. Hebrew Poetry is primarily rhymed _____ _____ .

2.   The two main ways of conveying thought in Hebrew poetry are _____ and figures of _____ .

3.   List the Poetical Books of the Bible:_____ _____

_____ _____ _____

4.   The Book of _____ was assembled as a prayer and hymn book after the exile for use in the second _____ .

5.   There are 50 psalms with unknown authors. Of the seven known contributing authors, _____ wrote the greatest number.

6.   There are _____ New Testament quotations from the Book of Psalms.

Using Table 8-1, Selected Messianic Passages Found in Psalms, answer the next 2 questions about the Messiah:

7.   What did they give me for my thirst? _____

8.   How many of His bones were broken? _____

9.   In Hebrew Poetry, the classification of the Book of Job is commonly referred to as _____ _____ .

10.   Job deals with what age old question?

_____

11.   T / F   The word "ecclesiastes" means teacher, preacher or one who convenes over or leads an assembly.

12.   The Book of Ecclesiastes deals with the meaning and satisfaction of life. The book states that the author is _____ _____ .

Using Table 8-3, Selected Verses from Ecclesiastes, answer the next 3 questions about Ecclesiastes:

13.   There is an appointed time for _____ .

14.   What is better than good ointment? _____

15.   You should remember your Creator in what days? _____

16.   The Book of Proverbs is composed of _____ _____ and general _____ _____ _____ .

17.   T / F   Proverbs states: "Fear of the Lord is the beginning of knowledge."

18.   _____ is obtained from God through a right relationship with Him.

Using Table 8-4, Selected Proverbs, answer the next 4 questions about Proverbs:

19.   From what part of your produce should you honor the Lord?_____

20.   A prudent wife is from the _____ .

21.   By what two things is a house built and established?

       _____   _____

22.   Why do you not boast about tomorrow?

       _____   _____

23.   The Bible character, Jonah, is most often associated with what creature?

       _____

24.   T / F   Jonah is a simple narrative in chronological order.

25.   Ruth is a _____ girl who married a Jew.

26.   The story of Ruth demonstrates that God cares for _____ .

27.   Ruth is listed in the genealogy of _____ as the grandmother of King David.

Talk The Talk

Psalms was the hymn and praise book of the Jewish people. This tradition follows into Christianity also.

A.   *Which psalms or portions of psalms are most familiar or meaningful to you?*

B.   *Why?*

The Book of Job has often been called a literary masterpiece. It raises the issue of the nature of human suffering.

C.   *Discuss your thoughts about why righteous, faithful, good people suffer.*

D.   *Can you recall a time when you personally struggled with the question of "why" there is suffering in our world? What was the conflict or event surrounding your struggle with this issue?*

The Book of Jonah demonstrates that God cares for all of the peoples of the world and reaches out to them. The actions of God's messenger also demonstrate that extreme righteousness leads to prejudice. Jonah wanted to see himself proved right, even at the expense of a large population being destroyed.

E.   *When have you experienced a joyful feeling at the expense of others?*

F.   *Has righteousness ever led you to prejudice?*

Walk The Walk

Read Proverbs 1:7.   This verse is sometimes considered the perspective for understanding all of the proverbs. In modern times, the concept of "fearing the Lord" is often met with a rebuttal of "God is a God of love and understanding and is not to be feared." The Bible is explicit that there are consequences for our actions, some of which are to be feared.

G.   *Using the definition of fear as "a reverence, respect and understanding that we must be obedient to God's will," how can you mesh the concepts of fearing the Lord and a God of love?*

H.   *How will your relationship with God change?*

Chapter 9
Time Between the Testaments
and
Introduction to the New Testament

TIME BETWEEN THE TESTAMENTS

The interval between the final prophet, Malachi, and the birth of Christ is called the intertestamental period. This four-century time period is also often referred to as the "silent years." Although there was not a writing prophet during this period, much literature was composed and many events transpired which helped form the Jewish way of thinking. Central to this thinking was the expectation of the coming Messiah and the rising of the Jewish nation once again to a place of world prominence.

Political Periods

The complete history of this time period is quite complicated; however, a very basic understanding can be gained by breaking the time into four major periods. Each of these periods can be defined by the power that governed Judah and the adjacent nations.

I. Completion of the Persian Period   (432-331 B.C.)

Persian rule began in 538 B.C. when King Cyrus of Persia defeated the Babylonian Empire and gave the great decree that allowed the Jews to return to their homeland, where they rebuilt the temple and ultimately the city of Jerusalem. The writings of the Old Testament ended with Nehemiah's second trip from Persia (Babylon) to Judah and the work of the final prophet, Malachi. Persian rule continued for approximately 100 years after these events.

For the most part, the Persian rulers allowed the Jews to practice their religion without intervention and the time was basically peaceful. However, during this period Judah was ruled internally by the high priest. This practice changed the priesthood to more of a political office and less of a religious duty or calling.

II. Greek Period (331-167 B.C.)

In 336 B.C., at the age of 20, Alexander the Great took command of the Greek army. By 331 B.C., he gained full control over the Persian Empire and basically ruled the entire world. Alexander did three things which had far reaching effects on the lands which he conquered. First, he introduced Greek ideas and culture into the new territories. Second, he built new Greek cities and colonies. Third, he spread the Greek language until it became the universal language for several centuries to follow. These steps together form the process of Hellenization.

Alexander did not seek to make the Jews change their religion. In fact, he granted them exemption from some tribute and actually encouraged them to settle in Alexandria, the Egyptian city which he built.

Alexander died in 323 B.C., and his empire was divided among five of his generals. Judah and adjacent areas, collectively referred to as Palestine, were a point of contention for the generals who ruled Egypt and Babylonia. Both generals and their successors wanted to control this area, which was a crossroads for trade and travel. During the majority of this time, the Jews continued to enjoy a somewhat peaceful existence despite the contention. Synagogues were built in Jewish settlements in Egypt, and the city of Alexandria became an influential center for Judaism. Also during this time period, the Septuagint, the Greek translation of the Scriptures, was made in Alexandria at the request of the ruler of Egypt, Ptolemy II (Philadelphus), son of one of the Greek generals under Alexander.

In 190 B.C., wars and politics in other parts of the Greek empire caused the Jews to be taxed heavily and to be required to more fully accept Hellenization. By 175 B.C., the situation had deteriorated even more. The Jews had themselves split into two groups. One encouraged Hellenization and the other remained orthodox. Antiochus IV, the new Greek ruler, sided with the Jews who chose to Hellenize. He became violently bitter toward the orthodox Jews, and sought to exterminate them and their religion.

In 168 B.C., Antiochus declared Judaism illegal, marched on Jerusalem and allowed his troops to kill many Jews. He sought to burn all of the copies of the Law and made possession of a copy a capital offense. Circumcision was forbidden; the Sabbath was not to be observed, and the temple was plundered. Antiochus was so bitter and determined to destroy Judaism that he sacrificed swine on the altar of the temple.

III. The Period of Jewish Independence   (167-63 B.C.)

Resistance to the harsh Greek rule was passive for only a short period of time. In 167 B.C., the Greeks required the Jews to offer sacrifices to pagan gods. In a supervised ceremony, an aged Jewish priest named Mattathias not only refused to offer the sacrifice, he killed the presiding Greek officer as well as a young Jew who collaborated with the Greeks by volunteering to offer the sacrifice. This action started a full scale rebellion. Mattathias and his sons fled to the hills and organized the orthodox Jews. After Mattathias' death, his son Judas, who was nicknamed Maccabeus, led the guerrilla war. After three years the Maccabees gained control of Jerusalem, forced a treaty, and cleansed and rededicated the temple. *(This is the reason for the festival of Hanukkah.)*

Judas Maccabeus brought the priests and civil authorities together and set the stage for a 100-year line of priest-rulers. Although the nation was once again independent, it was in a constant state of internal turmoil.

IV. The Roman Period   (63 B.C. - New Testament)

In 63 B.C., Palestine was conquered by the Romans under the leadership of Pompey. Under Roman rule the Jews were allowed to continue their religious practices; however, they were forced to pay heavy taxes.

For 33 years of this period, Herod, known as Herod the Great, was the puppet ruler for Rome. Herod did try to keep peace in the kingdom by lowering some taxation for the Jews and remodeling the temple. Still, Herod is known as one of the cruelest rulers of all time. Jews despised him for his continual efforts to Hellenize the country. Herod died soon after the time of Jesus' birth, but Roman rule continued into the period of Jesus' ministry and the Herodian family of rulers remained in power throughout the New Testament.

Diagram 9-1, Political Powers Between the Testaments, is located on the following page. It provides a simplified graphical view of the political powers during the intertestamental period.

POLITICAL POWERS BETWEEN THE TESTAMENTS

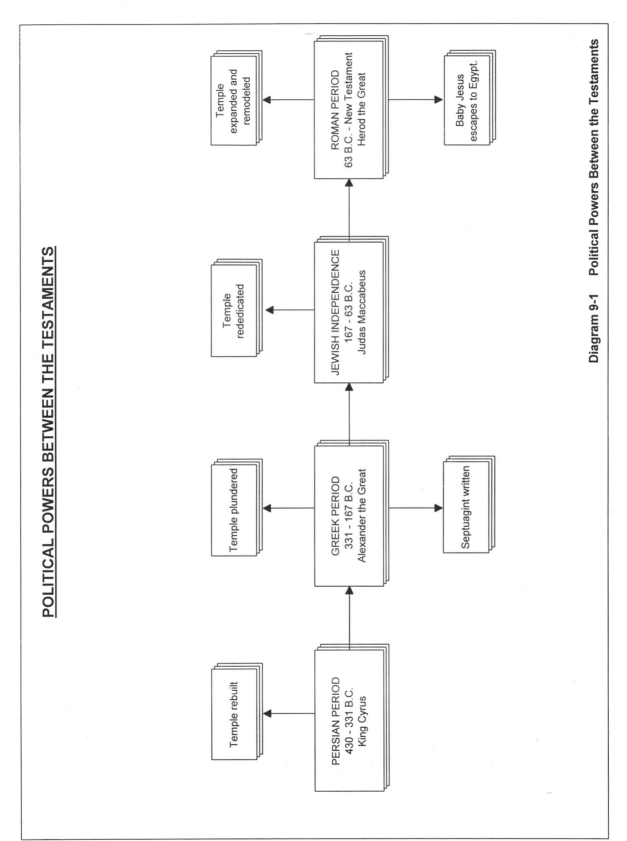

Diagram 9-1   Political Powers Between the Testaments

Jewish Religious Groups

As a direct result of Alexander the Great and his effective program to Hellenize the world, the thinking of the Near East was permanently changed. The Jews themselves were split between newer ideas brought by the Greek influence and the orthodox practices and thinking of their ancestors. This clash gave rise to a number of Jewish sects or groups, which had a major impact on the religious practices in the time of the New Testament. The six most familiar and significant sects or groups are listed in the following table.

Table 9-1   Jewish Religious and Political Groups

Group	Description
Essenes	The Essenes are not specifically mentioned in the Bible, but this group had significant impact on Judaism as indicated in the Dead Sea Scrolls and other historical documents. Like the Pharisees, the Essenes were opposed to Hellenistic changes; however, they totally withdrew from society. They felt that they were the true Israelites. They believed the Messiah would come to them.
Herodians	Herodians were more of a political party than a religious sect. Their name was taken from Herod the Great, and they felt that the best interest of the Jews would be served by cooperating with the Roman government.
Pharisees	Pharisees descended from the orthodox group that fought Hellenism. They believed in the doctrine of resurrection. In addition to believing in the Law of Moses, they also accepted the prophetic writings and oral traditions. The term "Pharisees" may have derived from a Hebrew word meaning "separatist." The Pharisees were very powerful in matters of Jewish law and religious practices.
Sadducees	The Sadducees denied the authority of tradition and believed only in the Law of Moses, the first five books of the Old Testament. They did not believe in the doctrines of resurrection, angels or spirits. Sadducees were normally wealthy people who held important positions and accepted Hellenism.
Scribes	The Scribes were more of a profession than a sect. They copied the Law and consequently became experts in matters of the Law. They taught the Law and were often in agreement with the Pharisees in opposing Jesus.
Zealots	The Zealots were a small political group of the Jewish population that wanted to overthrow any oppressing foreign government, especially the Romans in Palestine.

Writings During the Intertestamental Period

The Jews produced a great deal of very important written information during the intertestamental time period. These writings can be broken into major groups as listed in the following table.

Table 9-2   Intertestamental Writings

Writing	Description
Apocrypha	Apocrypha means "things which are hidden" and is composed of 15 books written by the Jews between the Old and New Testaments. The writings have never been considered part of the Hebrew Scripture. They were ultimately preserved by Christians, not by the Jews. The Apocrypha contains historical, wisdom, devotional and apocalyptic literature.
Pseudepigrapha	The Pseudepigrapha is a collection of 52 writings in two volumes. The content includes wisdom, apocalyptic and devotional literature.
Qumran Scrolls (Dead Sea Scrolls)	Near the end of 1946 a shepherd discovered a number of clay jars in a cave located approximately one mile from the Dead Sea. The jars contained well-preserved scrolls of leather, papyrus and parchment. In the following years, scrolls were discovered in at least 11 caves in the area. The discovery included the oldest known Old Testament manuscripts, non-Biblical Jewish writings, and writings from the group of Qumran Jews who lived there from about 130 B.C. to 70 A.D. Most scholars agree that the monastery at Qumran near the caves was the center for the Essenes.
Septuagint	The Greek ruler of Egypt, Ptolemy II (Philadelphus), requested that the Jews in Alexandria make a Greek translation of the Hebrew Scriptures. Tradition says that 72 Jewish scholars made the first translation in 70 days, hence the name Septuagint, from the Latin word "Septuaginta" for 70. The common abbreviation for Septuagint is simply LXX. The Septuagint was in common use in New Testament times.

THE NEW TESTAMENT

It is appropriate to again review and reflect upon the definition of testament:

Testament is another word for covenant. The definition of a covenant is a pact, treaty, alliance, or agreement between two parties of equal or unequal authority. The covenant can either be accepted or rejected, but it cannot be changed.

The Old Testament hinged upon God's dealings with his people and their acceptance and obedience to the covenant given through Moses on Mt. Sinai.

After a 2,000 year history of calling to and leading His chosen people, God sent His son, Jesus Christ, the long awaited Messiah, to extend the New Covenant to all nations. The New Covenant or Testament asserts a personal relationship between God and all humanity through Jesus Christ. **Plainly stated, God's free gift of grace and salvation is offered to all who accept Jesus Christ as the Son of God and believe.**

Table 9-3   Structure of the New Testament

Number of Books	27
Attributed Number of Authors	8, possibly 9
Approximate Number of Old Testament Quotes	There are 250 to 300 direct quotations. The total number, including indirect or partial quotations ,is more than 1,000.
Time Span of Writing	50 years *(roughly 50 to 100 A.D.)*

The 27 books of the New Testament fall into four natural divisions, as shown in the following table.

Table 9-4   Division of the New Testament Books

The Gospels	The Gospels provide four separate descriptions of the life and ministry of Jesus Christ.
The Book of Acts	The Book of Acts traces the beginnings of the church and the spread of Christianity.
The Letters	The 21 Letters, or Epistles, are addressed to both churches and individuals. These Letters provide instruction and teach Christian doctrine.
The Revelation of John	The Revelation of John is a visionary book written in apocalyptic literature style that describes the ultimate triumph of Jesus Christ.

Authorship

Traditionally, the 27 books of the New Testament are attributed to eight or possibly nine authors. The Books of Luke and Acts comprise the largest amount of pages by a single author, whereas the 13 letters of Paul, are the greatest number of books attributed to a single author.

By the second century A.D., a significant debate had surfaced among scholars concerning the exact identity of several of the authors of the New Testament books. These arguments have continued throughout the centuries and are still significant and sometimes emotional issues for modern day Bible scholars.

The arguments stem from obvious differences in writing style, vocabulary, language, and content. The custom of pseudonymous authorship was also widespread and accepted in ancient days. This was the practice of signing the name of a well-known teacher or mentor to work that was actually done by a follower or student. The authorships most often debated center around the writings of Paul, Peter and John.

It is neither the intent nor within the scope of this course to address such scholarly issues that have remained unresolved for centuries. This type of issue in no way lessens the importance or value of the writings and is best left to scholars for debate. In this study the traditional attributed author of each book will be cited.

Time of Writing

Unlike the books of the Old Testament, which were written over a span of many centuries, the New Testament books were completed in a short period of time, probably between 50 A.D. and 100 A.D. The subject matter of the books addressed current issues about Jesus, how He lived and taught, and how His followers must now conduct their lives. These issues were so paramount and so much a part of current daily life that little thought must have been given to the history which was being made.

The Gospel of Luke and the Book of Acts are practically the only books that are purposeful about providing dates and history of the type the modern reader is accustomed to seeing. Most of the New Testament books were not dated; consequently, there is considerable debate among scholars as to the order in which many of the books were written. However, for all but the most in-depth Bible study, the time of writing is simply a matter of general interest.

Political Structure and Chronology of the New Testament Period

The political structure of the New Testament period is not simple. Clearly the Roman Empire ruled the world, and the current Roman emperor or Caesar was ultimately in charge; however, kings were often placed to rule over certain areas within the empire. In turn governors, sometimes called prefects or procurators, were placed in charge of smaller areas within the king's domain. Many times, as can be evidenced in the gospels, it appears that there was not a clear power structure or chain of command under this system.

To provide an overview of the period, a table is presented which includes some of the various political leaders of the times as well as major events. Also included are several of the New Testament books which have more firmly established dates.

Table 9-5   Chronology and Selected Events in the New Testament Period

Date	Roman Emperors	Herods (Kings & Rulers)	Selected Governors of Judea	Selected Events	Selected New Testament Books
B.C.					
10	Augustus ↑	Herod the Great ↑			
- 0 -		Archelaus		Birth of Jesus	
10	Tiberius	Philip			
20		Herod Antipas	Pontius Pilate	Preaching of John the Baptist	
30	Gaius Caligula			Ministry of Jesus Crucifixion and Resurrection	
40	Claudius	Herod Agrippa I		Conversion of Paul Paul's First Journey	
50	Nero	Herod Agrippa II	Felix	Paul's Second Journey Paul's Third Journey	I & II Thessalonians I & II Corinthians
60	Galba, Otho Vitellius, Vespasian		Festus	Paul's trip to Rome	Romans Prison Letters Mark
70				Jerusalem and the Temple Destroyed	
80	Titus Domitian				Matthew Luke & Acts
90	Nerva				John
100	Trajan				
A.D.					

In the table below, the books of the New Testament are listed in the order in which they appear in the Bible. Their traditional author and the audience to whom they were generally addressed is listed. A brief summary statement of the main subject or thought of the book is also included. Please remember this table is very condensed and a broad range of views concerning these topics exists.

Table 9-6   Basic Information on the Books of the New Testament

Book	Traditional Authorship	Addressee	Main Subject or Thought
Matthew	Matthew	Jewish reader	Matthew is first of the synoptics and is the second longest of the four gospels. It contains 128 Old Testament references and clearly relates to the Jewish reader that Jesus is the long awaited Messiah.
Mark	John Mark	Christians familiar with Greek	Mark is the second of the synoptics and the shortest of the four gospels. Most scholars believe it was the first gospel written. Mark omits many of the details which would be of interest to Jews and moves rapidly into the death and resurrection of Jesus.
Luke	Luke	Gentiles	Luke is the third of the synoptics and is the longest and most detailed of the four gospels. Luke carefully covers the entire life and ministry of Jesus and presents Jesus as the Savior of all people.
John	John	Christians	John is constructed around seven individual miracles with a long discourse concerning each event. Almost one half of John is devoted to the final week of Jesus' life. With the use of the "I am" statements, John stresses that Jesus, the Messiah, is the Son of God and actually God Himself.

Acts	Luke	Gentiles	The Book of Acts chronicles the 30 year history of the spread of Christianity. Acts begins with the ascension of Christ and ends with Paul's journey to Rome, the capital of the world.
Romans	Paul	Christians in Rome	Romans is a formal letter which sets forth Christian doctrine. It is very theological and discusses such subjects as salvation, justification by faith, service, sin and spiritual gifts.
I Corinthians	Paul	Christians in Corinth	First Corinthians is a very practical letter which deals with spiritual and moral problems faced by a congregation of new believers still living in a very corrupt and pagan environment.
II Corinthians	Paul	Christians in Corinth	Second Corinthians was written to express joy and confidence in the Corinthians after Paul received favorable reports that they had come through a time of crisis. He also discussed finances and defended his own authority in the letter.
Galatians	Paul	Christians in a five city region in Asia Minor	The letter to the Galatians was sent to resolve the conflict over whether or not Gentiles must first become Jews before they become Christians. The doctrine of justification by faith, not by human effort, is also strongly presented.
Ephesians	Paul*	Area around Ephesus	Ephesians is a theological letter intended to be circulated to several churches as a doctrinal statement. Major topics include Christ as the head of the Church and the Church as the building and temple of God.
Philippians	Paul	Church at Philippi	Philippians is Paul's most cordial letter written to a church. This letter is very uplifting and full of joy, despite the fact that Paul is in prison.

Book	Author	Recipient	Description
Colossians	Paul*	Church at Colosse	Colossians was written to insist that only Christian doctrine was to be followed. Jewish legalism, Greek philosophy and pagan practices were being combined with church teachings.
I Thessalonians	Paul	Church at Thessalonica	First Thessalonians was written to address confusion about death, resurrection and the second coming of Christ. It also encouraged the church to stand strong against the opposition which they faced. Paul visited this church only a short time, and he felt he had not left the church with strong leadership.
II Thessalonians	Paul*	Church at Thessalonica	Second Thessalonians was sent to further clarify the second coming of Christ and to explain that its time was not at hand and that life must go on in the meantime.
I Timothy	Paul*	Timothy	First Timothy is a pastoral letter which contains requirements for ministers and gives guidance for church administration. Various subjects, such as qualifications for officials, worship, caring for widows and the use of money are discussed.
II Timothy	Paul*	Timothy	Second Timothy is a pastoral letter which passionately sets forth the characteristics, concerns and duties of a good soldier of Christ.
Titus	Paul*	Titus	The Letter to Titus provides qualifications for church leaders, gives conduct instruction for various ages and calls for living in response to God's grace.
Philemon	Paul	Philemon, a member of the Church at Colosse	The Letter to Philemon is Paul's most personal letter. It is literally a letter of intercession to be delivered by Onesimus, a runaway slave, to Philemon, his master. Its message is also intended as a standard of behavior for other slaves and slave owners.

Hebrews	Unknown	Unknown *(perhaps Jewish Christians)*	Hebrews is a letter of unknown origin to an unknown readership. However, the readers were clearly very familiar with the Jewish faith. The letter emphatically shows Christ to be superior to the Old Testament. Hebrews contains 29 Old Testament quotes and 53 allusions to passages which prove Christ's superiority to the old covenant.
James	James	Jewish Christians	James is a very practical letter which addresses Christian conduct in everyday work and life. This book is often considered controversial because it emphasizes good works so strongly.
I Peter	Peter	Christians in Asia Minor	The main theme of First Peter is clearly stated in verse 5:12, "The true grace of God" shows up in the life of a believer.
II Peter	Peter*	Christians in Asia Minor	Second Peter points out the truth of Christianity and calls for faith. The letter warns against false teachers and goes into detail denouncing and describing them.
I John	John	Christians near Ephesus	First John is actually a type of written sermon. The writing is filled with contrasts between good and evil and warns against the false teachings which were attacking the church during this time period.
II John	John	Church near Ephesus	Second John is a very short letter which states that Christians must obey Christ's commandments and teachings.
III John	John	An individual named Gaius	Third John is a short personal letter with instructions regarding accepting and providing hospitality to traveling preachers.

Jude	Jude	Christians troubled with false teachers	Jude is an urgent letter intended to be used to rid the churches of the numerous traveling ministers who had twisted and perverted the teachings of Christ.
Revelation	John	Seven Churches of Asia Minor	Revelation is an apocalyptic writing given to John in a vision. The ultimate victory of Christ and the Church is the central theme.

*Indicates that there is a significant debate among scholars regarding the exact authorship of the specified books. See the previous section on authorship for more information.

Read The Book

1.   The time interval between the Old and New Testament was _____
      centuries and is called the _____ period.

2.   List the four main political periods into which this time interval can be
      divided:

      I. _____   II. _____

      III. _____   IV. _____

3.   King Cyrus of _____ gave a decree which allowed the Jews to
      _____ to their homeland.

4.   T / F   The Persian rulers who succeeded King Cyrus also treated the Jews
             reasonably well.

5.   At the beginning of the Greek Period, how did Alexander the Great treat the
      Jews in general? _____

6.   In Alexandria, Egypt, what significant event occurred in the history of the
      Bible (as a written document) during the Greek Period?
      _____

7.   T / F   Through the end of the Greek Period the Jews were treated well.

8.   What was the nickname of the Jewish guerilla leader who gained control of
      Jerusalem and brought about Jewish Independence? _____

9.   What is the common name for the yearly festival which commemorates the
      cleansing and rededication of the temple? _____

10.   During what period was Herod the Great a ruler over the Jews? _____

11.   T / F   The Jews were united in their thoughts about following the new concepts brought about by the Greek Hellenization of the world.

12.   Which Jewish group believed in the doctrine of resurrection, the Law of Moses, the prophetic writings and oral traditions? _____

13.   Which Jewish group <u>did not</u> believe in the doctrine of resurrection and believed only in the Law of Moses? _____

14.   What was the initial function or profession of the scribes?

        _____

15.   What did the profession of the scribes later develop into? _____

16.   T / F   The Jews produced very little written information during the Intertestamental Period.

Using Table 9-2, Intertestamental Writings, answer the next 2 questions concerning the intertestamental writings:

17.   Which of the writings were preserved by the Christians?_____

18.   What is the abbreviation for the Septuagint? _____

19.   The New Testament asserts a _____ _____ between God and all humanity through Jesus Christ.

20.   The books of the New Testament were written in a time span of approximately how many years? _____

21.   Who wrote the greatest amount of pages in the New Testament? _____

22.   T / F   During New Testament times, there was a straightforward political structure and a clear chain of command governing the Holy Land.

Using Table 9-5, Chronology and Selected Events in the New Testament Period, answer the following question:

23.   How many rulers named Herod are listed in this table during the New Testament period?

Using Table 9-6, Basic Information on the Books of the New Testament, answer the following questions:

24.   What letter is of unknown origin and addressed to an unknown readership? _____

25.   What letter is concerned with slaves and slave ownership? _____

Talk The Talk

Alexander the Great introduced many things to the ancient world. Among the most important were Greek culture and Greek as the universal language. In the new city of Alexandria, Egypt, the Greek translation of the Jewish Scripture (the Septuagint) was written. Previously, Jewish Scripture had only been written in the Hebrew language.

A.   *What avenues did this act open for the spread of Judaism and for the spread of Christianity centuries later?*

B.   *How could this act impact the writings of the New Testament?*

Using Table 9-2, Intertestamental Writings, answer the next three questions:

C.   *Which of these writings do you think have played a major role throughout history? Why?*

D.   *Which of these writings do you think played a major role in early church history?*

E.   *Do you think any of these writings have only played a role in modern history?*

Walk The Walk

Two centuries before Christ's birth, the Jews found themselves split over the issue of remaining orthodox or giving in to Greek influences. During the time of Christ, the Herodians took their very name from Herod, the leader whose leadership they felt was safer and more expedient to follow. During and immediately after Christ's ministry, thousands of Jews formed Christianity. Change and pressure to change is always present. The reasons for change and the results of change can be good or bad.

F.   *What are the motives for change in the above examples? What are the consequences of these changes?*

G.   *Sometimes change is brought about by simply ignoring Christian standards or values which you know to be right although they may be unpopular. How have you responded to such situations?*

H.   *From your perspective as a person of faith, list what you consider to be the primary values and standards for a follower of Jesus Christ. How do you rank them in order of importance?*

I.   *Which of the above values/standards are popular in our society? Why?*

Chapter 10
The Gospels - Why Four?

The first four books of the New Testament are called the gospels. The term gospel comes to us from the Anglo-Saxon word, "God-Spell," which means "Good News." The Good News is the Good News of Jesus Christ. These four books provide the details of His life, ministry, death, and resurrection.

The gospels, however, are not biographies or histories in the sense that one would expect to be written today. The gospels purposely tell the story of Christ in a manner to influence the reader and cause lives to be changed.

 John 20:31 states clearly, ***"But these are written that you may believe that Jesus is the Christ, the Son of God, and that by believing you may have life in his name."***

Oral Tradition to Written Word

Many scholars agree that the first gospel to be written was Mark, and it was not recorded until almost three decades after Jesus' ministry. The final gospel, John, was recorded six decades after Christ. There are several basic reasons for the long time span between the events and the recordings.

For centuries, the Jewish people relied upon oral traditions to preserve their history and their most important ideas and beliefs. Even as late as the time of Christ, in many people's eyes the oral word was still of more value than the written word. From Scripture we learn that most of the disciples were common people with minimum education and presumably with little, if any, writing skills. Jesus avoided any type of publicity, and we find no indication that he sought to have any recordings made. Finally, throughout Jesus' ministry and assuredly afterwards, it was clear that the people were expecting the end of the age to occur at any time. This common idea would give little reason to make any kind of permanent recordings.

As time passed, Christianity spread to a large geographical area and eyewitnesses to Christ's ministry were no longer present. The necessity for written accounts became clear.

Synoptic Gospels

Matthew, Mark and Luke are the synoptic gospels. All three of these gospels are very similar in their presentations of the life of Jesus, hence the word synoptic. Synoptic comes from the Greek word *"synoptikos"* which means "view together."

Each of these three gospels tell the story of Jesus by relating events, quotations, miracles, parables and other details in his ministry. Although the three are very similar in their structure and they all share similar information, their intended audiences are very different. Consequently, the driving themes and special interests of the books are different.

The Gospel of Matthew   *(Synoptic)*

The Gospel of Matthew seems to be written with the Jewish reader in mind, yet it is sensitive to the inclusion of the Gentile church. The Jews had been waiting for centuries for the Messiah; therefore, 128 Old Testament references are used to assure the readers that Christ fulfills the ancient prophecies. The genealogy and birth of Jesus is also a very important part of the book because of the Jewish audience. Similarly, because the Book of Matthew is geared toward the Jews, tradition suggests it was placed first among the gospels to act as a connection between the Old Testament and New Testament.

THEOLOGICALLY SPEAKING

The Gospel of Matthew is the gospel to the church. It is the only gospel to use the term "church"(16:18, 18:17), derived from the Greek word "ekklesia." It is also structured in such a fashion that it provides clear and coherent guidance to a community of believers.[1]

The Gospel of Mark *(Synoptic)*

The Gospel of Mark was written for readers who were already Christians and obviously read Greek. Tradition says it was primarily addressed to believers in Rome. Christ is portrayed as one whose divinity is not easily grasped even by his own disciples. Mark is the shortest and the fastest moving of the gospels. It has less than half of the Old Testament quotations of Matthew, does not relate the birth or genealogy of Christ and deals more with the actions of Jesus than his teachings.

THEOLOGICALLY SPEAKING

A unique characteristic of Mark's gospel is his fondness for the patterns of "threes." He groups together three seed parables (Mark 4:3-32), three popular opinions about John the Baptist (Mark 6:14-15), three popular opinions about Jesus (Mark 8:27-28), three predictions of Jesus' suffering and death (Mark 8:31, 9:31, 10:33-34), and the three denials of Jesus by his disciple, Peter (Mark 14:66-72).[2]

The Gospel of Luke *(Synoptic)*

The Gospel of Luke was written by a Gentile physician for the Gentiles. In a broad sense, the word Gentile means anyone who is not a Jew. This certainly included a large group of Greeks. In Luke's gospel, Christ often referred to himself as the Son of Man. This theme opens Christ to the entire world and still gives due credit to the Jewish heritage and fulfillment of the prophecies. Luke is the most detailed and comprehensive of the gospels.

THEOLOGICALLY SPEAKING

Luke is the only gospel that tells us of the early life and childhood of Jesus. Christ is often in the company of common everyday people who are not particularly religious or virtuous. His ministry is that of elevating the poor and disenfranchised. Jesus regularly celebrates life with friends.

In the first five chapters of Luke, we find Jesus calling disciples who are sinners (Luke 5:1-11) and tax collectors (Luke 5:27). Luke presents the reader with a Messiah who, like Moses, is rejected despite his offer of salvation.[3]

The Gospel of John

The Gospel of John was written for Christians and deals more with what Jesus said and taught and less with his day-to-day actions. The book is built around seven miracles, five of which are recorded nowhere else. John concentrates on these miracles, provides more of the detail of Jesus' teaching concerning them and is more theological, in general, than the synoptics.

John portrays Christ as the Son of God and emphasizes his physical existence, divine power and yet his human suffering. It has been said that if a person became interested in Christianity and was allowed to read only one book of the Bible, it should be the Gospel of John.

THEOLOGICALLY SPEAKING

John's gospel is very different from those of Matthew, Mark and Luke. Most Biblical scholars agree that the first three synoptic gospels probably used the same source for telling the story of Jesus's life and ministry; John adds to and changes some of the stories contained in the previous gospels.

Since the exodus, Jewish religious life had centered around the temple. After the fall of Israel to the Romans in 70 A.D., the temple in Jerusalem was destroyed. As a result, the Jewish approach to religion went from "temple-centered" to "synagogue-centered." Synagogues, which had traditionally served as religious schools, now became a places of prayer and worship as well. Because of the obvious threats to Judaism, becoming a Christian was strictly forbidden within the Hebrew community.

John's gospel presents Jesus as one who makes a definite break with the Old Testament's view of religious practice, for he Christianizes Jewish worship, customs and symbols. For example, the traditional Passover meal is converted to the sacrament of Holy Communion. Baptism, as an optional act

---

of religious purification, becomes a required initiation and symbol of commitment to a life of faith in Christ. Again and again, Jesus takes what was previously Jewish by nature and replaces it with a "new" Christian meaning and practice.

Anyone (especially a Jewish person) reading John's gospel within the early Christian community would find no question as to Jesus' purpose. Christ had come to replace the former Jewish way of practicing religion with a new, Christian way of experiencing faith and worship. This was not an attempt to communicate hostility toward Judaism, but was a way of drawing distinctions between the Jewish religion and the Christian religion.[4]

Comparison of the Four Gospels

To use a very broad and modernized analogy, the synoptic gospels of Matthew, Mark and Luke can be compared to three newspaper headlines and articles which report the facts of the same important story. The three articles are in three different editions of the paper and are aimed at three completely different groups of readers, so the emphasis is placed on things which are important to each respective group.

In this analogy, the Gospel of John can be viewed as the editorial. The facts and events of the story are already established and accepted. The editorial highlights and comments on specific happenings go into the underlying meanings and reasons.

Some differences between the four gospels are presented on the following comparison table. Studying the table will make many of the reasons for these differences evident.

Table 10-1   Comparison of the Four Gospels

	Matthew	Mark	Luke	John
	SYNOPTIC GOSPELS			
Order Written	Third	First	Second	Fourth
Apparent Intended Readership	Jewish background yet respectful of Gentiles	Christians familiar with Greek	Gentiles	Christians
Christmas Story	Yes	No	Yes	No
Old Testament Quotations	128	63	90-100	12
Miracles Recorded	20	18	20	7 (with discussion) 8 total
Parables	15	4	19	0
Childhood Stories of Jesus	no	no	yes	no

Read The Book

1.   The English word "gospel" means _____ _____ .

2.   For centuries, the Jewish people relied upon _____ _____ to preserve their history.

3.   List the three synoptic gospels.

      _____   _____   _____

4.   The word "synoptic" comes from the Greek word *"synoptikos"* which means "to _____ _____ ."

5.   The Gospel of Matthew is written with the _____ reader in mind.

6.   How many Old Testament references are used in Matthew? _____

7.   T / F   Mark is the shortest of the gospels and does not contain the Christmas story.

8.   Mark was written for readers who read what language? _____

9.   Luke is the most detailed and comprehensive of the gospels. What was Luke's occupation or profession? _____

10.   T / F   Luke was a Jew.

11.   How many miracles are highlighted in the Gospel of John? _____

12.   In general, John is more _____ than the other three gospels.

Talk The Talk

There are many reasons why Jesus' ministry was not chronologically documented and detailed as it happened. This is difficult for the modern reader in the information age to comprehend. Oral tradition plays a great role in the lack of written documentation concerning certain events in the history of the Jews and Christians.

A.   *Can you think of modern examples of oral tradition? Do you know certain readings or saying by memory, yet at this given moment you would not know exactly where they are written down?*

 We have learned that Matthew is geared toward the Jewish reader. Matthew is not only the first of the four gospels to appear, it is the first book to appear in the New Testament.

B.   *In what way(s) does the Gospel of Matthew serve as a bridge between the Old and New Testaments?*

As we reflect upon the intended readership of the different gospels, we recognize greatly varied backgrounds in both religion and culture.

C. *How could these backgrounds influence the authors' decisions to include such information as Christ's genealogy, the Christmas Story, etc?*

Luke is presumed to be a physician. In modern times we normally think of such a person as receiving a great deal of respect and being confident. In the "Theologically Speaking" section we learn that Luke seems to focus on everyday, common people and that he elevates the poor and disenfranchised.

D. *What factors other than profession might have influenced Luke's thinking as an author?*
    Hint: Was Luke a Jew?

Walk The Walk

The "Theologically Speaking" section concerning the Gospel of John paints a clear picture that there must be breaks with some of the old ideas and customs to allow new ideas to be fully accepted.

E.   *The more we study God's Holy Word, the more God speaks to us in many different ways. Do we have ideas, customs, habits, etc. that we must break in order to allow God to more fully come into our lives?*

NOTES

Chapter 11
Jesus
The Journeys - The Places - The People

Learning about Christ is clearly the ultimate purpose of our Bible study. However, just as it was necessary for God to nurture and prepare the children of Israel for 2,000 years before finally sending His Son, it was also necessary for us to study and understand the Old Testament in order to prepare our hearts and minds for learning about Jesus.

In Christ's own words, ***"Do not think that I have come to abolish the Law or the Prophets; I have not come to abolish them but to fulfill them."*** *Matthew 5:17*

Learning the gospels [no, learning to live as the gospels teach] is the supreme goal for every Christian. The examples and teachings of God's Son are the way to the Christian life. We must make a lifelong commitment to study, learn and pray in order that these teachings come into our hearts and serve as our daily guide. **Remember, this study provides only an overview of the life and ministry of Jesus.**

Prophecies About the Messiah

The coming of Christ fulfilled numerous Old Testament prophecies concerning the Messiah. These prophecies are located throughout the books of the Old Testament. According to how detailed the prophecies are, how they are broken down, and if they are repeated in other books, the number of prophecies can range from about 40 to over 100. The number of Old Testament books in which they are located can also vary accordingly, from one to over 20 books.

The subject matter of these prophecies covers the full range of Jesus' life and ministry. Some of these prophecies are very specific and predict details such as the location of Jesus' birth and his escape to Egypt as a baby. The prophecies also include John the Baptist and other specifics concerning Jesus' ministry. Some of the most interesting prophecies are from the Books of Isaiah and Psalms, which vividly foretell the elements of the crucifixion, death and resurrection of Christ.

The New Testament books which provide the majority of the fulfillment of these prophecies are Matthew, Mark, Luke and John, and the Book of Acts. The table on the following page presents some selected prophecies and their fulfillment.

Table 11-1   Selected Old Testament Prophecies Fulfilled by Jesus

Prophecy or Subject	Old Testament	New Testament
The Messiah will come from the tribe of Judah.	Genesis 49:10	Luke 3:33
Bethlehem will be the place of birth for the Messiah.	Micah 5:2	Luke 2:4-7
The Messiah will be born of a virgin.	Isaiah 7:14	Luke 1:26-31
The Messiah will be called out of Egypt.	Hosea 11:1	Matthew 2:14-15
Elijah will come before the Lord.	Malachi 4:5	Matthew 11:13-14
He will be declared the Son of God.	Psalms 2:7	Mark 1:11
His own people will reject Him.	Isaiah 53:3	John 1:11
The King will have a triumphant entry, riding on a donkey.	Zechariah 9:9	Mark 11:7-11
He will be betrayed for 30 pieces of silver.	Zechariah 11:12	Matthew 26:14-15
Lots will be cast for His clothes.	Psalms 22:18	John 19:24
He will be buried with the rich.	Isaiah 53:9	Matthew 27:57-60
He will be resurrected.	Psalms 16:10	Mark 16:6-7

Note: Several prophecies listed are linked to other Scriptures which may also predict and/or fulfill the prophecy.

The Homeland of Jesus

Jesus lived in Israel, the Promised Land of the Old Testament. In Jesus' day, Israel was under the rule of Rome and the entire area was referred to as Palestine. There were five major districts or regions that are significant with respect to the gospels.

The southern district was Judea, taking its name from the former nation of Judah. Judea was located to the west of the Dead Sea and the Jordan River. Jerusalem was located in Judea and was still the major city of the entire area. The temple, as well as several synagogues, was located in Jerusalem, the center of religion for the Jews.

Samaria was the district located directly to the north of Judea. The city of Samaria was the main city in that district and served as the religious center for the Samaritan people. Seven centuries after the fall of the northern kingdom of Israel, the Samaritan people were still considered an intermingled and impure race and continued to be looked down upon by the Jews.

The district of Galilee bordered Samaria on the north and surrounded the west coast of the Sea of Galilee. Jesus' hometown of Nazareth was located in Galilee. The people of Galilee had a slightly noticeable dialect. References are made in the gospels to the recognizable speech differences of the people from Galilee.

The two other districts of interest to the gospel reader are the Decapolis and Perea. The Decapolis was located almost entirely east of the Jordan River and was named because of the 10 predominately Greek city states in the area. Perea was located entirely east of the Jordan River and is not mentioned by name in the Scripture, instead it is referred to as "beyond the Jordan."

Map 11-1, Regions of Palestine During the Time of Christ, is located on the following page. It provides approximate outlines of these regions or districts. The exact boundaries of the regions are uncertain and often vary in different Bible maps.

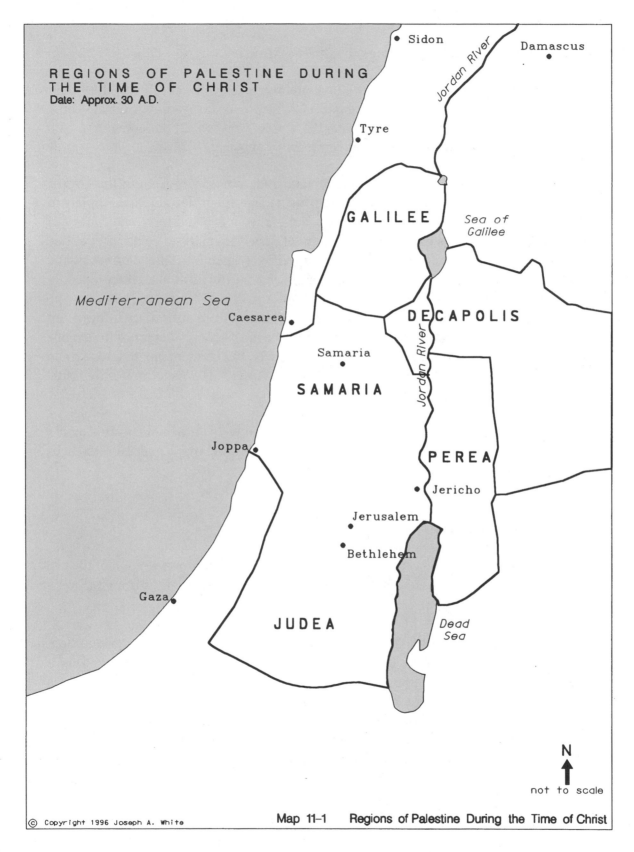

REGIONS OF PALESTINE DURING
THE TIME OF CHRIST
Date: Approx. 30 A.D.

Sidon

Damascus

Jordan River

Tyre

GALILEE

Sea of
Galilee

Mediterranean Sea

Caesarea

DECAPOLIS

Jordan River

Samaria

SAMARIA

Joppa

PEREA

Jericho

Jerusalem

Bethlehem

Gaza

JUDEA

Dead
Sea

N

N

not to scale

Map 11-1   Regions of Palestine During the Time of Christ

Exact Chronology and Locations in Christ's Ministry

We have already learned that early Christians were very much influenced by their history of oral tradition and their feeling that Christ would soon return. Consequently, when the gospels were finally recorded, the writers were still more concerned with what events happened than when and where they happened.

This unusual criterion has in no way diminished the power and truth of the Gospel message. Its only real effect has been to provide significant latitude for scholars to theorize the exact length of Jesus' ministry and the sequence and location of many of the events. Arguments exist for the duration of Jesus' ministry to be as short as one year and as long as four. The Gospel of John specifically mentions three Passovers, and many scholars place the length of Jesus' ministry at a little more than three years.

In general, where an event occurred is known primarily from subsidiary information given about the event itself. Scholars determine the most probable order of the events, which may be listed in from one to four of the gospels, and then attempt to trace a route that Jesus may have followed on that particular journey. The exact routes of Jesus' journeys are also open to discussion.

In this chapter and the next, we will focus on the most well-known events in Christ's ministry and convey this information as simply as possible, using general references with respect to both time and location.

The Journeys of Jesus

Even in terms of ancient days, Jesus' travel was limited. With the exception of the trip to Egypt when Jesus was an infant, he was never more than 100 miles from his home in Nazareth.

In some countries this would not have been unusual; however, throughout ancient history, Palestine has been located between world powers and has served as a crossroads for travel and commerce. A section of the famous King's Highway bisects Palestine by paralleling the Jordan River on the east bank and extending from the city of Damascus to the Gulf of Aqaba on the Red Sea. The King's Highway was a major caravan route, and has been in continuous use for over 3,000 years. The following table provides brief descriptions of Jesus' major travels.

Table 11-2   The Journeys of Jesus

Event	Description	Distance or Area
Birth of Jesus	Mary and Joseph were traveling from Nazareth to Bethlehem for a census when Jesus was born.	This trip was about 75 miles one way.
Escape to Egypt	Soon after the birth of Jesus, the family was forced to flee from Palestine to Egypt in order to escape from King Herod.	This trip was approximately 350 miles one way depending upon the exact route taken and the destination in Egypt.
The Passover as a child	As a child and youth, Jesus possibly made more than the one recorded Passover trip from Nazareth to Jerusalem.	This was a 60 to 70 mile trip, one way.
Early Ministry	The events in Jesus' early ministry were very diverse and led him from Galilee to Jerusalem and back with many detours along the way.	The total extent of this journey was from the north end of the Sea of Galilee south to Jerusalem. A distance of about 100 miles excluding the side trips.
Galilean Ministry	The Galilean ministry was conducted primarily in an area around the shoreline and immediately west of the Sea of Galilee.	This area was approximately 20 miles east to west and 20 miles north to south.
Judean and Perean Ministry	This ministry was conducted in Judea, the region around Jerusalem, and in the area immediately east of the Jordan called Perea.	This area was about 30 miles east to west and 20 miles north to south.
Entire Ministry	Jesus' entire ministry was conducted in the heart of the Jordan Valley. His recorded travels were bounded on the south by the Dead Sea and reached the Mediterranean coast near the towns of Tyre and Sidon to the north.	This area was approximately 50 miles east to west and 150 miles north to south.

Map 11-2, Escape to Egypt, and **Map 11-3, Journeys of Jesus,** are located on the following pages. They provide an idea of how far Jesus traveled in His escape to Egypt as a child and the limits of the Galilean and Judean/Perean ministries.

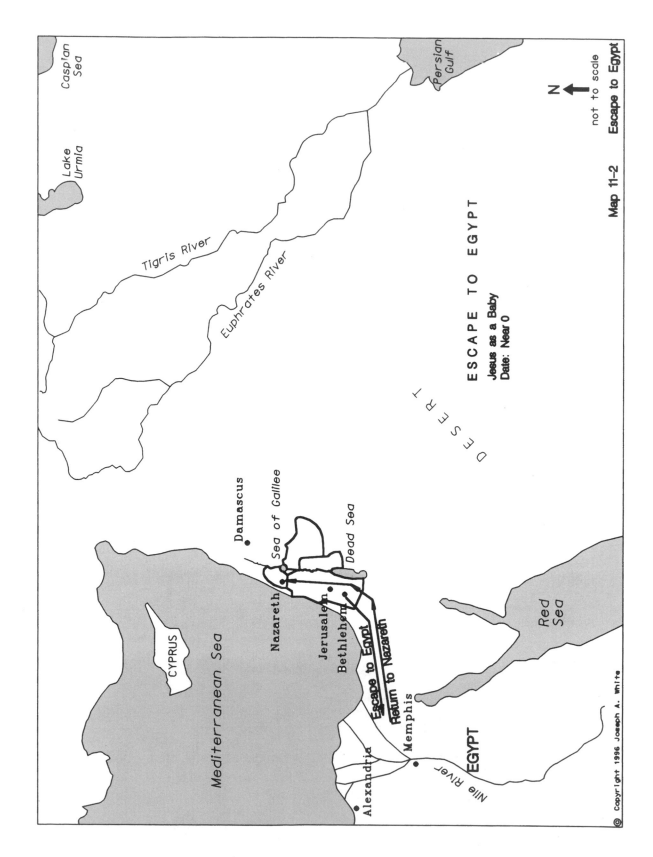

ESCAPE TO EGYPT

Jesus as a Baby
Date: Near 0

Map 11-2   **Escape to Egypt**

not to scale

Caspian Sea

Lake Urmia

Tigris River

Euphrates River

Persian Gulf

DESERT

Damascus

Sea of Galilee

Dead Sea

Nazareth

Jerusalem

Bethlehem

Escape to Egypt

Return to Nazareth

Memphis

Mediterranean Sea

CYPRUS

Alexandria

Nile River

EGYPT

Red Sea

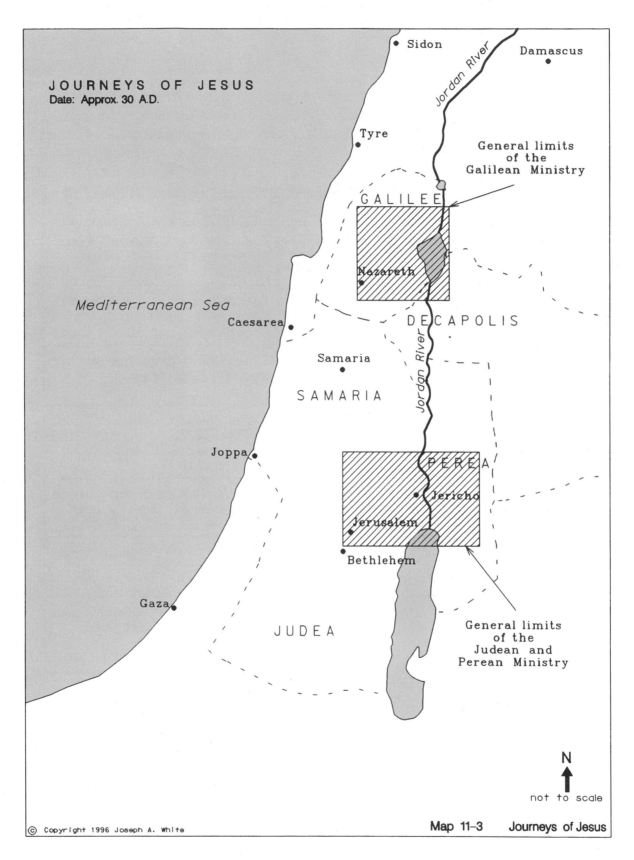

JOURNEYS OF JESUS
Date: Approx. 30 A.D.

Sidon

Damascus

Tyre

General limits
of the
Galilean Ministry

G A L I L E E

Nazareth

Mediterranean Sea

Caesarea

D E C A P O L I S

Samaria

S A M A R I A

Joppa

P E R E A

Jericho

Jerusalem

Bethlehem

General limits
of the
Judean and
Perean Ministry

Gaza

J U D E A

Jordan River

N

N

not to scale

Map 11-3   Journeys of Jesus

The Places in Jesus' Ministry

The following table lists some selected places in Jesus' life and ministry. Most of the places are best associated with the significant events that occurred there. Although the purpose of the table is to define the place, it is set up in chronological order of events for convenience of the user.

Table 11-3   Selected Places in Jesus' Life and Ministry, Arranged by Order of Event

Event	Scripture	Location	Description
Announcement of Jesus' Birth	Luke 1	Nazareth	Town in the region of lower Galilee, 15 miles west of Sea of Galilee.
Birth of Jesus	Luke 2	Bethlehem	Town with many Biblical references located five miles southwest of Jerusalem.
Childhood home	Matthew 2 Luke 2	Nazareth	Small village in Jesus' time with only one spring for water supply.
Jesus' Baptism	Matthew 3 Mark 1 Luke 3 John 1	Jordan River	The location is thought to be on the south end of the river near the Dead Sea in the region of Perea.
Jesus' first miracle	John 2	Cana	Small town in Galilee, thought to be located five miles to the northeast of Nazareth.
Samaritan woman at the well	John 4	Jacob's Well	Water well located in the Samaritan town of Sychar.
Four fishermen become disciples	Matthew 4 Mark 1 Luke 5	Sea of Galilee	Fresh water lake around which a great deal of Jesus' ministry occurred.
Sermon on the Mount	Matthew 5-7 Luke 6	Near Capernaum	Exact mountain location is unknown. Capernaum was a town located on the north end of the Sea of Galilee.
Boy raised from the dead	Luke 7	Nain	Small town in region of southwest Galilee.

Feeding of the 5,000	Matthew 14 Mark 6 Luke 9 John 6	Near Bethsaida	Small town located on the Sea of Galilee.
Jesus walks on the water	Matthew 14 Mark 6 John 6	Sea of Galilee	North end of the Sea of Galilee
Feeding of the 4,000	Matthew 15 Mark 8	Decapolis	Region southeast of Sea of Galilee originally named for 10 cities which were strong in Greek influence.
Jesus visited the temple	As a baby, as a youth and multiple times during his ministry.	Jerusalem	Major city 18 miles west of the Dead Sea which was the center of Jewish religious life.
Peter realized that Jesus was Christ	Matthew 16 Mark 8 Luke 9	Caesarea Philippi	Historical city located near the most northern extent of Jesus' journeys. Known for pagan worship
Lazarus was raised from the dead	John 11	Bethany	Town located two miles southeast of Jerusalem on the Mount of Olives. Home of Martha, Mary and Lazarus.
Zacchaeus climbed the sycamore tree to see Jesus.	Luke 19	Jericho	An oasis city, 800 feet below sea level, near the north end of the Dead Sea. Possibly the oldest city in the world.
Jesus' final week of ministry	The later chapters of all four Gospels.	Jerusalem	Chief city of Palestine. Also called the "City of David."
Jesus appeared to two apostles	Mark 16 Luke 24	Road to Emmaus	Emmaus was a village about seven miles from Jerusalem. The name means "hot baths." The exact location is unknown.
Jesus appeared to seven apostles	John 21	Shore of the Sea of Galilee	Home area for several of the apostles.
The ascension into heaven	Mark 16 Luke 24 Acts 1	Mount of Olives	A ridge with four summits located east of Jerusalem.

The following table also describes places in Jesus' ministry; however, most of these are either associated with multiple events or they are points which are difficult to place on a map. This table is set up in alphabetical order without reference to events.

Table 11-4   Places in Jesus' Ministry, an Alphabetical Listing

Place or Location	Description
Calvary	The place where Jesus was crucified, from the Latin word "calvaria" which means "skull." *Also see Golgotha.*
Capernaum	Town on the northwest shore of the Sea of Galilee which was Jesus' headquarters during his ministry in that area.
Galilee	In Roman times, one of the main geographic divisions of Palestine. Galilee was the area west of the Sea of Galilee.
Garden of Gethsemane	The garden on the Mount of Olives was where Jesus was arrested.
Golgotha	The place where Jesus was crucified, the Hebrew word for "skull" or "place of the skull." *Also see Calvary.*
Judea	In Roman times, one of the main geographic divisions of Palestine. Judea was the area around Jerusalem.
Mount Hermon	Mountain, 9,000 foot in elevation, which is located 30 miles north of the Sea of Galilee. Possible site of the Mountain of Transfiguration.
Palestine	The Holy Land. In Roman days the area was divided into Galilee, Samaria, Judea, Decapolis and Perea.
Perea	One of the five regions of Palestine in the Roman days. The name Perea is not used in the Bible. The area is east of the Jordan River and is simply referred to as "beyond the Jordan."
Samaria	In Roman times, one of the main geographic divisions of Palestine. Samaria was south of the Sea of Galilee and north of the Dead Sea.

Synagogue	Local Jewish building for religious education and worship. The temple in Jerusalem remained the center for sacrificial worship. Jesus taught and worshiped in many local synagogues. Synagogue can also mean the community of believers that worship at the building.
The Temple	The temple in Jerusalem was the center of the Jewish religious life. The actual structure was the replacement for Solomon's Temple which had recently been remodeled extensively by King Herod the Great as an appeasement for the Jews.
Tyre	City on the Mediterranean Sea. Jesus visited the region around the city, and this was the northern geographical limit of his ministry.
Upper Room	Room on the second floor of a building where Jesus ate "The Last Supper," a Passover meal with his 12 apostles.

Map 11-4, Selected Places in the Life of Jesus, located on the following page exhibits many of the places listed in the two previous tables.

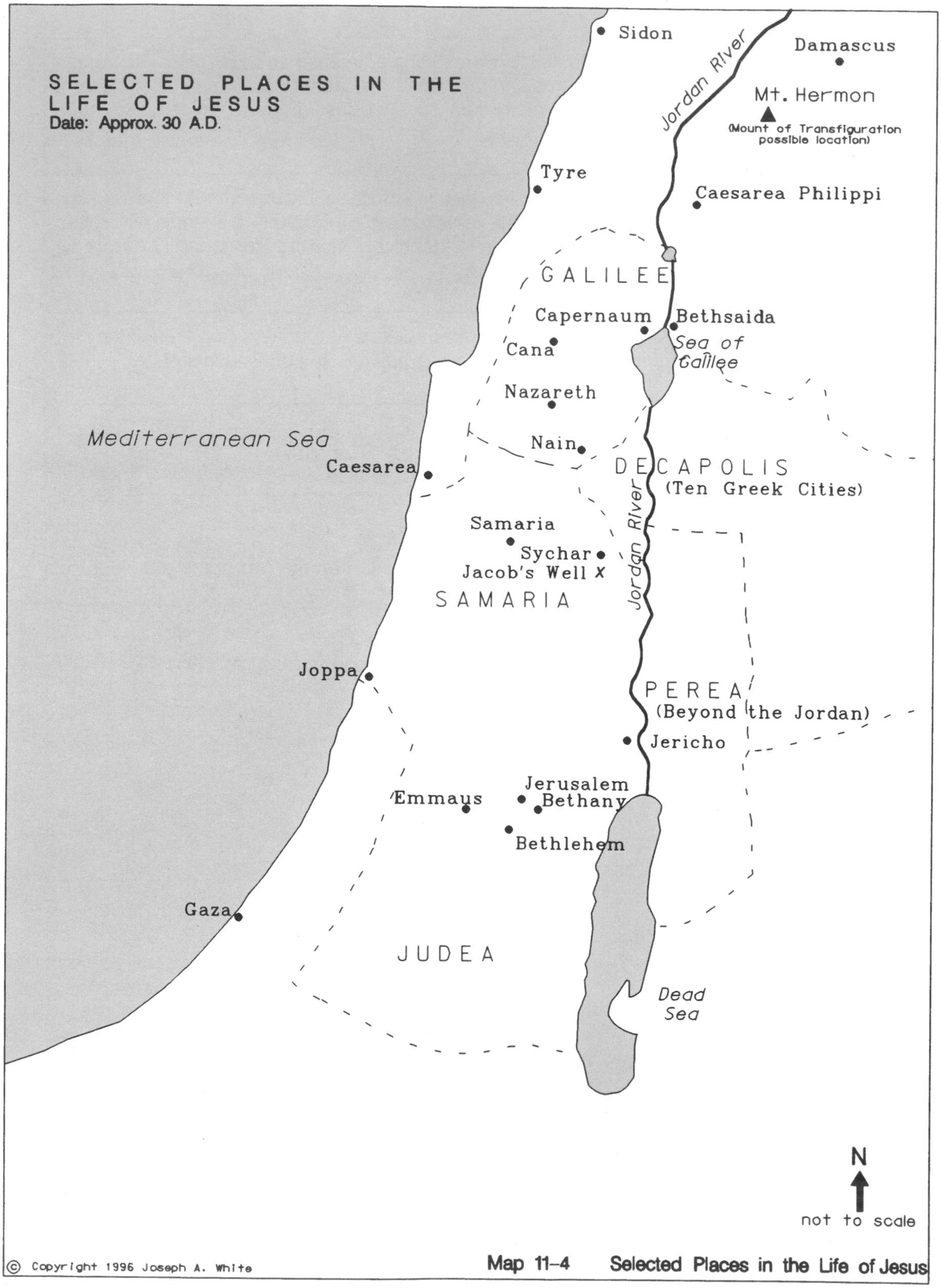

SELECTED PLACES IN THE
LIFE OF JESUS
Date: Approx. 30 A.D.

• Sidon

Jordan River

Damascus •

Mt. Hermon ▲
(Mount of Transfiguration
possible location)

Tyre •

Caesarea Philippi •

G A L I L E E

Capernaum •   • Bethsaida

Cana •

*Sea of
Galilee*

Nazareth •

Mediterranean Sea

Nain •

D E C A P O L I S
(Ten Greek Cities)

Caesarea •

Jordan River

Samaria •

Sychar •

Jacob's Well **X**

S A M A R I A

Joppa •

P E R E A
(Beyond the Jordan)

• Jericho

Emmaus •

Jerusalem •
Bethany •

Bethlehem •

Gaza •

J U D E A

*Dead
Sea*

N

N
not to scale

Map 11–4   Selected Places in the Life of Jesus

© Copyright 1996 Joseph A. White

The People in Jesus' Life and Ministry

People are what Jesus' ministry is all about, both then and now. Without expressly attempting to convey the situation, the gospel accounts paint a clear picture that, from the very beginning of Jesus' ministry, he was surrounded by people and actually had to seek solitude and private time to teach his disciples.

Considering Jesus' constant interaction with countless people, it is interesting to note that there are very few actual names or even specific descriptions of individuals listed in the gospels. In no way does this reflect that his ministry was insensitive to the individual. It only points out that Jesus alone was sufficient to accomplish God's promise of the New Covenant.

The following table contains most of the major characters in the gospels. They are listed in the basic order of their appearance with their first Scriptural location also being given.

Table 11-5   Familiar Characters in the Gospels

Name	First Scripture Location	Description
Caesar Augustus	Luke 2	Roman emperor who called for the census at the time of Jesus' birth.
Mary*	Matthew 1 Mark 6 Luke 1	Mother of Jesus.
Joseph*	Matthew 1 Luke 1 John 1	Husband of Mary.
Elizabeth	Luke 1	Mother of John the Baptist.
Zacharias (Zachariah NIV)	Luke 1	Priest who was the father of John the Baptist.
Gabriel	Luke 1	Angel that delivered birth messages to Mary about Jesus and to Zacharias about John the Baptist.

John the Baptist	Matthew 3 Mark 1 Luke 1 John 1	Jesus' cousin, who was a divine forerunner of the Messiah.
Herod* the Great	Matthew 2 Luke 1	Cruel ruler who controlled all of Palestine. He was considered king of the Jews and was known for remodeling the temple and trying to kill the Christ child.
Centurion	Matthew 8 Mark 15 Luke 7	Roman officer with 100 soldiers in his command. Jesus healed a centurion's servant.
Jairus	(Matthew 9) Mark 5 Luke 8	Synagogue leader in Capernaum whose daughter Jesus raised from the dead.
Mary*	Luke 10 John 11	Close friend of Jesus, sister of Martha and Lazarus. Mary anointed Jesus with costly oil.
Martha	Luke 10 John 11	Close friend of Jesus, sister of Mary and Lazarus.
Lazarus*	John 11	Close friend of Jesus, brother of Mary and Martha, Jesus raised Lazarus from the dead.
Mary* Magdalene	Matthew 27 Mark 15 Luke 8 John 19	Mary, the lady from whom Jesus cast out seven demons.
Mary*	Matthew 27 Mark 15 Luke 24	Mary, a follower of Jesus, who is identified as the mother of the disciple called James the Less.
Mary*	John 19	Mary who witnessed Jesus' crucifixion. Only identified as the wife of Clopas. *(Also spelled Cleopas and Cleophas)*
Zacchaeus	Luke 19	Tax collector that climbed a tree to see Jesus.
Caesar Tiberius	Matthew 22 Mark 12 Luke 20 John 19	Adopted son of Augustus Caesar, the Roman Emperor during Jesus' ministry.

Lazarus* the beggar	Luke 16	One of the main characters in Jesus' story about the rich man and the beggar.
Beelzebub *(spelling varies)*	Matthew 10 Mark 3 Luke 11	Name that means "Lord of the Flies," and is connected with the worship of Baal. The Jews used the word as a title for Satan.
Caiaphas	Matthew 26 Luke 3 John 11	Jewish ruling high priest who plotted against Jesus.
Herod* Antipas, the tetrarch	Matthew 14 Mark 6 Luke 3	Ruler of one fourth of Palestine, the Galilee region. He ordered John the Baptist beheaded and Jesus was sent before him by Pilate. Antipas was the son of Herod the Great.
Pontius Pilate	Matthew 27 Mark 15 Luke 3 John 18	Roman governor of Judea who tried and sentenced Jesus.
Barabbas	Matthew 27 Mark 15 Luke 23 John 18	Known criminal that was released at the request of the crowd instead of Jesus.
Simon of Cyrene	Matthew 27 Mark 15 Luke 23	Stranger who was forced to carry Jesus' cross.
Joseph* of Arimathea	Matthew 27 Mark 15 Luke 23 John 19	Rich man who donated the tomb for Jesus.
Nicodemus	John 3, 7 & 19	Jewish ruler who sought Jesus at night to learn from him. He later helped with Jesus' burial.

* Denotes that more than one person by that name is listed in the table.

John the Baptist

John the Baptist was the son of Zachariah the priest, and he was also Jesus' cousin. John was the fulfillment of the prophecy that the great prophet Elijah would return before the Messiah would come. For the Jews this was one of the key considerations in determining that the Messiah had indeed arrived. All four of the gospels include an introduction to John the Baptist with emphasis on the nature and purpose of his ministry. They also include quotes like the following from the Book of Isaiah, chapter 40, concerning John the Baptist:

"A voice of one calling in the desert, 'Prepare the way for the Lord, make straight paths for him.'"   *Matthew 3:3b*

The Twelve Apostles

The country in which Jesus lived was the crossroads of civilization. Jerusalem, the major city which he knew so well, was home to some of the most scholarly and learned men in the entire ancient world. Jesus chose only a small number of workers to personally prepare for the colossal mission of carrying His message to the whole world. Jesus realized that a message this important could only be carried in the heart and soul, and that scholarliness and formal training were not mandatory prerequisites for apostles. The first workers were not the elite people of the times, but were everyday common folks.

The list of the 12 apostles is located in four places in the New Testament; Matthew 10, Mark 3, Luke 6 and Acts 1. Each of the four lists presents a slightly different order of names with the exception that all begin with Peter and end with Judas Iscariot. It has been suggested by many that there were 12 apostles to symbolize the 12 tribes of Israel.

The words "disciple" and "apostle" are often used interchangeably and normally without confusion; however, there is an interesting distinction between the two words. In simplest terms, a disciple is a follower, while an apostle is a follower or disciple who has been given specific authority by the teacher. All three of the gospels make this distinction in some form before the names of the 12 are listed. For example, Luke makes the following distinction:

"When morning came, he called his disciples to him and chose twelve of them, whom he also designated apostles."   *Luke 6:13*

The following table lists the apostles, their known occupations and additional information concerning them.

Table 11-6   The Twelve Apostles of Christ

Apostle	Occupation	Additional Information
Simon Peter	Fisherman	Also called Cephas Brother of Andrew, son of Jonah Peter was married and is the apostle most often mentioned in the gospels. Leader of the early church in Jerusalem
Andrew	Fisherman	Brother of Simon Peter Former disciple of John the Baptist
James	Fisherman	Son of Zebedee Brother of John *(probably the elder)* Also called one of the "Sons of Thunder"
John	Fisherman	Son of Zebedee Brother of James Also called one of the "Sons of Thunder"
Philip		A former disciple of John the Baptist
Bartholomew		Possibly also called Nathanael
Thomas		Also called Didymus
Matthew	Tax collector	Also called Levi
James		Son of Alphaeus Sometimes called "James the Less"
Thaddaeus		Also called "Judas, son of James"
Simon		Referred to as "Simon the Zealot" * or "Simon the Canaanite"
Judas Iscariot **		The treasurer of the apostles The betrayer of Jesus

* Zealot, a political party that wanted to overthrow the Roman government.
**Judas Iscariot was replaced by Matthias

Read The Book

1. At a minimum, the coming of the Messiah fulfilled how many Old Testament prophecies? _____

2. From what tribe would the Messiah come? _____

3. The Messiah would be betrayed for how much? _____

4. In Jesus' time, the land of Israel was under Roman rule and the entire area was referred to as _____ .

5. Palestine was divided in _____ regions with Jesus' hometown of Nazareth being located in _____ .

Using Map 11-1, Regions of Palestine During the Time of Christ, answer the next question:

6. What area or region is located directly between the city of Jerusalem and the region of Galilee?_____

7. Many scholars place the length of Jesus' ministry at slightly longer than _____ years.

8. With the exception of the escape to Egypt as a baby, Jesus never traveled farther than approximately _____ miles from his home in Nazareth.

9. Why were Joseph and Mary traveling when Jesus was born?

    _____

10. As a youth, to what city did Jesus travel to celebrate the Passover? _____

11. The Galilean Ministry was conducted in a small area around the Sea of Galilee and immediately to the west. What are the approximate distances north to south and east to west of the limits of this ministry? _____ _____

Using Map 11-3, Journeys of Jesus, answer the next question:

12. What major city was included within the Judean and Perean Ministry? _____

13. In what stream or river was Jesus baptized? _____ _____ .

14. Jesus performed His first miracle in a small town named Cana. What event was Jesus attending? _____

15. T / F   There was more than one event at which Jesus fed a multitude.

16. Near the town of Jericho, who climbed a sycamore tree in order to see Jesus? _____

17. The ascension of Jesus into heaven occurred on the _____ __ _____ which is located near Jerusalem .

18. What is the commonly used Latin variation for the word "skull?" _____
What is the Hebrew word for "skull?" _____

19. Where was Jesus arrested? _____ ____ _____

20.   What were the local Jewish buildings for religious education and worship called? _____

21.   T / F   There was only one temple and it was located in Jerusalem.

22.   The room in which Jesus and his 12 apostles ate "The Last Supper" is commonly called the _____ _____ .

Using Map 11-4, Selected Places in Jesus' Life, answer the next question:

23.   Jesus often visited his friends Lazarus, Mary and Martha, in the small village of _____ , which is located near Jerusalem.

24.   How many women named Mary are mentioned in the gospels? _____

25.   There are two people by this name in the gospels; one is a beggar, the other is a close friend of Jesus and brother of Mary and Martha. _____

26.   John the Baptist, the divine forerunner of the Messiah, was also Jesus' _____ .

27.   Four books of the New Testament provide a list of the 12 apostles. In all four lists, which apostle is named first and which is named last?

        _____   _____

28.   At least two of the 12 apostles were former disciples of whom?

        _____ _____ _____

Talk The Talk

When Jesus spoke of the Scriptures we now call the Old Testament, He said He did not come to abolish but to fulfill the Law. Also, the New Testament very deliberately includes numerous statements showing that Christ fulfilled the Old Testament prophecies about the Messiah.

A.   *Why do you think Jesus was concerned that the Old Testament not be discredited or diminished in any way?*

B.   *You may have heard opinions expressed that the Old Testament is only history and has very little to do with being a Christian today. In what ways is this opinion substantiated or challenged, considering the many fulfillments of prophecy and Old Testament quotes found in the New Testament?*

With the exception of His escape to Egypt as a baby, Jesus never traveled more 100 miles from His home. A search of the gospels will reveal only a few dozen names involved with Jesus' ministry, none of which were important worldly figures of the era.

C.   *Considering the divine mission to bring the Good News to the entire world, why do you think Jesus' ministry was centralized in such a small area and directed to so limited a group of people?*

The list of the 12 apostles is found in four places in the New Testament. Each time Peter is listed first and Judas Iscariot is listed last.

D.   *Why do you think the listings are this way?*

E.   *Why were such common individuals chosen to be apostles? Why do you think there were 12?*

Walk The Walk

A small group of people in a tiny geographical area was selected to spread Christianity. They were no doubt ill-prepared and underequipped. Yet, Christianity spread like wildfire.

F.   *You are a disciple of Christ. In today's modern world of technology and communication, how well are we equipped as compared to the original few who were selected?*

G.   *What kind of obligation do you have to spread the Word and how will you utilize the tools which you have?*

Chapter 12
Jesus
The Events - The Teachings - The Miracles

Jesus' life and ministry can be traced through a series of between 175 and 200 individual events; these stand alone well-enough to be listed in standard tables commonly referred to as the "Harmony of the Gospels." In this study we will be limited to a small number of these events. The selection of these particular events is in no way an indication that they are of more significance or of any greater lesson value than the others. They have been selected simply because the reader may be familiar with these events and they serve as time guideposts in the life and ministry of Christ.

This chapter will be subdivided into the following six time periods:

> THE BIRTH AND CHILDHOOD OF JESUS
> THE EARLY MINISTRY
> FROM THE FIRST TO THE SECOND PASSOVER
> FROM THE SECOND TO THE THIRD PASSOVER
> FROM THE THIRD TO THE LAST PASSOVER
> THE FINAL WEEK

THE BIRTH AND CHILDHOOD OF JESUS

The first two chapters of the Gospels of Matthew and Luke contain the announcement and details of the birth of Jesus. Luke also gives the announcement and birth of Jesus' cousin and divine forerunner, John the Baptist. Careful reading of the two gospels will reveal some subtle differences in the actual accounts and the modern commercialized version of the Christmas story. The following table gives a brief description of selected events.

Table 12-1   Birth and Childhood of Jesus

Scripture	Event
Luke 1	The angel Gabriel appeared to Zacharias the priest and announced that John the Baptist would be born. Because of his unbelief, Zacharias would be unable to speak until his son John was born. This event fittingly occurred in the temple in Jerusalem.

Matthew 1 Luke 1	Six months later, Gabriel appeared to Mary at Nazareth and told her that Jesus would be born. The angel later appeared to Joseph.
Luke 2	When the Christ child was born in Bethlehem, the angels made the announcement to the shepherds. As prescribed by law, the rite of circumcision was performed on the eighth day. The child was presented in the temple 33 days later. *(Lev. 12:3-4)*
Matthew 2	The wise men visited the Christ child in a house in Bethlehem. The number of three wise men is surmised only from the three gifts. Each gift was symbolic of the future; gold for a king, frankincense for purity and myrrh for embalming.
Matthew 2	Jesus' family fled to Egypt to escape King Herod and eventually returned to Nazareth. Both of these events were at the direction of an angel. *As a practical matter, one might wonder how a poor young family was financially able to make such a journey. The gifts of the magi may have had a purpose other than symbolism.*
Luke 2	Each year Jesus' parents went to Jerusalem during the Feast of the Passover. At the age of 12, Jesus accompanied his parents on the trip. He remained in the temple three days, talking to and questioning the teachers in a manner which was considered amazing.

THE EARLY MINISTRY

The Baptism of Jesus

After Jesus' visit to the temple at age 12, the Bible provides no other information about his youth. The third chapter of Luke gives specific information about the political leaders at the time John the Baptist and Jesus started their ministries. This information, combined with the knowledge of the political leaders at the time of Jesus' birth, indicates that approximately 18 years elapsed between Jesus' first trip to the temple and the beginning of his ministry. It follows that his approximate age was 30.

Jesus' ministry began with His baptism in the Jordan River by John the Baptist. The synoptic Gospels of Matthew, Mark and Luke give slightly varied accounts of the actual baptism; however, all three detail that the heavens opened, the Holy Spirit descended upon Jesus like a dove and the voice of God said a version of, *"This is my*

beloved Son, in whom I am well pleased." The Gospel of John does not include the actual account of Jesus' baptism. However, John the Baptist is quoted concerning the event and the fact that Jesus is indeed the Son of God.

The Temptation of Jesus

The synoptic Gospels next give the account of Jesus being led into the wilderness and tempted by the devil for 40 days. Matthew and Luke both give a significant amount of dialogue between the devil and Jesus concerning the temptation. The devil attempted to make Christ sin, and each time Christ withstood him and answered with powerful Old Testament Scriptures. It is interesting to note that the devil also quoted portions of Scripture when it was to his advantage.

THEOLOGICALLY SPEAKING

Traditionally, temptation has been viewed as an expression of human weakness. We are tempted at our point of weakness. Yet, the reverse is the case. We are not tempted to do that which we cannot do (weakness). We are tempted to do that which we can do (strength). In fact, what we are usually tempted to do is rationalized as being "good," not evil.

Jesus is tempted at his point of strength under the disguise of "doing good." What transpires in his temptations is not a test of his weakness but proves to be a statement as to the nature of his purpose and ministry.

Jesus is invited to turn stones into bread, and you can almost hear every starving person in the world say, "Stones to bread? Please, Jesus, be the kind of Messiah that focuses on the feeding of those who suffer from physical hunger." Yet, He chooses a different path of spiritual nourishment which moves His followers to always address the physical needs of God's children around the world.

He is tempted with the ultimate political power over the world. One can almost hear the voices of those who have suffered at the hands of graft and political corruption saying, "Jesus, in charge of all political power? Please, Jesus, rule the world with justice and grace and honesty." Yet, he chooses a different direction and refuses such a role in his ministry.

He is tempted to cast himself down from the highest point of the temple, only to be saved by angels. One can almost hear people saying, "Please, Jesus,

---

do something like that and have an altar call, and everyone will follow you forever." Yet he chooses a different direction and refuses to manipulate people's trust through frivolous miracles or trickery...regardless of how effective they might be.

The narrative of Jesus' temptation is a story about "knowing who you are and focusing on life's purpose." Jesus will not use food for those who hunger, political power for those who need justice, or miracles for those who are easily impressed, as motivations for following him. It is an invitation to all of us to, like Jesus, know who we are and live life with integrity and faith.[1]

FROM THE FIRST TO THE SECOND PASSOVER

Soon after the temptation, Jesus chose several of the early disciples and performed his first miracle of turning water into wine at the wedding feast in Cana. Shortly thereafter, He traveled to Jerusalem for the Passover. While in Jerusalem, Jesus overturned the money changers' tables and drove them out of the temple. He then ministered and taught His disciples in Judea. Upon learning that John the Baptist was imprisoned, He withdrew to Galilee. On the way to Galilee, Jesus passed through Samaria and encountered the Samaritan woman at the well. Once in Galilee, Jesus started his public ministry in that area.

Details and Customs of the Times

Some interesting details in the Scriptures are often missed by the modern reader because we are unaware of the customs of the times. For example, in the previous paragraph the key events involving the wine, the moneychangers and the trip through Samaria are all linked to customs of the day.

The best wine at a feast was always served first and the lesser quality was used last. Jesus caused this sequence to be reversed, as explained in the Scriptures. Next, why was Jesus so angry at the money changers and traders? Jews came from all over the world for the Passover in Jerusalem. Therefore, they had to exchange their currency and purchase animals for sacrifice. This practice of exchange and purchase was a business and should not have been conducted in the temple. Also, it was often further corrupted by the practice of rejecting local Jew's sacrifices and demanding that their blemished animals be exchanged for so-called unblemished animals, at a profit of course.

The third custom, which might go unnoticed, is the fact that most Jews would choose to travel a longer route around Samaria rather than to go through the region. The simple statement that Jesus passed through Samaria has a strong meaning in itself. The Scriptures make powerful statements with only a few words. Footnotes and Bible commentaries can often provide enlightening detail.

FROM THE SECOND TO THE THIRD PASSOVER

With the coming of the second Passover season of His ministry, Jesus again returned to Jerusalem for the celebration. While in Jerusalem, he healed a man at the pool near Bethesda, declared Himself equal with God and thus caused the Jews to seek to kill Him. Shortly thereafter he returned to Galilee and began what is known as His main Galilean ministry.

The Sermon on the Mount

Matthew chapters 5 through 7 and Luke chapter 6 contain one of the best known of all of Jesus' teachings, the Sermon on the Mount. This sermon was delivered to a large group of followers that tradition says, was gathered on a mountain west of the Sea of Galilee. The sermon showed believers the way to live a Christ-like life.

The sermon began with the Beatitudes, a group of short statements that all begin with "blessed are," which means "happy are." Jesus next addressed the Old Testament laws and gave clarifications and examples for each one. The sermon then moved to the actual practice of living a Christian life and covered a wide variety of subjects, such as worry, prayer, giving and, finally, the famous Golden Rule. The conclusion to the sermon uses examples that contrast the way to destruction and the way to life.

Although the sermon is located in the beginning of Matthew and a reduced version in the first part of Luke, the actual time of delivery is well into Jesus' second year of ministry. The physical location of this long and powerful sermon at the beginning of the New Testament clearly shows the reader that Jesus was teaching with authority and proclaiming a new and very personal message to each individual.

```
THEOLOGICALLY SPEAKING

Many scholars believe that the Sermon on the Mount is actually a condensed
form of a collection of sermons which Jesus preached to large crowds of
common everyday people.
```

The Sermon by the Sea

A short time after the famous Sermon on the Mount, Jesus was teaching by the Sea of Galilee and the crowd became so large he eventually preached from a fishing boat slightly offshore. This event became known as the Sermon by the Sea and is identified with parables. Telling parables was one of Jesus' favorite methods of teaching.

A parable can be defined in many ways. The simplest is to call it an earthly story with a heavenly meaning. Many of these parables had a double meaning, one obvious meaning addressing the present and another addressing the future in an often inconspicuous manner. Another important point concerning parables is that hearers must interpret their meanings. The utilization of parables allowed Jesus to safely and tactfully make his points and to sometimes predict the future in an often hostile environment. The following table lists the parables of Jesus.

Table 12-2   The Parables of Jesus*

#	Title	Matthew	Mark	Luke
1	The Sower	13:5	4:3	8:4
2	The Tares	13:24		
3	The Mustard Seed	13:31	4:31	13:18
4	The Leaven	13:33		13:21
5	The Hidden Treasure	13:44		
6	The Pearl of Great Value	13:45		
7	The Dragnet for Fish	13:47		
8	The One Lost Sheep	18:12		15:3
9	The Unmerciful Servant	18:23		

10	The Workers in the Vineyard	20:1		
11	The Two Sons	21:28		
12	The Wicked Vine-growers	21:33	12:1	20:9
13	The Wedding Feast for the King's Son	22:2		
14	The Wise and Foolish Maidens	25:1		
15	The Talents	25:14		
16	The Seed Growing Secretly		4:26	
17	The Two Debtors and the Creditor			7:41
18	The Good Samaritan			10:30
19	A Friend in Need at Midnight			11:5
20	The Rich Fool			12:16
21	The Barren Fig Tree			13:6
22	The Great Supper			14:16
23	The Lost Money			15:8
24	The Prodigal Son			15:11
25	The Unjust Steward			16:1
26	The Rich Man and Lazarus the Beggar			16:19
27	The Unworthy Servants			17:7
28	The Persistent Widow and Unjust Judge			18:1
29	The Pharisee and the Tax Collector			18:9
30	The Ten Minas			19:11

*The exact number of parables identified in the gospels varies with the definition used for parable. Some scholars include several other teachings of Christ. Consequently, the number of parables in those respective tables ranges up to 50.

Near the end of the year between the second and third Passovers Jesus taught a great multitude, and that evening He miraculously fed more than 5,000 people. He then dismissed the crowd, sent the disciples ahead of Him in a boat and later came to the disciples walking upon the water of the Sea of Galilee.

FROM THE THIRD TO THE LAST PASSOVER

Soon after the third Passover and another miraculous feeding of 4,000 people, Peter recognized the obvious that Jesus was the Messiah, the Son of God. Jesus then disclosed to the disciples the future concerning His death and resurrection. The disciples were shocked, yet they still did not fully understand the truth.

Six days later Jesus took Peter, James and John with him to a high mountain where Jesus was transfigured before them and Elijah and Moses both appeared. This event, referred to as the Mount of Transfiguration, was dramatically concluded as God spoke to His beloved Son.

Toward the coming of the final Passover, Jesus learned of the sickness of his friend Lazarus, the brother of Mary and Martha. Jesus did not immediately travel to their home and when He arrived, Lazarus was already dead and placed in a tomb. Jesus was so deeply moved that he wept. Jesus then commanded Lazarus to rise from the dead and come out of the tomb, which he did.

On Jesus' last journey to Jerusalem, a crowd was forming to see Jesus as he passed by, and a small tax collector named Zaccheus climbed a sycamore tree in order to see the Christ. Jesus commanded him to come down and went to Zaccheus' house for a meal.

The Miracles of Jesus

The miracles of Jesus were clearly a sign that He was indeed the Son of God. They were performed at various locations and times throughout His ministry and involved a variety of people. Although there was and still is no limit to the power of Christ, a common link which was mentioned in the majority of the miracle stories was the faith of the person involved in the miracle.

Scholars identify between 30 and 40 separate miracles interspersed in the four gospels. It is also stated in all four of the gospels that Jesus performed many other healings and miracles that are not individually recorded.

Although it is evident that Jesus was driven by divine compassion for the people, His mission was to bring the New Covenant to the entire world for the present and all future generations. Consequently, there seemed to have been a practical limit to the number of miracles He chose to perform and many times He simply avoided the masses.

✝

The miracles have a broad range of teaching applications. Of the 35 miracles listed in the following table, nine controlled nature (N), six cured people with demons (D), 17 cured the human body (B) and three raised people from death (R).

Table 12-3   The Miracles of Jesus

#	Type	Miracle	Matt.	Mark	Luke	John
1	N	Turning water into wine at a wedding feast in Cana				2:1
2	N	Calming the storm on the Sea of Galilee	8:23	4:35	8:22	
3	N	Feeding the 5,000	14:13	6:35	9:12	6:1
4	N	Jesus walking on the Sea of Galilee	14:25	6:47		6:19
5	N	Feeding the 4,000	15:32	8:1		
6	N	Jesus paying taxes with money from a fish's mouth	17:24			
7	N	Withering the fig tree	21:18	11:12		
8	N	Miraculous catch of fish at the time the disciples were called			5:4	
9	N	Miraculously catching the fish after the Resurrection				21:1
10	D	Sending demons into a herd of swine	8:28	5:1	8:26	
11	D	Curing a demon-possessed mute man	9:32			
12	D	Curing a demon-possessed blind and mute man	12:22		11:14	
13	D	Healing a Canaanite woman's demon-possessed daughter	15:21	7:24		
14	D	Healing a boy with demonic seizures (the disciples could not)	17:14	9:14	9:38	
15	D	Healing of a man with an unclean spirit at the synagogue		1:23	4:33	
16	B	Healing a leper	8:2	1:40	5:12	

17	B	Healing the Roman centurion's servant of paralysis	8:5		7:1	
18	B	Curing Peter's mother-in-law of a fever	8:14	1:30	4:38	
19	B	Healing a paralytic in Capernaum	9:2	2:1	5:18	
20	B	Healing the woman that touched his cloak	9:20	5:25	8:43	
21	B	Healing two blind men	9:27			
22	B	Healing a man with a withered hand on the Sabbath	12:9	3:1	6:6	
23	B	Healing the blind near Jericho	20:30	10:46	18:35	
24	B	Healing of a deaf mute in the region of the Decapolis		7:31		
25	B	Healing of a blind man at Bethsaida		8:22		
26	B	Curing of a woman who was bent double for 18 years			13:11	
27	B	Healing of a man with dropsy on the Sabbath			14:1	
28	B	The healing of ten lepers (only one thanks Jesus)			17:11	
29	B	Restoring the slave's ear during the arrest of Jesus			22:49	
30	B	Healing of a royal official's son in Capernaum				4:46
31	B	Healing of a man who had been sick for 38 years at the pool at Bethesda				5:1
32	B	Healing the man that was born blind				9:1
33	R	Raising Jairus' daughter from the dead	9:18	5:22	8:40	
34	R	Raising the widow's son at Nain			7:11	
35	R	Raising Lazarus from the dead				11:43

THE FINAL WEEK

The last week of Jesus' life and ministry is not a week of unfortunate events or a case of being at the wrong place at the wrong time as it might appear on the surface. Many of the major events that comprise the last week were predicted by Old Testament prophets centuries before. Even though Jesus knew what was going to happen, and had explained things in detail to His apostles, He continued His ministry.

The Gospels of Matthew and Mark devote one third of their pages to the final week. Luke uses one fourth and John dedicates one half of his entire writing to this momentous event. For a full week there are many important events which occur leading up to the trial, crucifixion and resurrection. The table below is very condensed, and lists only a representative number of the events.

Table 12-4   Events of Holy Week

Jewish Day*	Event	Matt	Mark	Luke	John
Sabbath (Saturday)	Angry Jews sought Jesus in Jerusalem. Jesus was anointed by Mary while still in Bethany. *(or possibly on the third day)*	26:6	14:3		11:55 12:1
	Many Jews came to Bethany to see Jesus and Lazarus.				12:9
First Day (Sunday)	Jesus made a triumphant entry into Jerusalem with palm branches waving. Jesus returned to Bethany in the evening.	21:1	11:1	19:29	12:12
Second Day (Monday)	On His return to Jerusalem, Jesus cursed the fig tree. He again cleansed the temple by overturning the moneychanger's tables. Jesus returned to Bethany in the evening.	21:12	11:12	19:45	

Third Day (Tuesday)	On His return to Jerusalem, the fig tree was withered.	21:20	11:20		
	Jesus taught in the temple.	21:23	11:27	20:1	
	The Pharisees and Herodians tried to trap Jesus with His own words.	22:15	12:13	20:20	
	The Sadducees were against Jesus because of the resurrection.	22:23	12:18	20:27	
	Jesus replied to a lawyer about the greatest commandment.	22:35	12:28		
	Jesus warned against the teachings of the scribes and Pharisees. Jesus mourned for Jerusalem.	23:1	12:38	20:45	
Fourth Day (Wed.)	Jesus announced His upcoming betrayal and crucifixion. The Sanhedrin craftily consulted to have Jesus killed.	26:1	14:1	22:1	12:36
Fifth Day (Thursday)	Two disciples were sent by Jesus into Jerusalem to prepare for the Passover.	26:17	14:12	22:7	
Sixth Day (Friday)	The Last Supper	26:26	14:22	22:15	

A Jewish day (24 hour period) began at sunset. Days were further subdivided into two 12 hour periods. (see Matthew 27:45 and John 11:9)

Diagram 12-1, Selected Events of Holy Week, is located on the following page. It provides a graphical representation of the basic events which occurred during the first six days of the last week.

✝

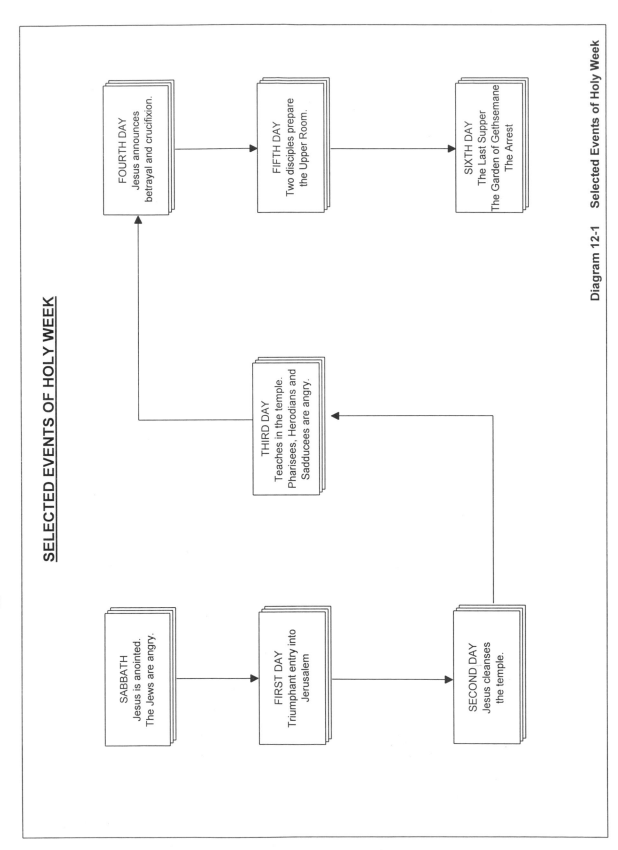

SELECTED EVENTS OF HOLY WEEK

FOURTH DAY
Jesus announces betrayal and crucifixion.

FIFTH DAY
Two disciples prepare the Upper Room.

SIXTH DAY
The Last Supper
The Garden of Gethsemane
The Arrest

THIRD DAY
Teaches in the temple. Pharisees, Herodians and Sadducees are angry.

SABBATH
Jesus is anointed. The Jews are angry.

FIRST DAY
Triumphant entry into Jerusalem

SECOND DAY
Jesus cleanses the temple.

Diagram 12-1   Selected Events of Holy Week

The Last Supper

The meal that Jesus and His 12 apostles shared in the upper room was the Passover meal. This was Jesus' last meal before His death and resurrection. It is commonly known as the Last Supper or the Lord's Supper.

Thirteen hundred years prior to Jesus' ministry, God saved His chosen people from the tenth and final plague which would come upon the Egyptian nation by instituting the Passover. By preparing a special meal and observing a particular ceremony the people of Israel would be "passed over" by the plague of death. This celebration became the most important event of the year for the Jews.

As Jesus ate His last meal and gave final instructions to the disciples, He purposefully began a ritual that Christians would regularly celebrate for the next 2,000 years. At the Last Supper, Jesus gave the familiar instructions which we hear in communion service today about the bread and the wine representing His blood and His body and He plainly stated, *"Do This in Remembrance of Me."*

There are many parallels in the Bible, but few so striking as those between the requirements and conditions of the sacrificial lamb for the Passover and of Jesus Christ as the sacrifice for the sins of the entire world. Both sacrifices were perfect, had their blood shed, had no bones broken and were killed. However, the sacrificial lamb was a yearly requirement. Jesus would serve as a one-time sacrifice, sufficient for the sins of the entire world.

Table 12-4   (continued)

Day	Event	Matt.	Mark	Luke	John
Sixth Day (cont.) (Friday)	The words of the Lord's Supper were given. *(also found in I Cor. 11:23)*	26:26	14:22	22:15	
	At night, Jesus prayed in the Garden of Gethsemane.	26:30	14:26	22:39	18:1
	The betrayal and arrest of Jesus.	26:47	14:43	22:47	18:2
	That same night, Jesus was brought before Annas, father-in-law of the high priest.				18:13

	At dawn, Jesus was brought before Caiaphas, the high priest and the Sanhedrin. Jewish law prohibited the court from meeting at night.	26:57	14:53	22:54	18:24
	Jesus was brought before Pilate, the Roman governor.	27:2	15:1	23:1	18:28
	Pilate sent Jesus before Herod the ruler of Galilee, the home region of Jesus.			23:6	
	Herod mocked Jesus and sent Him back to Pilate.			23:11	
	Pilate released Barabbas and sentenced Jesus.	27:26	15:15	23:18	18:40 19:16
	Jesus was crucified at Golgotha, called the place of the skull.	27:33	15:22	23:33	19:17
	Jesus died.	27:45	15:33	23:44	19:28
	Jesus was buried.	27:57	15:42	23:50	19:38
Seventh Day (Saturday)	Pilate placed a guard and set a seal upon the entrance of the tomb.	27:62			

Diagram 12-2, The Arrest to the Resurrection, is located on the following page. It provides a graphical representation of the arrest, trials, crucifixion and resurrection of Jesus.

THE ARREST TO THE RESURRECTION

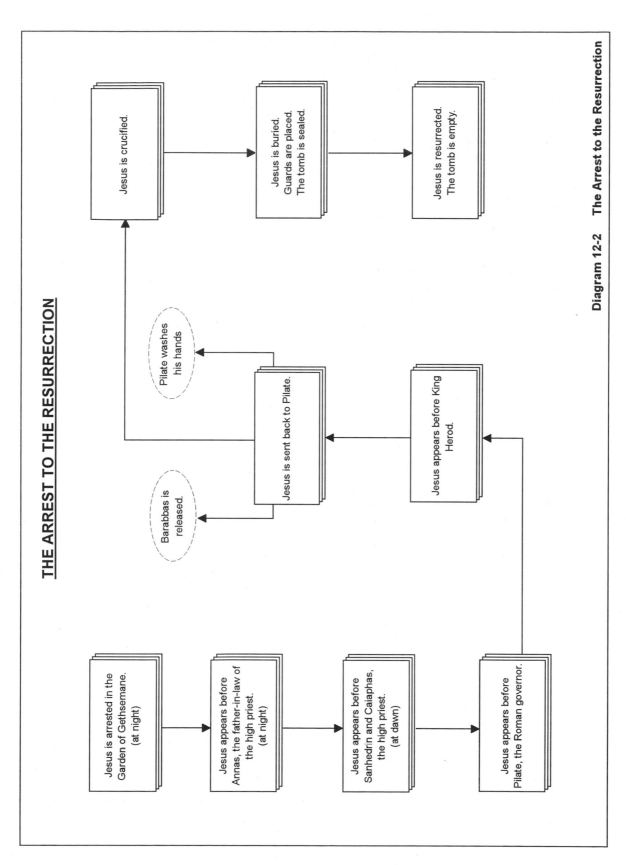

Jesus is crucified.

Jesus is buried. Guards are placed. The tomb is sealed.

Jesus is resurrected. The tomb is empty.

Pilate washes his hands

Jesus is sent back to Pilate.

Jesus appears before King Herod.

Barabbas is released.

Jesus is arrested in the Garden of Gethsemane. (at night)

Jesus appears before Annas, the father-in-law of the high priest. (at night)

Jesus appears before Sanhedrin and Caiaphas, the high priest. (at dawn)

Jesus appears before Pilate, the Roman governor.

Diagram 12-2   The Arrest to the Resurrection

Specific Prophecies Fulfilled

The betrayal, trial and crucifixion of Jesus fulfilled between 15 and 20 Old Testament prophecies. These Messianic prophecies are located primarily in the Books of Psalms, Zechariah and Isaiah. Several are very general in nature, such as He would be rejected by the Jews; however, the majority are strikingly precise. For instance, He would be betrayed for 30 pieces of silver, He would be silent before His accusers, He would be spat on and struck, His hands and feet would be pierced, lots would be cast for His clothes, His side would be pierced and He would be buried with the rich.

The Resurrection, Appearances and Ascension

The final chapter of the three synoptic gospels and the last two chapters of John provide the details of the resurrection, appearances and ascension of Christ. Each of the gospels furnish slightly varied accounts, but the message is clearly the same: Jesus was resurrected from the dead, appeared numerous times to many different individuals, and after 40 days He ascended into heaven.

Each of the gospels begins its account with the empty tomb and angels (or divine messengers) announcing that Jesus has been raised from the dead. The gospels continue with documentation of the appearances of the risen Christ. There are approximately 10 separate appearances of Christ that can be identified in the four gospels and in First Corinthians. These appearances are physically located around Jerusalem, on the road to Emmaus, and in the region of Galilee. They include Jesus revealing Himself to the woman at the tomb, to the disciples individually and twice before them as a group, and to a crowd of more than 500 described in First Corinthians. After the ascension, Jesus also revealed Himself to the Apostle Paul.

Mark states that Jesus was received up into Heaven. Luke states that Jesus blessed them and parted from them and they rejoiced. In the Book of Acts, Luke goes on to give a full account of the Lord's ascension into heaven from the Mount of Olivet which is near Jerusalem. Christ's final instructions to the apostles may best be summed up in the closing verses of Matthew by what is commonly known as the Great Commission:

"All authority in heaven and on earth has been given to me. Therefore go and make disciples of all nations, baptizing them in the name of the Father and of the Son and of the Holy Spirit, and teaching them to obey everything I have commanded you. And surely I am with you always, to the very end of the age."

Matthew 28:18b-20

Read The Book

1.   The angel, Gabriel, appeared to three people in order to announce the births of John the Baptist and Jesus. Who were these people? _____

_____   _____

2.   Jesus was born in a stable, yet where did the wise men visit him? _____

3.   Jesus was _____ years of age when he talked with and questioned the teachers in the temple.

4.   All four Gospels state that this person baptized Jesus.

_____ _____ _____

5.   In the various accounts of Jesus' baptism:
What opened?   _____
What descended?   _____
Who spoke?   _____

6.   In the wilderness, when Jesus was tempted by the devil, the devil quoted _____ .

7.   T / F   It was not the function of the money changers that made Jesus angry. The problem was that they were in the temple.

8.   The subject of the Sermon on the _____ is how to live a Christ-like life.

9.   The short statements known as the Beatitudes all begin with what two words?

_____ _____

✝

10.   In what was Jesus sitting when he gave the Sermon by the Sea? _____

11.   The Sermon by the Sea is identified with _____.

12.   T / F   One characteristic of a parable is that it does not have to be interpreted by the hearer.

Using Table 12-2, The Parables of Jesus, answer the next question:

13.   How many parables are:

found in the Gospel of John?   _____

found in the Gospel of Mark?   _____

common to Matthew, Mark and Luke?   _____

14.   Who accompanied Jesus to the Mount of Transfiguration?

_____   _____   _____

15.   Who divinely appeared on the Mount of Transfiguration before God concluded the event by speaking from the heavens? _____ _____

16.   T / F   All of the miracles and healings performed by Jesus are individually recorded in the gospels.

Using Table 12-3, The Miracles of Jesus, answer the next 3 questions:

17.   How many recorded incidences are there in which Jesus raised someone from the dead? _____

18.   In one particular healing, Jesus sent demons into a herd of _____ .

19.   List the four major types of miracles according to this table.

   _____   _____

   _____   _____

20.   Who anointed Jesus at the beginning of the final week? _____

21.   During part of the week, Jesus left Jerusalem in the evening and spent the night in what small town? _____

22.   Jesus' last Passover meal is commonly known as _____ _____ _____.

23.   T / F   Jesus was arrested during the day in the Garden of Gethsemane.

24.   Jesus appeared how many times before Pilate and Herod?
   Pilate _____   Herod _____

25.   Jesus was crucified at a place slightly outside of Jerusalem called _____.

26.   What two measures were taken to secure the tomb in which Jesus' body was placed?_____

   _____

27.   After Jesus' resurrection, but before His ascension, approximately how many recorded appearances do we find in the New Testament? _____

†

28.   How long was the time period between Jesus' resurrection and His ascension into heaven? _____

29.   T / F   The Book of First Corinthians states that the resurrected Christ appeared to a group of over 500 people.

30.   Part of Christ's final instructions to the apostles is known as _____ _____ _____ .

†

Talk The Talk

The Christmas story is told in Matthew and Luke. The commercialized version of the story combines elements of both Luke and Matthew.

A.   *Read chapter 2 of both Matthew and Luke. With regard to the characters in the typical nativity, what discrepancies do you detect?*

B.   *What conclusions can you draw when you consider the magi, the star, and the order to kill male children 2 and under?*

C.   *The tradition of three magi clearly comes from the three gifts. What new thoughts or feelings do you have about the Christmas story considering the symbolic purpose and value of the three gifts?*

✝

The "Theologically Speaking" section deals with the temptation of Jesus. For many this section adds a whole new dimension to the idea of temptation.

D.   *Looking at temptation from this new perspective, do you recall a time when you felt temptation to do what was a strength?*

E.   *What are your views on this new way to understand temptation?*

F.   *List your greatest temptations. How do you deal with them?*

✝

The Passover, Holy Communion, the Passover lamb and Christ as the sacrificial lamb are all integral to each other.

G.   *How are these connected to each other?*

H.   *How are these still connected to Christians today?*

✝

Walk The Walk

Read the Great Commission which is located at the end of the Gospel of Matthew. This commission speaks to all Christians.

I.   *As disciples of Christ, what are the four actions we are commissioned to perform?*

J.   *How are you now better enabled to carry out some of these actions than before you started this Bible study? How will you carry out the commission?*

NOTES

✝

Chapter 13
Christianity Spreads and the Church Begins

The Book of Acts is the primary record of the beginning of the Church and the subsequent spread of Christianity. It can be said that the Book of Acts explains the formation of Christianity much like the Books of Genesis and Exodus explain the formation of the Hebrew nation.

The Book of Acts was written by Luke, a Gentile physician and known companion of Saint Paul. The first sentence in the book makes reference to his earlier work, The Gospel of Luke. Luke never mentions his own name in the writing; however, in chapter 16 he clearly changes the writing tense to first person when he joins the party on the second missionary journey. The combined pages of the Gospel of Luke and the Book of Acts make Luke the major contributor, page-wise, to the New Testament.

Acts begins with the ascension of Christ and covers approximately the next 30 years. The exact starting date is debated and varies from 30 to 33 A.D. For the purposes of this study, 30 A.D. will be used as the date.

Major Characters And Important Names

The first 12 chapters of Acts follow several important figures. After chapter 12, the Apostle Paul is the predominate figure. The major characters in the Book of Acts and some key individuals who later become important in other New Testament books are given in the following table. The chapter in which characters are first introduced is listed.

THEOLOGICALLY SPEAKING

The Acts of the Apostles, and the Gospel according to Luke, both written by Luke, comprise close to one fourth of the New Testament. The primary purpose of the Gospel of Luke is to detail the life of Jesus; the Book of Acts continues and fulfills the story of the gospel.

Acts begins with the small band of faithful people who are still left after the death, resurrection, and ascension of Christ, and tells how they were filled with God's Holy Spirit and spread the good news of Christ throughout the world. Acts tells us how the Christian church moves from the city of

Jerusalem to encompass the world. It is within the context of the evolution of this original movement of Christianity that Luke introduces us to his hero, Paul, who will emerge as the primary leader within the early church. Paul will direct and enable the church to move from a "Jewish Christian Church," which incorrectly views Christianity as an enlightened sect of Judaism, to become a religion which believes that Christ's love is for the Jew and the non-Jew alike. Paul leads the Christian church to see that Jesus' mission was not to develop a sect of the Jewish religion, but to establish a religion that is unique and independent unto itself and is offered to everyone.

Table 13-1   Major Characters in the Book of Acts

Character	Chapter first named	Description
Luke	n/a	Although Luke, the author of Acts, does not name himself in the text, he was a known companion of Paul for several years. The words "us" and "we" are used in his writings.
Peter	1	Simon Peter, the apostle, was founder of the Christian church among the Jews.
John	1	John, the apostle, was the brother of James.
James	1	James, the brother of John, was the first apostle to be martyred.
Barnabas	4	Barnabas was a Jewish Levite from Cyprus, who became a follower of Christ after hearing Peter and John preach. His conversion was very soon after Pentecost.
Stephen	6	Stephen was one of seven workers to be chosen by the 12 apostles to help administer and carry out the work of the early church. Stephen was the very first follower of Christ to be martyred.
Philip	6	Philip was one of the seven workers chosen along with Stephen. He later became a great evangelist.

Saul of Tarsus	7	Saul is the Hebrew name for Paul. Paul brought Christianity to the Gentiles and authored numerous books of the New Testament.
Cornelius	10	Cornelius was a Roman centurion and is known for being the first Gentile convert.
John Mark	12	John Mark was a young companion of Paul and Barnabas.
King Herod	12	Herod Agrippa I was the grandson of Herod the Great.
Silas	15	Silas was a companion of Paul on his second missionary journey.
Timothy	16	Timothy accompanied Paul on his second missionary journey. Timothy's mother was Jewish and his father was Greek. Paul later referred to him as " his child in the faith."
Felix	24	Felix was the Roman governor of the province of Judea who kept Paul jailed two years.
Festus	24-25	Festus was the Roman governor of the province of Judea who succeeded Felix. Under his administration Paul appealed to Caesar.
King Agrippa	25	Jewish King Agrippa is Herod Agrippa II, the great grandson of Herod the Great. He stated that Paul had done nothing wrong.

Places in Acts

The Book of Acts covers more geographical territory than any other book in the Bible. Acts records the journeys of the missionaries as the word of Christ spreads throughout Asia Minor, North Africa, Europe and to the very capital of the world, Rome. The following table describes some of the best-known places mentioned in the Book of Acts.

Table 13-2   Important Places in Acts

Place	Description
Antioch	1. Sometimes called Pisidian Antioch. A city in southern Asia Minor where Paul visited on his missionary journeys, not to be confused with city of Antioch which was the capital of Syria. 2. The capital of the Roman province of Syria. The center for Paul's three missionary journeys, not to be confused with the city of Antioch in Asia Minor.
Caesarea	Coastal city in Palestine which was the home of Philip and the site of significant activity in Acts. Caesarea is not to be confused with Caesarea Philippi, an inland city near Mount Hermon where Jesus visited.
Corinth	City in Greece in which Paul founded a church.
Cyprus	An island in the east Mediterranean which was rich in copper. It was the home of many Jews, including Barnabas.
Damascus	A major city in Syria. Paul was in route to Damascus when his conversion experience occurred.
Ephesus	Capital city of the Roman province of Asia. Paul founded a church there.
Galatia	Territory in Asia Minor in which Paul founded several churches.
Jerusalem	Central city in Palestine where the church began on the day of Pentecost.
Joppa	Coastal city in Palestine where Peter visited and preached.
Macedonia	Roman colony in Europe located north of Greece in which Paul founded several churches.
Philippi	City in the Roman colony of Macedonia in which Paul founded a church.
Phoenicia	Country along the Mediterranean coast just to the north of the Sea of Galilee. In Old Testament times it was referred to as Canaan.

Samaria	Region of Palestine where the word of Christ was spread by Philip. The main city in that region is also named Samaria.
Syria	Large Roman province located north of Palestine.
Tarsus	City in southeast Asia Minor. Home of the Apostle Paul.
Thessalonica	Chief city in the Roman colony of Macedonia in which Paul founded a church.

The Major Stages in the Spread of Christianity

Scholars have most often divided the Book of Acts into six distinct portions or stages. These stages are natural divisions and are primarily dictated by the geographical areas where the Good News of Jesus Christ was being taken by the missionaries. As shown below, this chapter will be subdivided into similar stages with the addition of an introduction about Paul:

THE CHURCH AT JERUSALEM
CHRISTIANITY IN PALESTINE AND SYRIA
PAUL THE MISSIONARY
PAUL'S FIRST MISSIONARY JOURNEY
PAUL'S SECOND MISSIONARY JOURNEY
PAUL'S THIRD MISSIONARY JOURNEY
PAUL'S ARREST AND JOURNEY TO ROME

THE CHURCH AT JERUSALEM

The numerous appearances and instructions given by the risen Lord which are found in the last chapters of the Gospels are summarized in the first chapter of Acts with the following Scripture:

"He appeared to them over a period of forty days and spoke about the kingdom of God. On one occasion, while he was eating with them, he gave them this command: 'Do not leave Jerusalem, but wait for the gift my Father promised, which you have heard me speak about. For John baptized with water, but in a few days you will be baptized with the Holy Spirit.'"

Acts 1:3b-5

Table 13-3   The Church at Jerusalem

Chapter	Event
	30 A.D.
1	**The Commission and Ascension** The risen Lord gathered the apostles together, promised them the power of the Holy Spirit and commissioned them to witness in Jerusalem, Judea, Samaria and even to the remotest parts of the earth. On the Mount of Olives, Jesus then ascended into heaven. As the apostles waited for the gift of the Holy Spirit, they choose Matthias as the replacement for Judas.
2	**Pentecost** As the apostles were gathered together, on the day of Pentecost, the Holy Spirit was poured out upon them as tongues of fire. They began to speak in other languages and witness to the other Jews who were gathered in Jerusalem from all over the world. Peter began to preach and explain the Good News of Jesus Christ. The result was that 3,000 individuals received the Word and were baptized that day alone. Pentecost is the birthday of the Church. *Pentecost is the Greek name for the Jewish Feast of Weeks. It is celebrated seven weeks (a week of weeks) or 50 days after the Passover.*

3	**Peter and John Attract Attention in Jerusalem** As Peter and John entered the temple to pray, Peter healed a man who had been lame from birth. Peter then preached to the crowd about Jesus, the risen Lord.
4	**The Beginning of Persecution** The Sadducees, who did not believe in life after death, were greatly offended and very angry because Peter and John were teaching about the resurrection of Jesus. Peter and John were arrested, jailed and later questioned by Annas the high priest, Caiaphas and other Jewish religious officials concerning healing the lame man and preaching about Jesus. They were ordered not to speak or teach in the name of Jesus and released.
4-5	**Continued Growth** The new church congregations voluntarily shared their property to support the work of the disciples. People came from nearby cities to be healed and to hear the Good News of Jesus. Multitudes of men and women were added to their number.
5	**Persecution Increases** The high priest and the Sadducees became so angry that Peter and the apostles were again arrested and jailed. An angel rescued them from jail, and they immediately began to preach again. They were arrested for a third time, flogged and ordered not to preach. Their response was, *"We must obey God rather than men,"* and they continued to preach and teach both in the temple and in houses.
6	**Workers Chosen** Seven devout individuals were chosen to aid the apostles in administrating the work of the church. Both Stephen and Philip were in this group.
	33 A.D.
6-7	**Stephen is Martyred** Stephen was full of grace and power and performed many signs and wonders. He was falsely accused by leaders of one of the synagogues in Jerusalem and was stoned to death. Saul of Tarsus was a witness to Stephen's stoning and was in full agreement. Stephen was the first Christian martyr.

CHRISTIANITY IN PALESTINE AND SYRIA

Persecution Causes the Word to be Spread

For the better part of three years, the apostles had spread the word of Jesus primarily in and around the city of Jerusalem without any documented effort of evangelizing elsewhere. The spread of the gospel outside of Jerusalem depended upon visitors being converted and carrying the Good News with them when they departed.

The public stoning of Stephen marked the establishment of full scale open persecution against the church. It also brought an end to limited localized evangelism, instead of forcing the believers to give up their faith, it simply caused many to leave Jerusalem and be scattered, thus the Good News of Jesus Christ was spread even more.

"But Saul began to destroy the church. Going from house to house, he dragged off men and women and put them in prison."　　　*Acts 8:3*

Table 13-4　Christianity in Palestine and Syria

Chapter	Event
8	**Philip Preaches** Philip traveled to the region of Samaria where he preached in the city of Samaria and in surrounding villages. Many who had been paralyzed and lame were healed and there was great rejoicing in the city. Peter and John later came from Jerusalem to help Philip in Samaria because of his great success. Philip next traveled on the Gaza road where he met and baptized an important official from Ethiopia who was journeying to Jerusalem to worship. Philip continued preaching the Gospel to the cities up the coast to Caesarea.
	34 A.D.
9	**Saul (Paul) is Converted** Saul of Tarsus, a devout Jew who hated the followers of Jesus, was traveling from Jerusalem to Damascus. He had documents from the high priest which gave him authority to arrest any followers of Jesus he could find and bring them back to Jerusalem. On the road, Saul was struck by a great light and the voice of Jesus spoke to him. Saul was converted and immediately began to preach in the synagogues of Damascus that Jesus was indeed the Christ. All who heard Saul were amazed that this was the same person who had persecuted the believers just a short time earlier. Saul continued to spread the word even more powerfully and to prove that Jesus was the Christ.

	37 A.D.
9	**Saul is Persecuted** *Verse 23 of chapter 9 in Acts states that, after many days, the Jews plotted against Saul. In Paul's Letter to the Galatians, he explained that he went to Arabia during this time. In this case, the phrase after many days actually means three years.* Being aware of the three year trip to Arabia, we can more clearly state that, after Saul returned to Damascus from Arabia, he began preaching again and the Jews then plotted to do away with him. When Saul learned of the plot, he escaped from Damascus by being lowered down the city wall in a basket. Saul next traveled to Jerusalem, where Barnabas introduced him to the apostles and explained his conversion experience. Saul then began to speak boldly in the name of the Lord in Jerusalem and the Jews there also plotted to kill him. He left for Caesarea and then continued on to his hometown of Tarsus where he stayed for several years in relative silence.
9	**Peter and the Gentiles** While Peter was traveling in the area west of Jerusalem toward the coastline, he visited the city of Joppa. While he was in Joppa, a very kind and godly lady who was a follower of Christ died. The many mourners told of all her acts of kindness and charity. Peter raised her from the dead. After this event, even more people became believers. One day while Peter was still in Joppa, he saw a vision concerning clean and unclean food. Immediately after the vision he was divinely called to Caesarea to the home of a Roman centurion named Cornelius. Cornelius had also seen a vision. Peter then realized the meaning of the vision: all people were clean and could enter into God's kingdom if they only believed. Peter then baptized Cornelius making him the first Gentile convert. *Peter was called from the seaport of Joppa to bring the New Covenant to the Gentiles in the city of Caesarea. Centuries earlier, the Old Testament prophet Jonah sailed from Joppa after being called to bring the Word of God to the Gentiles in the city of Nineveh.*
11	**Results of the Persecution** Due to the persecution in Jerusalem, the word of Jesus had now spread to Phoenicia, Cyprus and Antioch. Antioch, the capital of Syria, was a city with a population of 500,000 located near the Mediterranean coast 300 miles north of Jerusalem.

	43 A.D.
11	**Barnabas is Sent to Antioch** News of many Gentile believers in Antioch reached the church in Jerusalem and, consequently, Barnabas was sent to Antioch. There he found many believers, both Jew and Greek. Barnabas then went to Tarsus to find Saul and bring him back to Antioch. Together they taught in the church at Antioch for one year. It was at this time in Antioch that the followers of Christ were first called Christians.
	Mid 40's A.D.
11	**Barnabas and Saul Travel to Jerusalem** Due to a great famine, the church in Antioch decided to aid the church in Jerusalem. Barnabas and Saul were sent to Jerusalem to deliver the gift.
12	**Persecution Escalates in Jerusalem** James the brother of John was killed by King Herod Agrippa I. Although other Christians had been killed, this was the first of the apostles to die for Christianity. Because the murder of James pleased the Jewish leaders, Herod had Peter arrested, chained and jailed. Immediately before Peter was to appear before Herod and the Jewish people, he was rescued from prison by an angel and then safely traveled to Caesarea. *Agrippa was the grandson of Herod the Great who ruled when Jesus was born.*
12	**Barnabas and Saul Return to Antioch** Barnabas and Saul fulfilled their stewardship mission in Jerusalem and returned to the city of Antioch. They brought with them a young man by the name of John Mark.

Diagram 13-1, The Good News Spreads, is located on the following page. It provides a graphical representation of some major events in the early chapters of Acts.

THE GOOD NEWS SPREADS

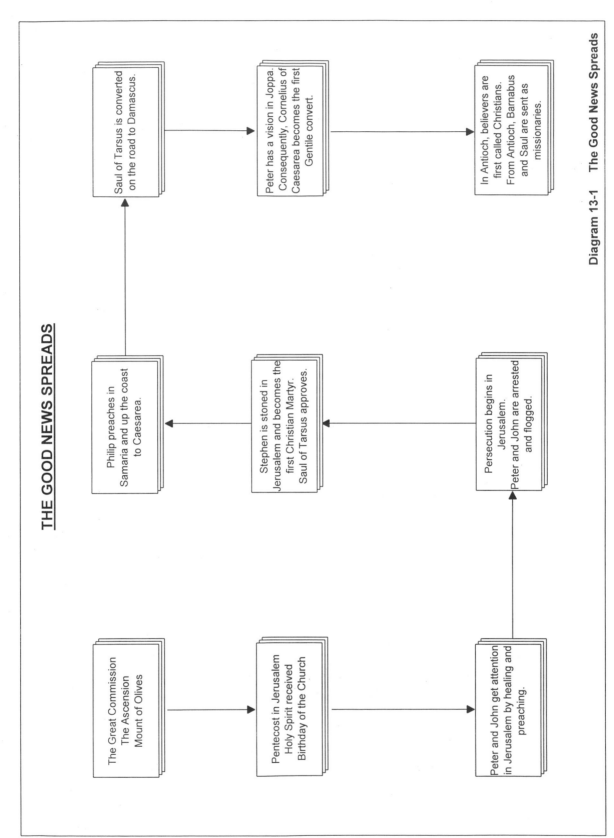

The Great Commission
The Ascension
Mount of Olives

Pentecost in Jerusalem
Holy Spirit received
Birthday of the Church

Peter and John get attention in Jerusalem by healing and preaching.

Persecution begins in Jerusalem.
Peter and John are arrested and flogged.

Stephen is stoned in Jerusalem and becomes the first Christian Martyr.
Saul of Tarsus approves.

Philip preaches in Samaria and up the coast to Caesarea.

Saul of Tarsus is converted on the road to Damascus.

Peter has a vision in Joppa. Consequently, Cornelius of Caesarea becomes the first Gentile convert.

In Antioch, believers are first called Christians. From Antioch, Barnabus and Saul are sent as missionaries.

Diagram 13-1   The Good News Spreads

PAUL THE MISSIONARY

Soon after the return of Barnabas and Saul to Antioch, the Holy Spirit came upon certain members of the church in Antioch and said the following:

"Set apart for me Barnabas and Saul for the work to which I have called them."
Acts 13:2b

Paul the Missionary to the Gentiles

Chapter 13 marks the point in the Scripture where Saul became the key figure in the remainder of the Book of Acts. Also in this chapter, Saul became known by his official Roman name, Paul. Paul's sole mission was to spread the Good News of Jesus Christ. Although he is known for bringing the gospel to the Gentiles, his method was not necessarily pointed in that singular direction.

As Paul traveled to new areas which were predominately Gentile, he sought out the small local Jewish inner community, in which there was normally a synagogue. Because Paul was a devout Jew, a Pharisee and a Roman citizen by birth, he was welcomed and immediately accepted with great credibility. Before the leaders in the local Jewish communities, Paul the distinguished Jew would begin to teach about Jesus Christ the Messiah.

More times than not Paul's words were rejected by the leading Jews, yet he continued to preach to all who would listen. This is where the Gentile believers became a key factor in the spread of Christianity. Many times the larger Gentile population was just as eager to receive the message of Christ as the small Jewish community was ready to reject it. Paul later wrote the following in his Letter to the Romans:

"I am not ashamed of the gospel, because it is the power of God for the salvation of everyone who believes: first for the Jew, then for the Gentile."   *Romans 1:16*

One must marvel at the continuity of God's plan and its implementation. The messenger to bring Christianity to these foreign lands was a devout Jew, who in the recent past had viciously fought against what he was presently risking his life to preach. Due to the combination of his distinctive Jewish background and Roman citizenship, Paul had credibility and could readily gain entry into these Jewish communities where few other individuals could have succeeded.

Equally important was the fact that there were small Jewish communities sprinkled throughout the civilized world. The very existence of these distant Jewish communities can be attributed to attempts to escape the persecution and exiles which God's people had endured in Old Testament times.

What previously appeared to be randomly scattered groups of refugee Jews now formed strategically placed stepping stones for the rapid spread of Christianity.

Details of Paul's Journeys

In a 13 year period, Paul traveled over 8,000 miles during his three missionary journeys and the trip to Rome. These travels and events are compressed into a very concise record in the Book of Acts. One brief passage of Scripture may be used to describe a journey that lasted for weeks or even months.

Paul's letters also include a significant amount of information about the routes and time frame of his journeys. Upon the completion of this study, if you want a more comprehensive understanding of the missionary journeys and the establishment of the churches, combine the information from Paul's letters with the information from Acts while referring to the maps.

PAUL'S FIRST MISSIONARY JOURNEY

Paul visited numerous cities on his journeys and started some type of church in a large number of these communities. To avoid complication, this study will list only a few of the churches.

Table 13-5   Paul's First Missionary Journey

Chapter	Event
	47 A.D.
13-15	**Barnabas, Saul and John Mark** Barnabas and Saul were sent out as missionaries by the church in Antioch. Apparently John Mark accompanied them as their assistant.
	The Journey They sailed first to the island of Cyprus and then traveled overland to the west end of the island. It was in this Gentile environment that Saul began to use his Roman or Gentile name, Paul. After this time, Paul's name was normally listed first in the scriptures and he clearly became the leader. They next sailed to Asia Minor. When they reached the coast, John Mark left them and returned to Jerusalem. They traveled inland and visited about six major cities in South Central Asia Minor. Some type of church was established at each location. They sailed from Asia Minor and returned directly to Antioch. Paul later addressed an epistle to the Galatia district.
	Length and Time The entire journey including land and sea travel was approximately 1,200 miles and took about two years.

Diagram 13-2, Paul's First Missionary Journey, is located on the following page. The diagram offers a graphical view of the journey.

Map 13-1, Paul's First Missionary Journey, is located on the page after the diagram. It presents a possible route of the journey. Only the major stops in the journey are shown.

PAUL'S FIRST MISSIONARY JOURNEY

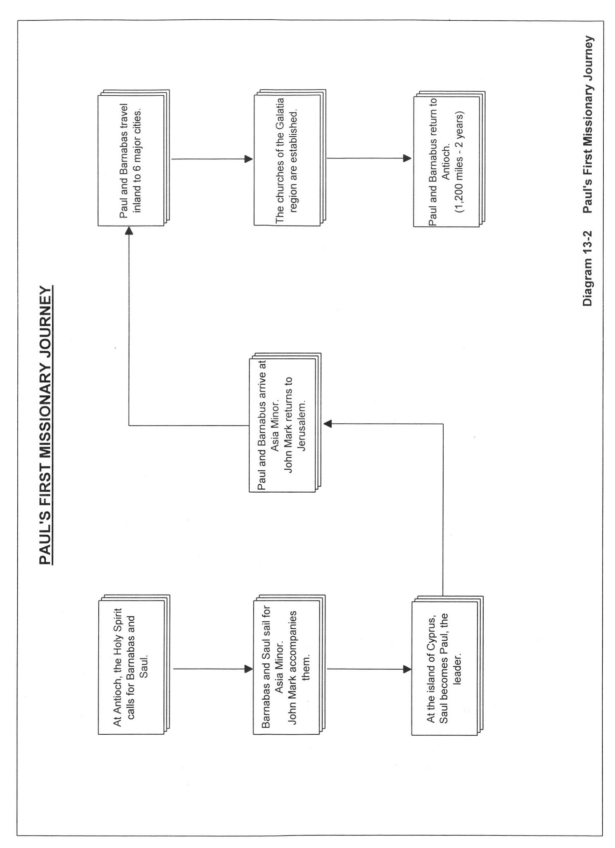

At Antioch, the Holy Spirit calls for Barnabas and Saul.

Barnabas and Saul sail for Asia Minor. John Mark accompanies them.

At the island of Cyprus, Saul becomes Paul, the leader.

Paul and Barnabus arrive at Asia Minor. John Mark returns to Jerusalem.

Paul and Barnabas travel inland to 6 major cities.

The churches of the Galatia region are established.

Paul and Barnabus return to Antioch. (1,200 miles - 2 years)

Diagram 13-2   Paul's First Missionary Journey

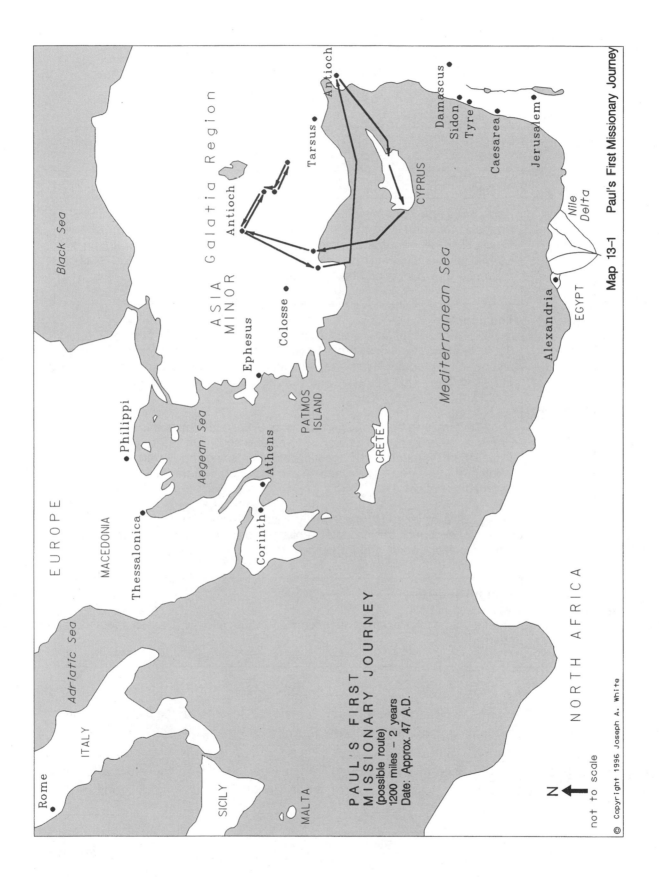

Map 13-1   Paul's First Missionary Journey

PAUL'S FIRST
MISSIONARY JOURNEY
(possible route)
1200 miles – 2 years
Date: Approx. 47 A.D.

N
not to scale

© copyright 1996 Joseph A. White

PAUL'S SECOND MISSIONARY JOURNEY

Table 13-6   Paul's Second Missionary Journey

Chapter	Event
	49 A.D.
15-18	**Paul, Silas and Timothy** Paul and Silas left Antioch and traveled overland through the center of Asia Minor. This allowed them to revisit the churches started on the first journey. Early in the journey, Paul met Timothy and he accompanied Paul and Silas on the rest of the journey and became Paul's faithful assistant.
	The Journey In Asia Minor, Paul saw a vision of a man that was calling him to Europe. Because of the vision, they crossed the Aegean Sea to Macedonia, a Roman colony in Europe. There they established the churches at Philippi and Thessalonica. This entrance into Europe was of major importance to the spread of Christianity. They then traveled south along the coast of Greece to Athens and on to Corinth where another important church was established. On the return trip, they established the church at Ephesus before crossing the Mediterranean and landing at Caesarea. They then visited the church at Jerusalem and finally returned to Antioch. There were at least 15 major points visited on this journey. Of particular interest, because of the later epistles, are the churches of Philippi, Thessalonica, Corinth and Ephesus.
	Length and Time The trip had a total length of approximately 2,500 miles and lasted about three years.

Diagram 13-3, Paul's Second Missionary Journey, is located on the following page. The diagram offers a graphical view of the journey.

Map 13-2, Paul's Second Missionary Journey, is located on the page after the diagram. It presents a possible route of the journey. Only the major stops in the journey are shown.

PAUL'S SECOND MISSIONARY JOURNEY

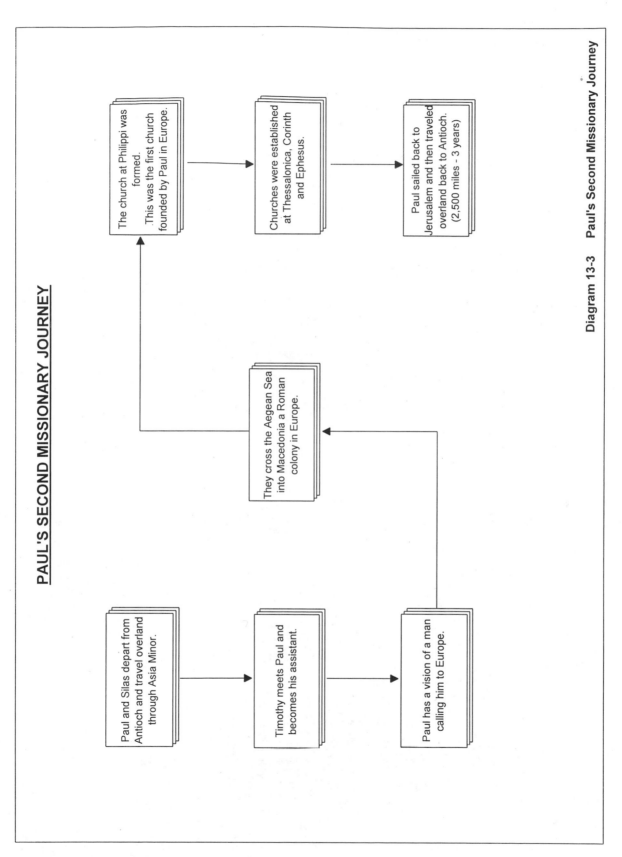

Paul and Silas depart from Antioch and travel overland through Asia Minor.

Timothy meets Paul and becomes his assistant.

Paul has a vision of a man calling him to Europe.

They cross the Aegean Sea into Macedonia a Roman colony in Europe.

The church at Philippi was formed. This was the first church founded by Paul in Europe.

Churches were established at Thessalonica, Corinth and Ephesus.

Paul sailed back to Jerusalem and then traveled overland back to Antioch. (2,500 miles - 3 years)

Diagram 13-3   **Paul's Second Missionary Journey**

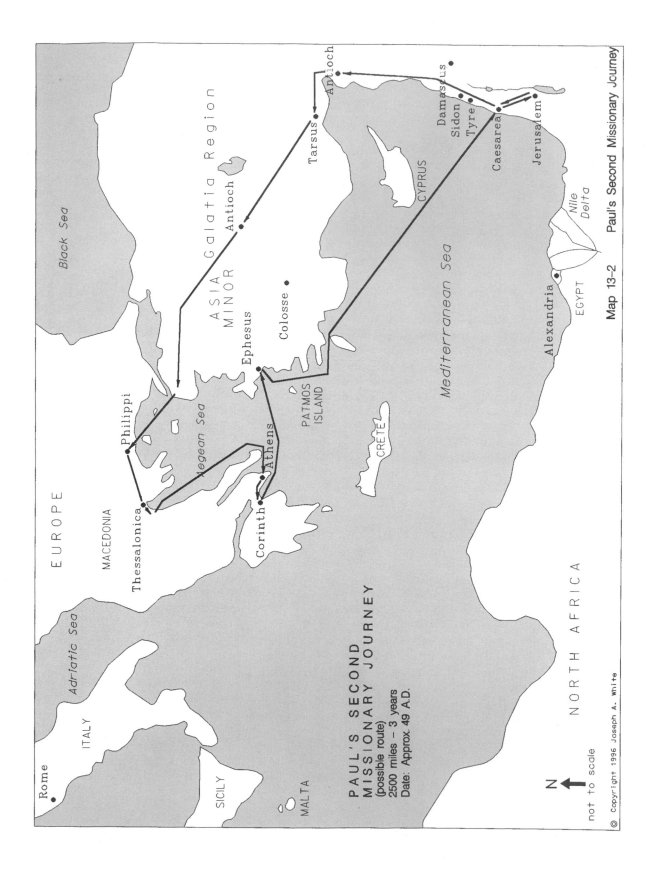

PAUL'S THIRD MISSIONARY JOURNEY

Table 13-7   Paul's Third Missionary Journey

Chapter	Event
	52 A.D.
18-21	**Paul and Timothy** Paul made much of this trip alone. He sent Timothy and other workers on various side trips while he preached and wrote in Ephesus.
	The Journey The third journey followed the same general route as the second and allowed Paul to revisit many of the young churches. Paul was very successful in Ephesus and worked there for approximately three years. To end the journey, Paul returned to Caesarea and visited in the house of Philip. There he was warned by the Holy Spirit that in Jerusalem he would be bound by the Jews and delivered into the hands of the Gentiles. However, Paul was not afraid and traveled on to Jerusalem.
	Length and Time The total journey covered more than 2,500 miles and lasted about four years.

Diagram 13-4, Paul's Third Missionary Journey, is located on the following page. The diagram offers a graphical view of the journey.

Map 13-3, Paul's Third Missionary Journey, is located on the page after the diagram. It presents a possible route of the journey. Only the major stops in the journey are shown.

PAUL'S THIRD MISSIONARY JOURNEY

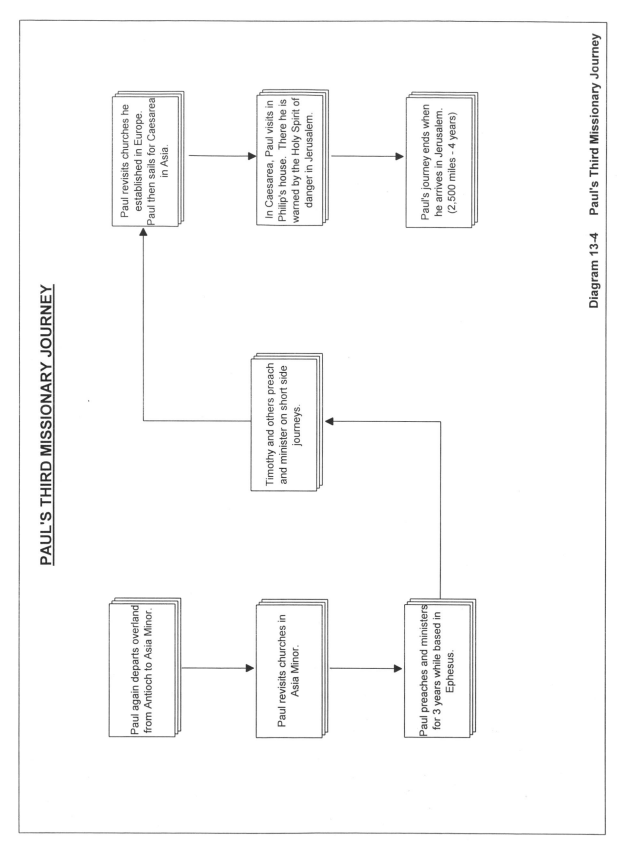

Paul again departs overland from Antioch to Asia Minor.

Paul revisits churches in Asia Minor.

Paul preaches and ministers for 3 years while based in Ephesus.

Timothy and others preach and minister on short side journeys.

Paul revisits churches he established in Europe. Paul then sails for Caesarea in Asia.

In Caesarea, Paul visits in Philip's house. There he is warned by the Holy Spirit of danger in Jerusalem.

Paul's journey ends when he arrives in Jerusalem. (2,500 miles - 4 years)

Diagram 13-4   Paul's Third Missionary Journey

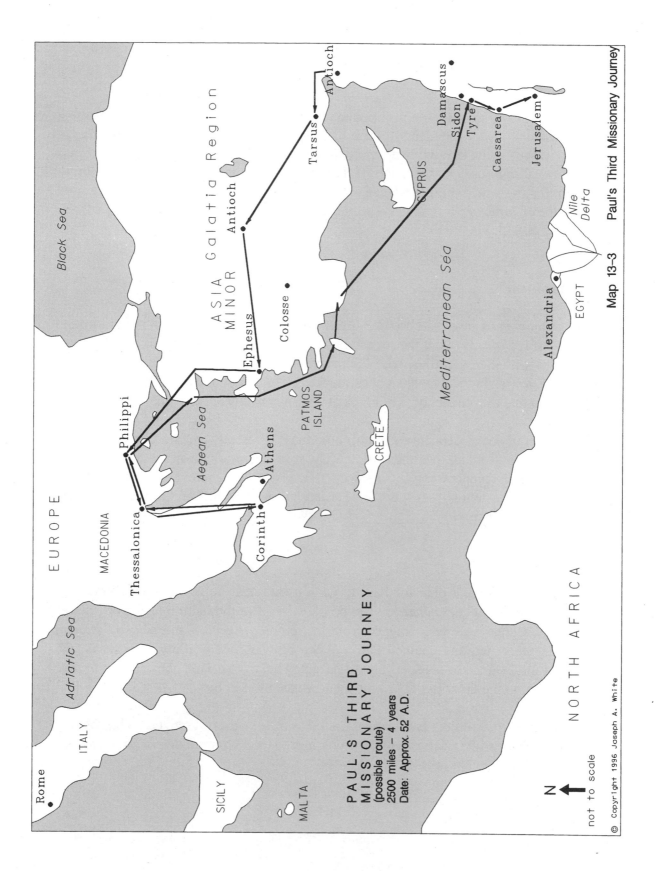

PAUL'S THIRD
MISSIONARY JOURNEY
(possible route)
2500 miles – 4 years
Date: Approx. 52 A.D.

Map 13-3   Paul's Third Missionary Journey

© copyright 1996 Joseph A. White

not to scale

PAUL'S ARREST AND JOURNEY TO ROME

After the third missionary journey, several disciples traveled with Paul from Caesarea to Jerusalem. All were clearly aware of the warning from the Holy Spirit of what would happen in the city and understood the dangers from the Jews in Jerusalem. Upon their arrival in Jerusalem, the elders of the church welcomed Paul and advised him of the major problem which he faced. It dealt with reconciling a very delicate and complicated issue which had developed between many of the Jews and Gentiles who believed in Jesus.

The Problem

A large number of Jews had become Christians and yet wanted to also remain true to their heritage by following the Jewish laws. To this Paul fully agreed. On the other hand, the Christian Gentiles, who Paul represented, did not know or care anything about the Jewish laws. They had been introduced to Christianity on the basis of faith alone. To this the leaders of the church at Jerusalem fully agreed.

This matter was very delicate and highly emotional. Presently in Jerusalem, there were groups of Jews from all over the world. Many were misinformed and very angry about Paul's teachings concerning this subject. There was also the ever-present group of Jews that flatly denied Jesus as the Messiah and would stop at nothing to halt the spread of Christianity.

The Plan Fails

The elders set forth a plan for Paul to demonstrate that he had not abandoned his heritage and did not ask other Jews to do likewise. But the faction against Paul was already too great. He was dragged from the temple by a mob and beaten. Roman soldiers intervened and chained Paul. When he was finally allowed to speak, the Jewish mob listened to his speech until he stated he had a divine commission to take the Gospel to the Gentiles. The mob again wanted to kill him.

By this time, the soldiers had learned Paul was a Roman-born citizen. The soldiers feared for Paul's life and immediately took him to their commander.

Table 13-8   Paul's Trials and Travel to Rome

Chapter	Event
	56 A.D.
23	**Before the Sanhedrin** After Paul was rescued from the mob by the Roman soldiers, he was placed under arrest and taken before the Sanhedrin. Paul, being a shrewd Pharisee, caused such a division between the Pharisees and the Sadducees that the Romans transferred him to Caesarea for his own safety. The Jewish charges against him were changed. They were never very substantial. Paul stated that he was being persecuted for two reasons, and these were the driving reasons of his ministry: 1. His call to the Gentiles. 2. His belief in the resurrection.
24	**Before Governor Felix** Paul defended his case before Governor Felix in Caesarea. He was kept prisoner by Felix for two years. Felix liked Paul and talked with him often; however, he also wanted to keep the Jews happy; therefore, Paul remained in prison.
	58 A.D.
25	**Before Governor Festus** A new governor, Festus, was appointed. Since he also wished to please the Jews, he planned to have Paul's trial 65 miles away in Jerusalem. At this point, Paul exercised his right as a Roman citizen to personally appeal to Caesar. This meant that Paul must now be transported to Rome in order to appear before Caesar.
25-26	**Before King Herod** The Jewish king, Herod Agrippa II, came to visit the new governor, Festus, and asked to hear Paul. He understood Paul's preaching; recognized the Jew-versus-Gentile issue and realized that the Jews simply wanted to stop Paul's ministry. Herod stated that Paul had done nothing wrong and could have gone free had he not appealed to Caesar.

	59 A.D.
27-28	**The Voyage to Rome** Although Paul sailed for Rome under guard, he was treated very well by the Roman centurion. They made several stops along the way, and were eventually shipwrecked on the island of Malta. In 60 A.D., after a 2,000 mile trip, they finally arrived in Rome. Paul was under "house arrest" in his own rented quarters for two years. In these quarters, he met with the leading Jews of Rome, wrote several of his letters and continued to spread the Good News of Jesus Christ.

The Final Days of Paul

There are several theories about Paul's final imprisonment. One theory states that Paul was released for a short period of time before being arrested again and finally executed. Another theory states that he was released and went on to do missionary work in Spain as he had previously planned. However, most scholars think that shortly after his documented two years of confinement in Rome, the situation deteriorated, and he was executed in the next outbreak of Christian persecution.

Diagram 13-5, Paul's Journey to Rome, is located on the following page. The diagram offers a graphical view of the events of and leading up to the journey.

Map 13-4, Paul's Journey to Rome, is located on the page after the diagram. It presents a possible route of the voyage.

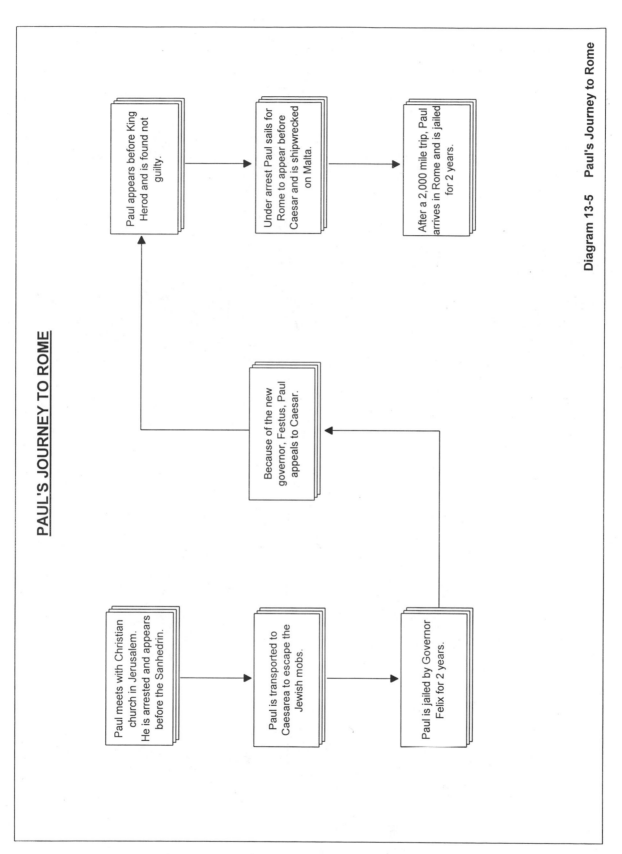

PAUL'S JOURNEY TO ROME

Paul meets with Christian church in Jerusalem. He is arrested and appears before the Sanhedrin.

Paul is transported to Caesarea to escape the Jewish mobs.

Paul is jailed by Governor Felix for 2 years.

Because of the new governor, Festus, Paul appeals to Caesar.

Paul appears before King Herod and is found not guilty.

Under arrest Paul sails for Rome to appear before Caesar and is shipwrecked on Malta.

After a 2,000 mile trip, Paul arrives in Rome and is jailed for 2 years.

Diagram 13-5   Paul's Journey to Rome

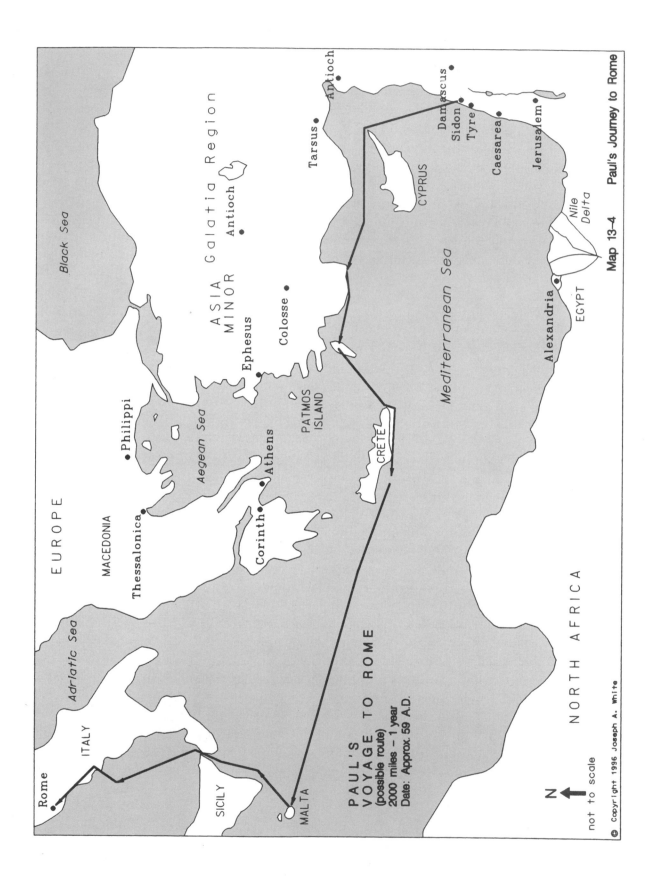

PAUL'S VOYAGE TO ROME
(possible route)
2000 miles – 1 year
Date: Approx. 59 A.D.

Map 13–4   Paul's Journey to Rome

not to scale

Read The Book

1. The Acts of the Apostles was written by _____ .

2. Acts covers a period of time of approximately how many years? _____

3. The Book of Acts can be divided into two main parts:
    The first _____ chapters follow several important figures.
    The later chapters focus on the_____ _____ .

4. Who was the <u>first</u> of the 12 <u>apostles</u> to be martyred? _____

5. Of the seven workers chosen by the apostles:
    Who was the first Christian martyr?   _____
    Who became a great evangelist?   _____

6. How many King Herods are in Acts? _____

7. Christianity began in Southwest Asia. Acts records its spread to Asia Minor
    and to the continents of _____ and _____ .

8. T / F   There are two cities named Antioch referenced in Acts, one of which
             was the center for Paul's missionary journeys.

9. Jesus told the apostles to not leave Jerusalem. John baptized with water, but
    soon they would be baptized with the _____ _____.

10. Before His ascension, the risen Lord commissioned the apostles to witness in
    Jerusalem, Judea, Samaria and where else?

    _____

11.   On this day the Holy Spirit came upon the apostles and it became known as the birthday of the Church. _____

12.   T / F   On Pentecost, 3,000 people believed and were baptized.

13.   The beginning of persecution of the followers of Christ started with the arrest of which two apostles? _____ and _____

14.   After the first arrest, Peter and the apostles continued to preach and were again jailed. This time they were rescued by an _____ .

15.   T / F   After their rescue, they were arrested a third time and then flogged.

16.   What significant person in the history of the church witnessed the stoning of Stephen? _____ __ _____

17.   On the road to _____ Saul was struck by a great light and heard the voice of _____ speaking to him.

18.   After Saul's conversion experience, he journeyed to Arabia, and later returned to Damascus. He was persecuted in Damascus and escaped from the city by being lowered in a _____ .

19.   After escaping from Damascus, Paul traveled to Jerusalem where he met with the _____ .

20.   In Jerusalem, the Jews plotted to_____ Saul; therefore, he returned to his hometown of Tarsus.

21. While in the town of Joppa, _____ had a divine vision in which he was called to travel to Caesarea and visit in the home of _____ .

22. The subject of the vision at Joppa was _____ and _____ food; however, the food was only symbolic and Peter realized that all people were _____ and could enter the kingdom of God if they believed.

23. When this Roman centurion was baptized, he became the first _____ convert.

24. T / F   It was in the Syrian city of Antioch that believers were first called Christians.

25. As persecution escalated in Jerusalem, the following events happened:
    The Apostle _____ was killed by Herod.
    The Apostle _____ was again rescued by an angel.

26. The Holy Spirit told the church at Antioch to set apart whom?
    _____ and _____

27. In 13 years, Paul traveled approximately how many miles in his three journeys? _____

28. Who did not complete the first missionary journey? _____ _____

29. T / F   Paul's first journey was the shortest in distance of the three.

30. On the second missionary journey, Paul was accompanied by which two individuals?_____ _____

31.   While in Asia Minor, Paul saw a vision of a man. What was this man doing?

_____

32.   List the four churches established during the second missionary journey to which letters were later addressed.

_____   _____

_____   _____

33.   T / F   The third missionary journey followed the same general route as the first.

34.   Approximately how many miles were traveled and how long did the third missionary journey last?_____   _____

35.   Paul was arrested in _____ upon his return from the third journey.

36.   After his arrest, Paul was moved from Jerusalem to Caesarea for his own safety. He remained under arrest for over two years by order of what two governors?   _____ and _____

37.   Paul was shipwrecked on the island of _____ during his voyage to Rome.

38.   Paul was under "_____ _____" for two years in Rome.

Talk The Talk

On the day of Pentecost the Holy Spirit was poured upon the apostles as tongues of fire and they began to speak other languages.

A.   *What immediate purpose did the apostles speaking in other languages serve?*

Approximately three years after Pentecost, the persecution of believers began to develop in Jerusalem.

B.   *Did this persecution help or hinder the spread of Christianity?*

As Paul traveled, three main factors allowed him to establish credibility and gain an audience in the local Jewish communities.

C.   *What were these factors and how did they help Paul?*

Early in the first missionary journey two significant changes are seen in the Scripture regarding Saul's name.

D.   *What were these changes and why did they occur?*

Walk The Walk

Persecution of Christians is seen throughout the Book of Acts. Religious persecution has continued throughout history, even to the present time.

E.   *Have you ever personally been the target of religious persecution?*

F.   *In the secular world, do we sometimes "duck" an issue or choose not to voice our true beliefs to avoid persecution?*

Chapter 14
The Letters of the Early Church

Of the 27 books which comprise the New Testament, 21 are letters, often called "epistles," which were written to churches or individuals. These letters teach Christian doctrine. This doctrine is set forth both in formal methods as found in the Letter to the Romans and in specific applications as found in the Letter to Philemon, which deals solely with the ownership of slaves. Although these letters comprise three fourths of the books of the New Testament, their combined number of pages makes up less than one third of the New Testament.

Letters in Ancient Days

The term "letter" is sometimes misleading for the Bible student. Today we think of a letter as a fairly short, rapidly transmitted document which is structured to include names, addresses, dates and signatures. In New Testament times, this was not necessarily the case. Although some ancient letters were much like our modern versions, the majority of the letters in the New Testament are more nearly in the format of a document which today might be presented in a seminar or lecture with the future intention of being used as reference material.

Authors and Dates of the Letters

Dates and addresses were often omitted from these letters, and sometimes even names were optional. In certain cases it was accepted practice to write under the name of another person. This practice was typically associated with students or followers of well-known teachers. The knowledge of the ancient style of letter writing, combined with the lack of privacy in the mail and the constant dangers of being persecuted because of one's Christian beliefs, gives us a much clearer understanding of why it is difficult, if not impossible, to determine exactly who wrote some of the church letters and when they were sent.

This chapter will be subdivided into the following three general divisions:

> THE LETTERS OF SAINT PAUL
> THE GENERAL LETTERS OR EPISTLES
> THE FINAL BOOK OF THE NEW TESTAMENT

THE LETTERS OF SAINT PAUL

The Book of Acts includes Paul's three missionary journeys and his voyage to Rome. As he traveled, Paul did three things: he set up new congregations, he visited churches that he had previously started, and he wrote letters. Although the purpose of the letters was always to provide instruction in the Christian faith, the letters themselves varied greatly and served many purposes.

> ### THEOLOGICALLY SPEAKING
>
> Without question Saint Paul was the most powerful voice in the Christian movement in explaining Jesus' story to the earliest converts. Paul took a hard-line stand "for" the inclusion of Gentiles (non-Jewish people) into the Christian Community. He continually speaks to this issue of God's grace being offered to <u>all</u> people. He understood his ministry as a response to God's calling, "that I might preach Him (Jesus) among the Gentiles." (Galatians 1:15).[1]

Greetings from Paul

Paul never ceased in his efforts to spread Christianity, neither did he cease in attempting to bridge the gap between the Jewish and Gentile Christian. This is evidenced even in the greetings which began each of his letters. Paul uses these words or a slight variation thereof for his greeting: *"Grace be to you, and peace, from God our Father, and from the Lord Jesus Christ."*

In this seemingly simple greeting, Paul combined important terms from both the Greek and the Hebrew letter writing tradition and transformed them into a new and distinctly

Christian greeting. The Greek word for "grace" was very much like the Greek word commonly used in a greeting. "Peace" was the usual greeting for Hebrews.

In the Christian tradition, we believe that grace is necessary for forgiveness and reconciliation. Peace is the condition of the heart after grace has done its work. Therefore, the greeting is always in that order, grace followed by peace.

The theological concept of grace was so important in Paul's teachings that he also ended all of his letters with another reminder of God's grace. His benediction was always some slightly varying form of "grace be with you."

Table 14-1   The Six Church Letters

Letter	Description
Romans	Rome was the capital of the Roman Empire, which included virtually all of the land around the entire Mediterranean Sea. During the time of the New Testament, Rome was the capital of the world. The Scriptures do not state anything about the establishments of or the workings of the church in Rome. It had clearly been in existence for some time when Paul wrote his Letter to the Romans from the city of Corinth during his third missionary journey. At that time Paul had never visited Rome, but the church there was widely known and was composed both of Jews and Gentiles. In the letter, Paul greeted many people that he obviously knew and he was aware that they met in various houses. Paul wrote the Letter to the Romans for very different reasons than his other letters. He was planning to visit Rome on his way to the eastern areas of the Roman Empire (Spain). The letter was written to request prayer for his problems in Jerusalem, tell the Romans he was coming, share his understanding of Christ, explain specific church problems, and enlist help in his new missionary venture. Romans is the most formal of Paul's letters. It systemically sets forth the doctrine of justification by faith and discusses a number of other basic Christian doctrines. *Romans has been called the most significant theological book ever written. Augustine of Hippo, Martin Luther and John Wesley all had profound religious experiences directly related to the reading and studying of Romans.*

I & II Corinthians	Corinth was a prosperous city in Southern Greece that was a hub of commerce and trade for Romans, Greeks, Jews and Egyptians. It was also very pagan and noted for everything sinful.
	On the second missionary journey, Paul went to Corinth after a very discouraging reception in the nearby city of Athens. He was later joined there by Timothy and Silas. Paul stayed in Corinth 18 months. The church consisted of people with both Jewish and Gentile backgrounds.
	Paul later wrote First Corinthians from the city of Ephesus. This letter is very practical. It is considered to be a casebook of theology for pastors. First Corinthians deals with spiritual and moral problems and questions. It also discusses gifts of the Holy Spirit, The Lord's Supper and the resurrection.
	After writing the first letter, Paul found it necessary to make a second hurried visit to try to solve problems in the church.
	He later wrote from Macedonia the second letter which was aimed at solving those problems of the church. Second Corinthians also encouraged the believers, discussed finances and defended Paul's own authority as an apostle.
	Paul later made a third visit to the church at Corinth.

THEOLOGICALLY SPEAKING

Without these two Corinthian letters, we would know far less than we do about the earliest examples of "Christianity at work." These letters provide a glimpse of a community typified by ambition, confusion, joy, desire, and enthusiasm.

Corinth, a port city with harbors to the east and north, had ships arriving from all around the Mediterranean World. Its transient population provided a convergence of many cultural, moral, and religious backgrounds. Corinth had a reputation for sexual immorality and could be typified as the "city of sin" of ancient Greece.[2]

| Galatians | Galatia described a region or area in Central Asia Minor and also a Roman province which included that region and an additional area to the south. Paul initially established churches in Galatia during his first missionary journey. He visited the region twice and possibly on all three journeys.

The Letter to the Galatians was written either immediately after Paul's first missionary journey or during his third journey. The time of writing depends upon which area of Galatia he was addressing.

Paul wrote to settle disputes that Gentiles must first become part of the Jewish faith before becoming Christian. In this letter, he references the fact that he corrected the Apostle Peter concerning the acceptance of the Gentiles. Paul firmly sets forth the doctrine of justification by faith in Jesus Christ. |

THEOLOGICALLY SPEAKING

The instruction set forth in Galatians was crucial for the new church since they were converted directly from paganism and knew nothing of Jewish background or Christian teaching.[3]

| I & II Thessalonians | Thessalonica was a major city in the Roman colony of Macedonia. The city was located on the northeast shore of the Aegean Sea. Thessalonica was the second place that the gospel was preached in Europe.

Paul, Silas and Timothy visited there on the second missionary journey. Paul was rejected by the Jewish leaders and forced to leave in a very short time. He later sent Timothy back to aid the believers. Consequently the church, composed primarily of Gentile believers, prospered.

Paul wrote the first letter very soon after he was forced to leave. His purpose was to dispel rumors that were started about him and to encourage the new believers not to revert back to their pagan ways.

The second letter was written shortly after the first to settle misunderstandings about the second coming of Christ and to inform the believers that daily life must go on in the meantime. |

THEOLOGICALLY SPEAKING

The Thessalonian letters are possibly the earliest writings of Christian literature. They are classic examples of Paul's instruction to the early Christian Church concerning its integrity and identity as a community of faith.[4]

The Prison Letters

Ephesians, Philippians, Colossians, and Philemon are often called the Prison Letters. Within each of the four letters, Paul identifies that he is a prisoner. Paul was initially arrested in Palestine, imprisoned for two years in the city of Caesarea and then transferred to Rome. There he remained a prisoner in his own quarters for an additional two years. The combined four years of imprisonment and the time under arrest during the voyage to Rome are documented in the Book of Acts. However, there is significant debate about the Roman imprisonment. Some scholars believe Paul was imprisoned only once in Rome, some feel he was released and soon imprisoned a second time, and yet others have additional theories.

Table 14-2   The Four Prison Letters

Letter	Description
Ephesians	Ephesus was the capital of the Roman province of Asia. It was a major seaport and trading center located on the west coast of Asia Minor. Paul visited Ephesus briefly on his second journey and stayed there for approximately three years on his third journey. During his second stay, Paul taught regularly and Christianity spread throughout the area. Ephesians is the least personal of Paul's letters. It was intended to be a circular type document to be shared with several churches. This is obvious because Paul uncharacteristically omitted names of his many friends in the church at Ephesus. Neither does he deal with specific problems of any individual church. Ephesians sets forth the basic concepts of the Christian faith. Paul knew that the new churches were constantly faced with the powerful influences of other religions and cultures. He was able to write a very strong, straightforward letter because he personally knew many of the leaders and believers in the area and understood their problems. The main theme of Ephesians is that it is God's purpose to establish the Church and that the Church is a place of reconciliation. This mandates that Christians must live a reconciled life.

| Philippians | Philippi was a small city in Eastern Macedonia Paul visited there on his second missionary journey. It was the site of the first church Paul established in Europe. Philippi apparently had no synagogue because Paul began his ministry there by preaching to women who had gathered on the river bank.

Paul again visited Philippi, at least briefly, on his third journey. Paul had a very warm and cordial relationship with the church. They had twice given Paul financial help in the past, and when they heard he was in prison they sent another gift. Paul was clearly in prison when he wrote this letter; however, there is great debate among scholars about when and where he was imprisoned

This letter is the most personal of Paul's letters to churches. The primary purpose of the letter was to send thanks for the third gift. The letter also addressed some of the problems that Paul knew existed in the church. The underlying theme in the letter is a plea for church unity and continued evangelism. Paul related several items such as the conversion of his captors, his own situation in prison, and examples that he and Timothy had set. |
| :--- | :--- |
| **Colossians** | Colosse was a small city in South Central Asia Minor near several other cities with church communities that had been established during Paul's journeys.

Although Paul had never visited the city of Colosse, the leader of that church knew Paul. He had either visited Paul in prison or had been imprisoned with Paul. In either case, in Rome he had personally reported the conditions and problems of the church directly to Paul.

The letter can be broken into two parts. The first portion is aimed against false teachings. Greek philosophy and pagan practices were being mixed with Christian teachings. The second portion is meant to uplift and encourage proper Christian living, which Paul considers necessary for those who wish to be mature in Christ.

Encouraging and facilitating Christian maturity is the main theme of this letter. |

Philemon	Philemon is the only letter of a private nature in the Bible, and it is the shortest of Paul's letters. It was written to an individual named Philemon, whom Paul apparently knew personally and had helped convert. He was a member of the church at Colossae and also a slave owner, which was not uncommon. Paul wrote the letter from prison in Rome on behalf of a slave who had run away from his master Philemon after stealing from him. The slave, who knew Paul, had become a Christian. He was now in Rome, and wished to return to his master although he had committed capital offenses according to Roman law. Paul wrote to Philemon asking him to forgive the slave, take him back and treat him as a Christian brother. The letter contains several elegant puns. One example is his play on the slave's name Onesimus, which means "useful." In verse 11 Paul says, ***"Formerly he was useless to you, but now he has become useful both to you and to me."***

The Three Pastoral Letters

The Pastoral Letters are so named because of their content. All three letters provide principles, guidelines and qualifications for pastors. The title *Pastoral Letters* also takes precedence over the place written.

Table 14-3   The Three Pastoral Letters

Letter	Description
I Timothy	Timothy was the son of a Gentile father and a believing Jewish mother. Paul passed through Timothy's hometown in Central Asia Minor early in his second missionary journey. Timothy joined Paul on the journey and soon became as a son to Paul. Timothy worked in whatever capacity he was needed. He accompanied Paul, was sent on various missions and was placed in charge of churches. Clearly, he was a key figure in carrying on Paul's missionary work. The first letter was written to encourage Timothy, who at that time was the pastor of the church in Ephesus. The leader of this church undoubtably had a great deal of responsibility for many of the other churches in that part of Asia Minor. The uplifting letter covers a wide variety of church topics, some of which are very specific. The theme of this letter might be the Christian challenge to "fight the good fight."

II Timothy	Second Timothy is the most personal of the pastoral letters. It conveys direct advice to Timothy concerning his responsibilities as pastor. He is told to not be ashamed of the testimony about Christ and to rekindle the gift of God. The theme of the letter may be considered "The Good Soldier of Jesus Christ." The body of the letter is filled with brief but powerful statements describing the many characteristics of such a soldier. Near the end of the letter is the familiar following verse: *"I have fought the good fight, I have finished the race, I have kept the faith."* <div align="right">*II Timothy 4:7*</div>
Titus	The person Titus is not mentioned in the Book of Acts; however, he is named in three of Paul's other letters. Titus was a Gentile that Paul must have converted early in his ministry. Titus traveled extensively with Paul and was sent on at least four trips to not only spread the Good News, but to use his administrative skills in the church organization. Titus was now pastor of the church on the island of Crete and was clearly facing opposition within the church. The letter was written to encourage Titus and also give him the power of written words from an authority for use in his ministry.

"All Scripture is God-breathed and is useful for teaching, rebuking, correcting and training in righteousness."

II Timothy 3:16

THE GENERAL LETTERS OR EPISTLES

The General Letters of the New Testament are composed of eight letters attributed to five authors.   The style of these letters varies greatly. The letters of Peter and Jude most closely follow the typical first century style of Paul. The Book of Hebrews begins like a sermon and ends like a letter. The Book of James somewhat parallels the wisdom writing of the Old Testament and the intertestamental period. Second and Third John follow a format very similar to the short Hellenistic letters of that time, and First John is closer to a sermon than a letter.

The General Letters of the New Testament are listed in the following table in the order that they appear in the Bible.

Table 14-4   The General Letters of the New Testament

Letter	Description
Hebrews	The author or location of writing of the Book of Hebrews is unknown. Obviously, this person had great literary skill and was very familiar with the Old Testament. The letter was written in a time when Christians faced great persecution. It is unclear what group the author was addressing, where they lived or their present spiritual condition. However, it appears that the recipients of the letter were presently facing persecution and were being pressured to deny the Christian faith. From the title it seems the addressees are Jewish Christians; however, many scholars feel that they may have been Gentile Christians. In either case, the unknown author provides a witness to the Christian experience which is clear and compelling. The main idea in the letter is that Jesus' coming fulfills the Old Testament predictions and hopes. Both the author and the readers were quite familiar with the Greek translation of the Old Testament (Septuagint). This is evidenced in the fact that there are 29 direct quotations and 53 allusions to Old Testament passages in the writing.
James	James is addressed to "the 12 tribes that are dispersed abroad," a designation for Christian believers everywhere. At this early date in Christianity, Jewish Christians comprised the majority of the community of believers. The purpose of the letter is very simple: to strongly encourage the practical aspects of Christian living. James tells how faith works in everyday life. In fact, scholars agree that the author's concerns are more practical and less theological than any other writing in the New Testament. The book is so strong about works and says so little about justification by faith that it has received a great deal of criticism. It is considered by some to be of lesser status than other letters in the New Testament.

I & II Peter	First Peter was written from Rome and refers to Rome as Babylon. This follows the theory of many scholars that Peter went to Rome, was a leader in the church there and was eventually martyred.
	The first letter is addressed to Christians scattered throughout Asia Minor. There was tremendous persecution from the pagan society in which most Christians lived and worked. Suffering is a major topic in this letter. The fiery ordeal mentioned in chapter 4 may possibly reference the insane Roman emperor, Nero, who literally burned Christians at night. Peter writes to encourage the believers and to assure them that even though they may suffer now they should live above such things and be assured of ultimate salvation.
	Second Peter has a significant style change and is not specifically addressed to any one person or group. This openness may mean the letter was intended for wider circulation or it may simply be the second letter to the same addresses as the first. This letter promotes faith in Christianity and denounces false teachers by identifying their conduct and characteristics.
I, II & III John	At the time of the writing of these three letters, Christianity was well over half a century old and was a powerful and established religion in many parts of the Roman Empire. However, there were still persecutions and organized attempts to dilute the Gospel by incorporating philosophies and pagan ideas into Christian beliefs.
	First John does not name its specific address, but is apparently intended as a circular type letter to the churches around Ephesus in Asia Minor. First John deals with the growing problem of the Gnostic teachings which were plaguing many churches at this date. The book uses numerous contrasts to make its points including the contrast of light and darkness which is reminiscent of the frequent use of the word "light" in the Gospel of John.
	Second John is addressed to "the chosen lady." There is much debate if this is a church near Ephesus, a person, or a family. Second John emphasizes the ultimate power of "truth." It warns of false teachers who can be recognized by their refusal to acknowledge Christ in the flesh. John states that these teachers should be rejected and closes the letter with hopes of personally visiting soon.
	Third John is a very personal letter addressed to an individual. It is a specific letter concerning a dispute about the reception and treatment of traveling Christian teachers and, like Second John, stresses "truth" as the aim of the Christian experience.

Jude	It is unknown to whom the Letter of Jude was written. It is obvious that the intended readers were being plagued with false teachers.
	Jude clearly states in the opening verses that he was planning to write a much different letter to discuss their common salvation, but now feels forced to write this letter addressing a specific problem instead.
	Clearly, ungodly people who were perverting the worship of God and denying Jesus had gained respectable positions in the readers' congregation. Jude had become aware of this happening, and the subject and purpose of the letter is to condemn such heretics in no uncertain terms and to call for the others to remain faithful.

THE FINAL BOOK OF THE NEW TESTAMENT

Persecution in Late New Testament Times

Much of the Book of Revelation deals with and is precipitated by persecution. Therefore, it is necessary to briefly review the level and type of persecution the Christians of this time period were facing. In the early decades of Christianity the majority of the persecution was suffered on a religious basis, primarily from the Jews rejecting Christianity. The Roman government had no real interest in suppressing Christianity other than to appease the Jews in Jerusalem and to keep a firm political grip upon the empire.

The Apostle Paul had even been protected by the Roman government on several occasions and urged Christians to obey its laws. There were only isolated cases of government persecution until A.D. 64, when Emperor Nero accused the Christians of burning Rome. This persecution was generally confined to Rome, and was based upon criminal, not religious, charges.

Since before the time of Christ, the emperors of Rome had been worshiped as gods. However, until Domitian came to the throne in 81 A.D., this practice was generally taken very loosely. Domitian made emperor worship the policy of Rome, and Christian beliefs came into direct conflict with government policy. In the early 90's A.D., Domitian launched programs throughout the entire empire to eliminate Christianity.

Apocalyptic Literature

Apocalyptic literature is difficult to define in concise terms. The word "apocalyptic" comes from the Greek verb *"apokalupto,"* which means "to uncover." The general term can be said to deal with the secret purposes of God.

There are several distinct characteristics of this type of literature. First, it is a product of times of extreme oppression and persecution, and is clearly marked by the era from which it was derived. It employs visions and prophecies. The terms it uses are very symbolic and are usually powerful and exaggerated for the purpose of making the point through extreme language. Apocalyptic literature often gives a negative view of the present world and yet expresses great hope for the future. It encourages the believers in times of hardship.

The later portion of the Old Testament Book of Daniel and all of Revelation are examples of apocalyptic literature.

Table 14- 5   The Book of Revelation

Book	Description
Revelation	The author of the Book of Revelation names himself simply as John. John states that he is a prisoner on the small island of Patmos off the coast of Asia Minor, near Ephesus. Scholars feel the book was either written on the island or at Ephesus, if John was indeed released. Revelation contains individual messages for seven of the major churches in Asia Minor. These churches are named in logical geographic order and the entire writing may have been intended as a circular type document to be shared with all of the churches.

The inspiration and direction to write the book was given to John in a divine vision while on the island.

Revelation is written in apocalyptic style and language. The writing can be divided into two distinct portions. The first three chapters deal with "things which are," and the remainder of the book deals with "things which will take place."

The complexity and very nature of the book give rise to great speculation and greatly varied interpretations of many parts of the writing. There are four principal viewpoints concerning the interpretation of this book. A very brief summary of these viewpoints follows:

Preterist	Prophecies that have been fulfilled in early history.
Historical	History as it unfolds from the writing until the end of time.
Idealist	Pictorial of principles without real events.
Futurist	Prophecy to be fulfilled in the future.

Regardless of the viewpoint taken, the main theme of Revelation is clear:

The Ultimate Triumph of Jesus Christ!

THEOLOGICALLY SPEAKING

The Revelation of John is easily manipulated into a kind of "fortune-teller's" book intended to foretell the exact date and historical occurrences surrounding the future arrival of Christ. Volumes and volumes of books, sermons, and teachings have focused in on this idea. Actually, Revelation is written to first century churches in an attempt to bring hope to those who are being persecuted and to those who suffer at the hands of oppression.

Revelation is written in a strange, symbol-centered literary style known as "apocalyptic literature." The language uses exaggerated images intended to show the great struggle between good and evil, and utilizes symbols to communicate hope over despair.

There is a wonderful story that illustrates the message of Revelation. Two very bright seminary students were walking down one of the halls of their school, when they noticed a janitor reading the Bible. One of the students asked the janitor, "Hey, what are you reading?" "Revelation," he replied. The students chuckled to themselves and one asked him, "Well, what does it say?" (For even the greatest minds have not agreed on Revelation). The janitor looked up at the students and said, "It says that, in the end, Jesus wins." In other words, when all is said and done, Revelation is primarily a message of hope to the whole of humanity.

It is appropriate to end this study with one of the best known verses of the entire Bible, yet few realize this wonderful verse is from the Book of Revelation.

"Here I am! I stand at the door and knock. If anyone hears my voice and opens the door, I will come in and eat with him, and he with me."

Revelation 3:20

Read The Book

1. In ancient letters, two and sometimes three components were often omitted or considered optional that modern writers would never imagine leaving out. What were these parts of the letter? _____
    _____   _____

2. In an effort to bring together Jewish and Gentile Christians, Paul's greetings combined the words "_____" from Greek and "_____" from Hebrew traditions.

3. How many letters are in the group commonly referred to as the "Church Letters?" _____

4. When Paul wrote the Letter to the Romans, he was on his _____ missionary journey in the city of _____.

5. T / F   Romans is an informal letter to a church which Paul had established on an earlier missionary journey.

6. T / F   The Book of Romans systematically sets forth Christian doctrine.

7. This city in Greece was a harbor for ships of many countries and was considered a pagan "city of sin." _____

8. After being rejected in the city of Athens, Paul established a church in Corinth and stayed there how many months? _____

9. T / F   First Corinthians is a very practical letter and is considered a casebook for pastors about theology.

10.   Paul's aim in his second letter to the Corinthians was to solve church
       _____ , encourage believers and discuss _____ .

11.   Galatia described both a _____ or area in Central Asia Minor and also
       a Roman _____ .

12.   In Galatians, Paul referenced correcting which apostle concerning the
       acceptance of Gentiles? _____

13.   In Galatians, Paul firmly sets forth the doctrine of _____
       by _____ in Jesus Christ.

14.   The city of Thessalonica was located on what continent? _____

15.   T / F   Upon Paul's initial arrival in Thessalonica, he was well-accepted.

16.   Who was directly responsible for the church initially prospering in
       Thessalonica? _____

17.   T / F   One of the purposes of the first letter to the Thessalonians was to
                 dispel rumors about Paul.

18.   Second Thessalonians was written to settle misunderstandings about the
       _____ _____ of Christ.

19.   List the letters which are often called "The Prison Letters."

       _____   _____

       _____   _____

20.   Ephesus was the capital of the Roman province of _____ . This city was located on the _____ coast of Asia Minor.

21.   The Letter to the Ephesians is the least _____ of Paul's letters because it was intended to be a _____ type document.

22.   The main theme of Ephesians is the following:
        It is God's purpose to establish the _____.
        The church is a place of _____.

23.   Philippi was the first church Paul established on which continent? _____

24.   Where and to whom did Paul begin preaching in Philippi?
        _____

25.   T / F   Paul started the church at Colossae.

26.   The letter to Philemon is not only the shortest of Paul's letters, it also holds what other unique distinction?
        _____

27.   What is the meaning of the name Onesimus? _____

28.   Name the three letters which are commonly referred to as the "Pastoral Letters."

        _____

        _____

        _____

29.   T / F   Paul met Timothy early in the second missionary journey.

30.   Second Timothy gives the characteristics of a _____ _____ of Jesus Christ.

31.   Where was Titus a pastor? _____

32.   How many books are there in the group commonly referred to as the "General Letters?" _____

33.   T / F   The letter to the Hebrews is addressed to Jews in Egypt.

34.   The main purpose of the Letter of James is to encourage the _____ _____ of Christian living.

35.   First Peter was written during a time of great suffering for the church and refers to Rome as what? _____

36.   How old was Christianity when the three letters of John were written? _____

37.   Which book of John is addressed to "the chosen lady?" _____

38.   By what were the readers of the Letter of Jude being plagued? _____ _____

39.   T / F   Revelation is the only example of apocalyptic literature in the Bible.

40.   No matter which of the _____ viewpoints of Revelation you consider, the main theme of Revelation is _____

_____.

Talk The Talk

Twenty-one of the 27 books of the New Testament are letters. We have learned that these letters are different from our letters of today.

A.   *List as many differences as you can think of between letters of today and the letters of New Testament times. Can you think of similarities?*

Paul set up the church at Corinth immediately after he was unsuccessful in nearby Athens. Corinth and Athens were both pagan cities, but Athens was a central place of learning, culture and education. Corinth, on the other hand, was a worldly "city of sin."

B.   *Does it not appear that the thinking scholarly population of Athens would be more interested in the story of Christ than the more worldly population of Corinth? Why was the reverse true?*

Paul wrote the Letter to the Galatians to settle a specific dispute about whether it was first necessary to become part of the Jewish faith before becoming a Christian. At this time, Christianity was being brought to areas with little or no Jewish background or influence as well as to areas with strong Jewish beliefs.

C. *Why was it so necessary to immediately set standards about the requirements and practices of Christianity in both extremes of the environments in which the Word was being spread?*

In one way or another, many of the letters in the New Testament set forth or explained the doctrine of justification by faith.

D. *Going back to your knowledge of ceremonies and laws in the Old Testament, list reasons you feel so much explanation and reinforcement was required to establish the concept of justification by faith in the New Testament.*

Walk The Walk

Without a doubt, no other book in the Bible is the subject of as much controversy as Revelation. Revelation is not intended to be a simple book; neither is the Bible intended to be a simple collections of books. However, the message of both is clear and can be summed up in a simple verse:

"Here I am! I stand at the door and knock. If anyone hears my voice and opens the door, I will come in and eat with him, and he with me."

Revelation 3:20

E.   *How will you be listening for the knock?*

F.   *How will you answer the voice and open the door?*

G.   *What will you offer the Christ?*

APPENDIX

GLOSSARY
of
Selected Religious Terms, Bible Names and Definitions

Aaron - Brother of Moses. Aaron served as spokesman for Moses and as the high priest.

Abel - Son of Adam and Eve. Killed by his brother Cain.

Abijam - Second king of Judah during the divided kingdom.

Abimelech - One of several Philistine kings. Possibly an official title for a king.

Abraham - Father of the Hebrew nation. God called him out of the land of Ur, changed his name from Abram to Abraham and made a covenant with him.

Abram - Original name of Abraham. Husband of Sarai. (Sarah)

Acts - Fifth book in the New Testament. Named for the acts or actions of the apostles.

Adam - The first man. Husband of Eve.

Ahab - Seventh king of Israel during the divided kingdom. Husband of Queen Jezebel.

Ahaz - Eleventh king (twelfth ruler) of Judah during the divided kingdom.

Ahaziah - 1. Sixth king of Judah during the divided kingdom. 2. Eighth king of Israel during the divided kingdom.

Alexander the Great - Leader who conquered the civilized world and sought to bring Greek culture to the entire world by the process referred to as Hellenization.

Alexandria - City in Egypt founded by Alexander the Great. After the exile, a strong Jewish community was established there.

Amaziah - Eighth king (ninth ruler) of Judah during the divided kingdom.

Ammonites - Nation of which Ben-ammi, son of Lot, is the father.

Amon - Fourteenth king (fifteenth ruler) of Judah during the divided kingdom.

Amos - Book in the Minor Prophets of the Old Testament. Amos was a sheepherder and dresser of figs.

Andrew - One of the 12 apostles. Andrew was a brother of Simon Peter.

Annas - Jewish high priest from 5 B.C. to 15 A.D. After leaving the position of high priest, he still exercised a great deal of power. He was the father-in-law of Caiaphas, who was the high priest during the trial of Jesus.

Anoint - The custom of placing oil on a person as a mark of respect. Both the words "Messiah" and "Christ" mean "anointed one."

Antioch - 1. Sometimes called Pisidian Antioch. A city in Southern Asia Minor where Paul visited on his missionary journeys. 2. The capital of the Roman province of Syria. The center for Paul's three missionary journeys.

Antiochus IV - Greek ruler in 175 B.C. who attempted to Hellenize the orthodox Jews and helped cause the Maccabean rebellion.

Apocalyptic - Dealing with the secret purposes of God. A type of writing or literature popular in the late Old Testament and New Testament times.

Apocrypha - Greek word meaning "things that are hidden." Fifteen Jewish books written primarily between the time of the Old and New Testament. These writings were not referred to by Jesus and have never been considered part of Hebrew Scripture. They were ultimately preserved by Christians.

Apostasy - Abandoning one's belief or faith.

Apostle - One sent forth, messenger. One chosen and sent with a special commission as the fully authorized representative of the sender. Used interchangeably with the word disciple; however, disciple describes a much broader group than just the 12 apostles of Jesus.

Arabia - Country located between the Red Sea and the Persian Gulf. Paul visited Arabia early in his ministry.

Arabs - Nation of which Ishmael, the son of Abraham and Hagar, is the father.

Aramaic - Language closely related to Hebrew which was common in Southwest Asia. Common language spoken in Palestine from post-exile times through New Testament times.

Archelaus - (Herod Archelaus). Roman ruler who was a son of Herod the Great.

Ark of the Covenant - Small chest constructed of wood and gold which contained the tablets of the Ten Commandments, Aaron's rod, manna and the book of the Law. Also called the ark of the Lord, ark of God and ark of the testimony.

Artaxerxes - Persian king that allowed Ezra and Nehemiah to return from the exile.

Asa - Third king of Judah during the divided kingdom.

Asher - One of the 12 sons of Jacob (Israel). Father and head of that respective tribe of Israel.

Assyria - Ancient country which was centered in Mesopotamia, north of Babylon. Nineveh was one of its capitals. Assyria was a world power during Old Testament times and eventually captured the northern kingdom of Israel.

Athaliah - Seventh ruler of the southern kingdom of Judah. Only ruling queen in the history of Judah or Israel. She murdered her family to obtain the position.

Augustine of Hippo - Early Christian church leader. Bishop of Hippo, 396-430 A.D. Underwent a profound experience after studying the Book of Romans.

Baal - Pagan gods, especially in the Old Testament. The word, "Baal" is used as a prefix to identify many individual pagan gods.

Baasha - Third king of Israel during the divided kingdom.

Babylon - Name of an ancient Mesopotamian country and its capital city, which was a world power in Old Testament times. Babylon came to power after Assyrian domination and was eventually taken over by the Persian empire. The southern kingdom of Judah was besieged by Babylon, Jerusalem was destroyed, and the people were taken into exile.

Barabbas - Known criminal who was released by request of the crowd instead of Jesus.

Barnabas - Jewish Levite that became a follower of Christ after hearing Peter and John preach. He later became a companion of Paul.

Bartholomew - One of the 12 apostles. Possibly also called Nathanael.

Bathsheba - One of the wives of King David. Mother of Solomon.

Beatitudes - A group of short statements that all begin with "Blessed are." The Beatitudes were spoken by Jesus in the Sermon on the Mount.

Beelzebub - Also Baalzebub. "Lord of the Flies". One of many derivatives of the name of the pagan god Baal. Also used to refer to the Devil.

Belshazzar - Last Babylonian ruler before the Persians conquered the empire.

Ben-ammi - Son of Lot. Ben-ammi is the father of the Ammonite nation.

Benjamin - One of the 12 sons of Jacob (Israel). Father and head of that respective tribe of Israel. Youngest of the 12 brothers.

Bethany - Small town located two miles southeast of Jerusalem where Jesus often stayed. Home of Martha, Mary and Lazarus.

Bethel - Town located slightly north of Jerusalem originally known as "Luz." Site of several significant Old Testament events.

Bethesda - Spring-fed pool in the northeastern section of Jerusalem.

Bethlehem - Town in Palestine which was the birthplace of Jesus. Bethlehem is located five miles southwest of Jerusalem.

Bethsaida - A town on the north side of the Sea of Galilee. Hometown of three of the disciples.

Bible - Formed from a Greek term meaning, "the little books." The word Bible was not commonly used until the fifth century A.D.

Bible Atlas - Atlas which contains various types of maps of the lands which are referenced in the Bible.

Bible Dictionary - A dictionary which defines Bible terms.

Caesar - Name of a Roman family. Title of Roman emperors after Julius Caesar.

Caesar Augustus - Roman emperor who called for the census at the time of Jesus' birth.

Caesar Tiberius - The Roman emperor during the ministry of Jesus.

Caesarea - Coastal city in Palestine which was the home of Philip and the site of significant activity in the Book of Acts.

Caesarea Philippi - Inland city in Palestine near Mount Hermon where Jesus visited.

Caiaphas - Jewish high priest who plotted against Jesus. Son-in-law of Annas the high priest.

Cain - Son of Adam and Eve. Cain killed his brother Abel.

Calvary - The Latin name for the place near the walls of Jerusalem where Jesus was crucified, from the Latin word "calvaria" which means skull. "Golgotha" is the Hebrew name which refers to the same place.

Cana - Small town in Galilee near Nazareth. Jesus' first miracle was performed at a wedding in Cana.

Canaan - The original name of the land of Palestine.

Canaanite Provinces - General term for the countries around Canaan, especially during the time of the entry of the Israelites into the Promised Land.

Canon - Derived from an ancient root word which means "reed." Latin for measuring line or rule. Canon refers to the Biblical books officially accepted as genuine by the church and governing religious body.

Capernaum - Town on the northwest shore of the Sea of Galilee. Jesus used Capernaum as his central point during the Galilean ministry.

Carchemish - Site of a major battle in ancient history. In 605 B.C. Egypt and Assyria were defeated by the Babylonian King Nebuchadnezzar.

Centurion - Roman army commander of 100 soldiers.

Chaldea - Country in Southern Mesopotamia of which Babylon was eventually the capital. Sometimes used interchangeably with Babylonia.

Chebar - River or canal in Babylon near which the prophet Ezekiel lived.

Christ - Anointed one. Greek word is "christos" for anointed.

Chronicles, I - Historical book in the Old Testament.

Chronicles, II - Historical Book in the Old Testament.

Chronological Bible - A Bible which is arranged in chronological order according to a specific time scheme selected by the editor.

City of David - Another name for Jerusalem

Claudius - Roman emperor during New Testament times.

Colosse - City in Roman province of Asia located on Western Asia Minor. Paul established a church in that city and later addressed a letter to the congregation.

Colossians - Book in the New Testament. One of Paul's letters.

Commentary - A text which provides additional meaning and or interpretation to selected portions of Scripture or specific chapter and verse.

Concordance - Indexes of various complexities which reference the chapter and verse location of major words of importance in the Bible.

Corinth - Prosperous city in Southern Greece that was a world trading center. Paul established a strong Gentile church in this pagan city and addressed two letters to the congregation.

Corinthians, I - Book in the New Testament. One of Paul's letters.

Corinthians, II - Book in the New Testament. One of Paul's letters.

Cornelius - A Roman centurion known for being the first Gentile to convert to Christianity.

Council of Carthage - The first church council to list together all 27 books of the New Testament as Scripture (397 A.D.).

Covenant - Pact, treaty, alliance, or agreement between two parties of equal or unequal authority. The covenant can either be accepted or rejected, but it cannot be changed.

Cyprus - Large island in the Eastern Mediterranean Sea. Cyprus was the home of Barnabas.

Cyrus - Founder of the Persian Empire. King Cyrus gave the original decree for the Jews to return from the exile.

Dagon - Ancient fertility god of the Philistines and other nations.

Damascus - A major city in the country of Syria. Damascus was important in both Old and New Testament times.

Dan - One of the 12 sons of Jacob (Israel). Father and head of that respective tribe of Israel.

Daniel - Major prophet in the Old Testament. Daniel lived in Babylon and served in the governments of the nations in power during the exile. Book in the Old Testament.

Darius I - Persian king who aided the Jews in rebuilding the temple.

David - Second king of the united kingdom. David succeeded King Saul and became Israel's greatest and most loved king.

Dead Sea Scrolls - Ancient scrolls discovered in 1947 which provide a copy of the complete Old Testament in Hebrew with the exception of the Book of Esther.

Deborah - Lady judge and prophetess of Israel. Composed a song of triumph.

Decapolis - Region in Eastern Palestine during late Old Testament and New Testament times which was originally named for the 10 Greek cities located there.

Delilah - Philistine woman who deceived Samson and caused his death.

Denarius or Denarri - A silver Roman coin which was the "penny" of the New Testament. One gold denarius was worth 25 silver denarii.

Deuteronomy - The name of the fifth book of the Old Testament which is the last of the five books of Moses. The name "Deuteronomy" refers to Second Law. The Law is set forth for the second time in this book.

Devil - Greek name meaning "slanderer." The enemy of humanity and God. Another name for Satan.

Disciple - Learner. A pupil or follower of some teacher. Sometimes it refers to the 12 apostles but more broadly simply to Christian followers.

Domitian - Roman emperor who launched a program in the early 90's A.D. to eliminate Christianity.

Dropsy - Symptom of a disease that caused fluid build-up or swelling in the body.

Ecbatana - Persian city in which King Cyrus issued the decree that allowed the Jews to return to Jerusalem.

Ecclesiastes - Book in the Old Testament. Ecclesiastes is part of the wisdom literature of the Old Testament. Ecclesiastes means preacher or official speaker in an assembly.

Ecclesiastical - Of the church, the organization of the church, or the clergy.

Edom - Name meaning "red." Country bordering Israel where Esau's descendants lived.

Edomites - Name of descendants of Esau.

Ekklesia - Greek word for church.

Elah - Fourth king of Israel during the divided kingdom.

Eli - Priest that young Samuel assisted. Eli failed to discipline his own sons.

Elijah - Powerful prophet who ministered to Israel during the divided kingdom. Elijah was taken to heaven by God. Elijah is not to be confused with his successor, Elisha.

Elisha - Prophet who was the successor to Elijah. Elisha worked more recorded miracles than anyone in the Bible other than Jesus.

Elizabeth - Wife of Zacharias the priest. Mother of John the Baptist.

Emmaus - Small village located approximately seven miles from Jerusalem. The exact location is unknown. After the resurrection, Jesus appeared to two of his disciples on the road to Emmaus.

Ephesians - Book in the New Testament. One of Paul's letters.

Ephesus - Capital of the Roman province of Asia. Ephesus was located on the west coast of Asia Minor. Paul established a church at Ephesus and addressed a letter to the congregation.

Epistles - Formal letters that teach Christian doctrine. The term epistle is used interchangeably with letter. Of the books of the New Testament, 21 of the 27 are epistles or letters.

Esau - Son of Isaac, twin brother of Jacob. Father of the Edomite nation.

Essenes - Jewish religious sect during the Intertestamental Period. Essenes are not mentioned in the Bible.

Esther - Jewish maiden during the exile who became a Persian queen. She remained faithful to God and saved the Jewish people. Book in the Old Testament.

Estienne, Robert - or Stephanus. Paris printer credited with printing the first Bible divided by both chapters and verses.

Etiology - A story which explains why something is "the way it is" when there is no explanation.

Euphrates River - Largest river in western Asia, located in ancient Mesopotamia.

Eve - The first woman. Wife of Adam.

Exodus - Name of the second book in the Old Testament. "A going out," from the Greek word, "exodos."

Ezekiel - Major prophet in the Old Testament. Ezekiel lived in rural area of Babylon and prophesied to the exiles. Book in the Old Testament.

Ezra - Jewish priest and scribe who returned from the exile and made religious reforms. Ezra worked closely with Nehemiah. One of the historical books of the Old Testament.

Felix - Roman governor of the province of Judea who kept Paul in jail for two years.

Festus - Roman governor of the province of Judea who succeeded Felix. Under his administration Paul appealed to Caesar.

Gabriel - Angel of God who announced the birth of both John the Baptist and Jesus.

Gad - One of the 12 sons of Jacob (Israel). Father and head of that respective tribe of Israel.

Gaius Caligula - Roman emperor during New Testament times.

Galatia - Galatia was a region or area in central Asia Minor. Galatia was also a Roman province which included the Galatia region and additional area to the south. Paul established a church in this area and addressed a letter to the congregation.

Galatians - Book in the New Testament. One of Paul's letters.

Galba - Roman emperor during New Testament times.

Galilee - The most northern of the three provinces of Palestine during the time of Christ. Galileans spoke with a distinctive accent and were disliked by the Jews of the southern regions of Palestine.

Garden of Gethsemane - Garden on the Mount of Olives where Jesus was arrested.

Gaza - Philistine city located 50 miles southwest of Jerusalem.

Genesis - Name of the first book in the Bible. Derived from a Greek word meaning "origin" or "beginning."

Gentile - General term for any non-Jewish person.

Gibeon - Town in Canaan located about six miles northwest of Jerusalem. The tabernacle was set up there.

Gideon - Powerful judge of Israel that won many military battles with a very small army of faithful soldiers.

Gnostics - Members of a powerful religious movement during the first three centuries A.D. that caused great problems in the early church. Gnostics believed salvation was obtained by possession of special knowledge. They thought of Jesus as "fully divine," yet denied his humanity. Due to their view of Christ only "pretending" to be human their views were rejected as unsound or heresy.

Golgotha - The Hebrew name "skull." The place near the walls of Jerusalem where Jesus was crucified. In Latin, "Calvary" refers to the same place.

Goliath - Philistine giant that David killed.

Gomorrah - Old Testament city which was destroyed by God because of its excessive wickedness. Gomorrah was near the city of Sodom.

Goshen - A region in the Nile delta where the family of Jacob settled.

Gospel - English word derived from Anglo-Saxon word "God spell," which meant "good news."

Grace - Undeserved love. In the New Testament the primary meaning is, God's unmerited favor toward humanity.

Greek - Term which is broadly used in New Testament descriptions. The word Greek may refer to a person from that country, a person who follows the culture of that country, the actual culture or the language itself.

Gulf of Aqaba - Gulf extending from the Red Sea which borders the eastern side of the Sinai Peninsula.

Gutenberg - Inventor of the printing press.

Habakkuk - Book in the Minor Prophets of the Old Testament.

Haggai - Book in the Minor Prophets of the Old Testament. Haggai encouraged rebuilding of the temple after the exile.

Hannah - Mother of Samuel. Hannah prayed to God for a baby and then dedicated the child to the service of the Lord.

Hanukkah - Jewish festival which commemorates the cleansing of the temple by Judas Maccabeus in 164 B.C. Also called the Feast of Dedication and Feast of Lights.

Harmony of the Gospels - A chronological list of events of the life of Jesus made by combining information from all four gospels.

Hebrew - A Gentile name for the descendants of Abraham. Used interchangeably with Israelites.

Hebrews - Title of the New Testament Book addressed only to the Hebrews. The author is unknown.

Hellenization - Organized method developed by Alexander the Great to spread Greek culture throughout the civilized world.

Heresy - Unsound religious teaching; theology which has been rejected by traditional, mainstream Jewish/Christian beliefs.

Herod Agrippa I - Grandson of Herod the Great. He executed the Apostle James and imprisoned the Apostle Peter.

Herod Agrippa II - Son of Agrippa I and grandson of Herod the Great. He listened to Paul's defense after Paul had appealed to Caesar.

Herod Antipas - Son of Herod the Great. He had John the Baptist beheaded and Jesus was sent before Herod during His trial.

Herod the Great - Powerful Jewish King that began remodeling the city of Jerusalem and the temple about 20 B.C. During the last years of his life, he tried to kill the Christ child.

Herodians - A Jewish party which was basically political in nature and felt the best interests of the Jews was to cooperate with the Roman government. Hence the name Herodians after King Herod.

Hezekiah - Twelfth king (thirteenth ruler) of Judah during the divided kingdom. Often referred to as good King Hezekiah.

Holy of Holies - The most sacred room in both the tabernacle and the temple. The ark of the covenant was in this room.

Hosea - Minor prophet in the Old Testament who compared his marriage to the relationship of Israel and God. Book in the Minor Prophets of the Old Testament.

Hoshea - Nineteenth king of Israel during the divided kingdom. Final king before the Assyrian exile or dispersion.

Idolatry - The worship of idols, including any image, person or object other than God.

Intertestamental Period - Interval between the final Old Testament prophet Malachi and the birth of Christ (4 B.C.).

Isaac - Son of Abraham and Sarah. Isaac became the father of the twins, Jacob and Esau.

Isaiah - Major prophet who ministered to the southern kingdom of Judah before the fall of Jerusalem. Isaiah wrote more about the Messiah than any other prophet. Book in the Old Testament.

Ishmael - Son of Abraham by Hagar. Many Arabs claim Ishmael as the father of the Arab nation.

Ishmaelites - Descendants of Ishmael. Joseph's brothers sold him to Ishmaelites. Often associated with Midianites.

Israel - Israel means "one who strives with God." God changed Jacob's name to Israel, hence the 12 sons of Jacob became the 12 tribes of Israel.

Issachar - One of the 12 sons of Jacob (Israel). Father and head of that respective tribe of Israel.

Jacob - Son of Isaac, twin brother of Esau. God later changed Jacob's name to Israel.

Jairus - Synagogue leader in Capernaum. Jesus raised his daughter from the dead.

James - 1. Book in the New Testament which is one of the general letters. 2. One of the 12 apostles. Son of Zebedee and brother of John the Apostle.

James the Less - One of the 12 apostles. Identified as the son of Alphaeus.

Jehoahaz - 1. Eleventh king of Israel during the divided kingdom. 2. Sixteenth king (seventeenth ruler) of Judah during the divided kingdom.

Jehoash - Twelfth king of Israel during the divided kingdom.

Jehoiakim - Seventeenth king (eighteenth ruler) of Judah during the divided kingdom. King of Judah when Nebuchadnezzar first invaded Jerusalem in 605 B.C.

Jehoichin - Young king of Judah who only reigned three months before Nebuchadnezzar staged his second invasion of Jerusalem in 597 B.C. Eighteenth king (nineteenth ruler) of Judah during the divided kingdom.

Jehoram - Fifth king of Judah during the divided kingdom.

Jehoshaphat - Fourth king of Judah during the divided kingdom.

Jehovah - English name for Yahweh.

Jehu - Tenth king of Israel during the divided kingdom.

Jeremiah - Major prophet who ministered to the southern kingdom of Judah before and during the fall of Jerusalem. Book in the Old Testament.

Jericho - One of the oldest cities in the world. There are actually three Jerichos located near each other; the Old Testament city, the New Testament city and modern Jericho. Joshua destroyed the Old Testament Jericho.

Jeroboam - Servant of King Solomon who became the first king of Israel in the divided kingdom.

Jeroboam II - Thirteenth king of Israel during the divided kingdom.

Jerome - Ancient church father who prepared the Latin Bible called the Vulgate.

Jerusalem - The central city in the entire Bible. The capital of the southern kingdom of Judah and site of the temple. Sometimes called the "City of David."

Jesse - Father of David.

Jesus - "Jesus" means savior. Greek equivalent of Joshua. In Hebrew Joshua means "Yahweh saves." Jesus was a common name in that day.

Jesus Christ - A combination of the given name Jesus and the title Christ. "Jesus Christ" appears only five times in the Gospels.

Jethro - A priest of Midian, father-in-law of Moses. Same as Reuel.

Jews - Name which referred to the people of Judah during the Babylonian exile. It was used to refer to all Israelites after the Babylonian exile.

Jezebel - Evil queen of the northern kingdom of Israel. Wife of King Ahab.

Joash - Seventh king (eighth ruler) of Judah during the divided kingdom. Joash became king at seven years of age and did "what was right in the eyes of the Lord."

Job - Main character of the Book of Job. Job is a book in the poetry section of the Old Testament.

Joel - Book in the Minor Prophets of the Old Testament.

John - One of the 12 apostles. Son of Zebedee and brother of James the Apostle. Tradition says John is the author of the Gospel of John and First, Second, & Third John and Revelation.

John, I - Book in the New Testament. One of the general letters.

John, II - Book in the New Testament. One of the general letters.

John, III - Book in the New Testament. One of the general letters.

John Mark - Young companion of Paul and Barnabas. He later wrote the Gospel of Mark.

John the Baptist - Cousin of Jesus and divine forerunner of the Christ.

Jonah - Minor prophet who is the main character in the Book of Jonah.

Joppa - City in Palestine on the Mediterranean coast.

Joram - Ninth king of Israel during the divided kingdom.

Jordan River - Major river that runs through Palestine, forms the Sea of Galilee and empties into the Dead Sea.

Joseph - 1 Next to the youngest of the 12 sons of Israel (Jacob). He was sold into Egyptian slavery by his brothers, became the assistant to pharaoh and saved the family of Israel. 2. The husband of Mary, mother of Jesus.

Joseph of Arimathea - Rich man who donated the tomb for Jesus.

Josephus - Famous Jewish general and historian of the first century who wrote extensively concerning the history of the Jews. Josephus is not mentioned in the Bible.

Joshua - Leader of the Israelites who succeeded Moses. Joshua was a powerful military leader and led the Israelites into the Promised Land. Book in the Old Testament.

Josiah - Fifteenth king (sixteenth ruler) of Judah during the divided kingdom. Josiah became king at eight years of age and was generally considered a good king.

Jotham - Tenth king (eleventh ruler) of Judah during the divided kingdom.

Judah - One of the 12 sons of Jacob (Israel). Father and head of that respective tribe of Israel. Leader among the 12 brothers. Tribe for which the southern kingdom was named.

Judaism - Religion of the Jews.

Judas Iscariot - One of the 12 apostles. The treasurer of the apostles and the betrayer of Jesus.

Judas Maccabee - or Maccabeus. Son of the aged Jewish priest Mattathias who started the Jewish revolt against the Greeks during the Intertestamental Period. Judas soon became the popular leader of the rebellion and was nicknamed Maccabee.

Jude - Brother of Jesus. Jude was also called Judas and is traditionally thought to be the author of the Book of Jude. Book in the New Testament which is one of the general letters.

Judea - Greek term, used especially by Romans, which referred to the area in Palestine where the nation of Judah returned after the exile.

Judges - Military, political and religious leaders in the Old Testament. Book in the Old Testament named for the men and women who ruled Israel.

King James Version - The popular revision of Tyndale's Bible which was made by order of King James in 1611.

Kings, I - Historical book in the Old Testament.

Kings, II - Historical book in the Old Testament.

King's Highway - Main north-south caravan route running from Damascus to the Gulf of Aqabah. This highway bisects Palestine and has been in continuous use for over 3,000 years.

Laban - Jacob's uncle who was the brother of his mother, Rebekah. Laban lived in the Padden-Aram (Mesopotamia).

Lamentations - Book in the Old Testament written by Jeremiah.

Land of Milk and Honey - Another name for Canaan or the Promised Land.

Law - Term which is loosely used to refer to the Ten Commandments, the first five books of the Old Testament, the complete Old Testament or God's will.

Lazarus - Close friend of Jesus who was the brother of Mary and Martha. Jesus raised Lazarus from the dead.

Lazarus the beggar - Central figure in Jesus' parable about the rich man and the beggar.

Levi - One of the 12 sons of Jacob (Israel). Father and head of that respective tribe of Israel. Tribe from which the priest came.

Levite - Descendants of the tribe of Levi appointed to assist in the duties of God. Priests were Levites, but Levites were not necessarily priests. The tribe was chosen because they stood with Moses against the supporters of the golden calf.

Leviticus - Name of the third book of the Old Testament which relates to the duties of the Levites.

Lot - Nephew of Abraham who was rescued before the cities of Sodom and Gomorrah were destroyed.

Luke - Gentile physician and companion of the Apostle Paul. Luke is the author of the Gospel of Luke and the Book of Acts. Book in the New Testament which is one of the four gospels.

Luther, Martin - Leader of the Reformation in Germany in the sixteenth century. Underwent a profound religious experience after studying the Book of Romans.

Maccabees - Immediate family and successors of Mattathias, an aged Jewish priest who started the Jewish revolt against the Greeks in 167 B.C.

Macedonia - A Roman colony in Europe located north of Greece. Philippi and Thessalonica are cities in Macedonia where Paul founded churches.

Major Prophets - The Old Testament prophets of Isaiah, Jeremiah, Ezekiel and Daniel. The term minor or major prophet refer only to the length of the book, not to its importance.

Malachi - Minor prophet of the Old Testament. Prophesied to Judah after the temple was rebuilt. Last book in the Old Testament.

Manasseh - Thirteenth king (fourteenth ruler) of Judah during the divided kingdom. Considered the most evil king of all of Judah's rulers.

Manna - Fine flaky bread divinely supplied from heaven which sustained the Israelites as they wandered in the wilderness.

Mark - Author of the book of Mark. Also called John Mark. Book in the New Testament which is one of the four gospels.

Martha - Close friend of Jesus who was the sister of Mary and Lazarus.

Mary - There are five women named Mary listed in the gospels. 1. Mary, mother of Jesus. 2. Mary, sister of Martha and Lazarus. 3. Mary Magdalene. 4. Mary, the mother of the disciple, James the Less. 5. Mary, identified only as the wife of Clopas.

Mattathias - Priest who was the founder of the Maccabee family. Revolted against the Greeks in 167 B.C.

Matthew - One of the 12 apostles also called Levi. Matthew was a tax collector. Attributed author of the Gospel of Matthew.

Matthias - Apostle that replaced Judas Iscariot.

Melchizedek - High priest of Salem (Jerusalem) to whom Abraham paid a tithe.

Menahem - Sixteenth king of Israel during the divided kingdom.

Mesopotamia - Area between the Tigris and Euphrates rivers which is often called the cradle of civilization. Modern day Iraq and Northeast Syria.

Messiah - Anointed one. Hebrew word for anointed one is "mashiah."

Micah - Book in the Minor Prophets of the Old Testament.

Midian - Father of the Midianite nation. Midian was the son of Abraham and Keturah.

Midian, Land of - Generally thought of as the eastern shore of the Gulf of Aqaba. In Arabia. No definite boundaries are given.

Midianites - Nomadic tribe which was often in conflict with the Israelites. Midianite traders were involved with Joseph being sold and taken to Egypt. Midianite are often associated with Ishmaelites.

Minor Prophets - Old Testament prophets of Hosea, Joel, Amos, Obadiah, Jonah, Micah, Nahum, Habakkuk, Zephaniah, Haggai, Zechariah and Malachi. The term minor or major prophet refers only to the length of the book, not to its importance.

Moab - Son of Lot. Descendants of Moab settled east of the Jordan River and were in constant turmoil with the Israelites.

Moabites - Nation of which Moab, the son of Lot, is the father.

Monarchy - A state in which the government is ruled by one person.

Moses - Leader of the Hebrews during the exodus, received the Ten Commandments directly from God and led the nation for 40 years in the wilderness.

Mount Hermon - The highest mountain in Palestine. The probable site of the mount of transfiguration.

Mount Horeb - Mount Sinai. Horeb is sometimes used interchangeable with Sinai.

Mount Moriah - Mountain near Jerusalem which was the site of Abraham's sacrifice and is most likely the location of Solomon's Temple.

Mount Nebo - One of the mountains from which Moses was allowed to view the promised land. The other nearby peak was Mount Pisgah.

Mount of Olives - A ridge of four summits located east of Jerusalem. The Garden of Gethsemane and the town of Bethany are located on its slopes. Jesus ascended into heaven on the Mount of Olives.

Mount Pisgah - Mountain peak near Mount Nebo.

Mount Sinai - Mountain on which Moses was given the Ten Commandments. Also called Mount Horeb.

Nadab - Second king of Israel during the divided kingdom.

Nahum - Book in the Minor Prophets of the Old Testament.

Nain - Small village in Galilee where Jesus raised the widow's son from the dead.

Naomi - Jewish mother-in-law of Ruth.

Naphtali - One of the 12 sons of Jacob (Israel). Father and head of that respective tribe of Israel.

Nathan - Prophet during the reign of King David and King Solomon. He both advised and rebuked King David.

Glossary

Nazareth - Small village in Palestine which was the childhood home of Jesus. Nazareth was located north of Jerusalem in the region of Galilee.

Nazarite - Consecrated. An Israelite who was consecrated and took a vow of separation. The separation vow normally included, no wine, not cutting the hair and avoiding contact with a dead body.

Nebuchadnezzar - Babylonian king who captured the southern kingdom of Judah, destroyed Jerusalem and carried the Jews into exile in Babylon.

Nehemiah - Jewish cupbearer to Persian King Artaxerxes. The king allowed Nehemiah to return to Jerusalem as governor and rebuild the city walls. Nehemiah worked extensively with Ezra.

Nero - Roman emperor whose persecution of Christians was limited primarily to the city of Rome. He accused the Christians of burning Rome.

Nerva - Roman emperor during New Testament times.

Nicodemus - Jewish ruler who sought Jesus at night to ask questions and learn from him. He later helped with Jesus' burial.

Nineveh - City in Mesopotamia which was at one time capital of the Assyrian Empire. Jonah was sent to Nineveh.

Noah - Faithful follower of God who built the ark before the great flood.

Numbers - Name of fourth book of Old Testament. So named because the Israelite fighting force was twice numbered. Hebrew title is "In the Wilderness" because the book describes wandering in the wilderness.

Obadiah - Book in the Minor Prophets of the Old Testament.

Omri - Sixth king of Israel during the divided kingdom.

Onesimus - Name which means, "useful." Name of the runaway slave who is the subject of Paul's Letter to Philemon.

Oral Tradition - The practice of handing down important information from one generation to the next by word of mouth.

Glossary

Orthodox - The practice of strictly observing Jewish rites and ceremonies.

Otho - Roman emperor during New Testament times.

Padden-Aram - or Padan-Aram. Another name for Mesopotamia.

Pagan - Refers to people, or religious practices which do not acknowledge the Bible.

Palestine - General name for the Holy Land. The name is derived from the original inhabitants, the Philistines. Also called land of Canaan, Israel and Judea.

Parable - Likeness. An earthly story with a heavenly meaning.

Paraphrase - A new statement of what the original author said using current language and yet conveying the same meaning.

Patmos - Small island in the Mediterranean Sea off the southwestern coast of Asia Minor.

Patriarch - Israel's founding fathers. Abraham, Isaac, Jacob and the 12 sons of Jacob (Israel) are considered the patriarchs of the nation of Israel.

Paul - The Apostle Paul, same as Saul of Tarsus. Paul was his Roman name. Paul wrote a greater number of books of the New Testament than other single author.

Pekah - Eighteenth king of Israel during the divided kingdom.

Pekahiah - Seventeenth king of Israel during the divided kingdom.

Pentateuch - First five books of the Old Testament. From two Greek words "penta" meaning five and "teuchos" meaning box, jar or scroll.

Pentecost - Pentecost means fiftieth day and is celebrated 50 days (a week of weeks) after the Passover. The Holy Spirit descended upon the apostles on the day of Pentecost.

Perea - Region in Palestine east of the Jordan River that Jesus visited. The word Perea is not used in the Bible it is simply referred to as "beyond the Jordan."

Perfect - Another name for a Roman governor or ruler.

Persia - Empire founded by Cyrus by defeating Media and Babylonia. At least four of its rulers were favorable to the Jews.

Peter - One of the 12 apostles. Also known as Simon Peter and Cephas. Traditionally thought to be the author of First and Second Peter.

Peter, I - Book in the New Testament. One of the general letters.

Peter, II - Book in the New Testament. One of the general letters.

Pharaoh - Title of the ruler of Egypt. There are at least 10 different pharaohs referenced in the Old Testament.

Pharisee - Prominent sect of Jews opposed to Jesus. They believed in both the oral and written law, resurrection of the body, immortality of the soul and reward or punishment based on works.

Philemon - Slave owner in church at Colossae to which Paul addressed a letter concerning the return of Philemon's runaway slave. Book in the New Testament which is one of Paul's letters.

Philip - 1. One of the 12 apostles. A former disciple of John the Baptist. 2. One of the seven workers chosen by the apostles to help administer the work of the early Church. He later became a great evangelist. 3. Roman ruler who was a son of Herod the Great.

Philippi - City in Europe located in the Roman colony of Macedonia. Paul founded a church there and later addressed a letter to its congregation.

Philippians - Book in the New Testament. One of Paul's letters.

Philistines - A nation of people that migrated to the coast of Canaan near the time of the Exodus. They were known as "the people of the sea" and were powerful warriors with a knowledge of metal working. They were in constant turmoil with the Israelites. The name "Palestine" is derived from Philistine.

Phoenicia - Country along the Mediterranean coast northwest of Palestine. It major cities were Tyre and Sidon. Phoenicia was known for shipbuilding and sailing.

Pompey - Roman ruler who took control of Palestine in 63 B.C.

Pontius Pilate - Roman governor of Judea who tried and sentenced Jesus.

Priest - Jewish personnel in charge of sacrifice and offering at worship places, particularly the tabernacle and later the temple. Priests were from the tribe of Levi, but not all Levites were priest.

Procurator - Another name for a Roman governor or ruler.

Promised Land - The land of Canaan, the land of milk and honey, settled by the Israelites after the exodus. The promised land was later known as Israel, Judea and finally as Palestine.

Prophet - A spokesman for God. Two aspects of a prophet's work in the Bible was forth telling the conditions of the present and foretelling certain events in the future.

Proverbs - Poetical book in the Old Testament. Proverbs are wise saying that reveal the truths of life.

Psalms - Poetical book in the Old Testament. The Book of Psalms was assembled and used as a prayer and worship book for the Jews after the exile.

Pseudepigrapha - Group of early Jewish writings which are not included in the Apocrypha or in Biblical writings.

Ptolemy Philadelphus - Ruler of Egypt who according to tradition requested that the Hebrew scriptures be translated into Greek. The result was the Septuagint.

Publican - Tax collector for the Roman government during the time of Jesus.

Qumran - Area near the northwest shore of the Dead Sea where the Dead Sea Scrolls were found.

Rabbis - Plural of Rabbi. "Master or great one." In the Old Testament, the word "Rabbi" designated a person of high rank. During Jesus' time it was a title of honor. By the second century A.D., the title was reserved for officially ordained teachers and masters of the law.

Rachel - Wife of Jacob, daughter of Laban.

Rameses - A city in ancient Egypt. The name of 11 pharaohs in ancient Egypt. Also spelled Ramses or Ramesses.

Rebekah - Wife of Isaac. Mother of Jacob and Esau.

Rehoboam - Son of King Solomon who became the first king of Judah in the divided kingdom.

Reuben - One of the 12 sons of Jacob (Israel). Father and head of that respective tribe of Israel. Eldest of the 12 brothers.

Reuel - A priest of Midian, father-in-law of Moses. Same as Jethro.

Revelation - Last book in the Bible. Derived from the Latin word "revelation" meaning revealing or disclosing. The only book in the New Testament which is exclusively prophetic or apocalyptic.

Revision - A rendering of the Bible which is derived by updating an existing translation.

Romans - Book in the New Testament. One of Paul's letters.

Rome - The capital city of the Roman Empire. In New Testament times Rome was the capital of the entire world.

Ruth - A young foreign girl who became a faithful Jew. Ruth is an ancestor of Jesus and the main character in the book of Ruth.

Sadducee - Jewish religious sect opposed to Jesus. They believed in only the written law, no resurrection of the body, and no life after death. They were a small group, but held high positions in the priesthood and basically controlled the activities in the temple.

Salvation - Deliverance from sin by God.

Samaria - Originally Samaria was another name for the northern kingdom of Israel. It later referred to a region between Galilee and Judea in New Testament times. Samaria is also the name of the city which was the capital of the northern kingdom of Israel.

Glossary

Samaritans - Inhabitants of the region of Samaria. After the exile, the Jews used the term with contempt to refer to the impure race of people in Samaria imported by the Assyrians.

Samson - Strong man who was a judge of Israel. Samson's exploits are among the most colorful of any in the Bible.

Samuel - Considered either the last judge or first prophet of Israel. Samuel was a faithful and powerful leader who advised both King Saul and King David.

Samuel, I - Historical book in the Old Testament.

Samuel, II - Historical book in the Old Testament.

Sanctify - To separate from the world and set apart for God.

Sanhedrin - Highest Jewish council or court. It was composed of 70 members who were primarily either priest or scribes plus the high priest who was the president. In general the priests were normally Sadducees and the scribes were Pharisees.

Sarah - Name of Abraham's wife, after God changed her name from Sarai.

Sarai - Original name of Sarah, Abraham's wife, before God changed her name.

Sargon II - Assyrian king who completed the final siege on the northern kingdom of Israel, destroyed the capital city of Samaria and dispersed the population.

Satan - Hebrew name for "adversary." The enemy of man and God.

Saul - First king of the united kingdom. Saul turned away from God and was eventually replaced by King David.

Saul of Tarsus - Another name for the Apostle Paul. Saul is the Hebrew name for Paul. Tarsus was Paul's home town.

Scribe - A person trained in writing and recording events. During the Babylonian Exile scribes became experts in the law. In New Testament times, a professional group of scribes who were experts in the written law. They were laymen and not priests.

Scroll - A book made of leather or papyrus rolled up on two poles.

Sea of Galilee - Major fresh water lake in Palestine formed by the Jordan River. Also knows as Lake Gennesaret, Sea of Tiberias and Lake Chinnereth.

Sects - Religious groups or parties with distinct doctrine, such as Pharisees or Sadducees.

Sennacherib - King of Assyria who attacked the southern kingdom of Judah under Good King Hezekiah, but God did not allow him to conquer the city of Jerusalem.

Septuagint - Title derived from Latin meaning "70." The oldest Greek translation of the Old Testament. Tradition says the Septuagint was completed in 70 days by 72 Jewish scholars for the King of Egypt in the third century B.C. This was the Scripture commonly used in Jesus' time. Consequently, the majority of Old Testament quotes found in today's New Testament were taken from the Septuagint. The name Septuagint is often abbreviated with the Roman numerals "LXX."

Shallum - Fifteenth king of Israel during the divided kingdom.

Shalmaneser III - King of Assyria to whom the northern kingdom of Israel was forced to pay tribute to a century before the final fall of the country.

Shalmaneser V - Assyrian king who started the final siege on the northern kingdom of Israel.

Shechem - Old Testament city about 40 miles north of Jerusalem.

Shekel - In the Old Testament, the term "shekel" refers to a unit of weight which was 0.4 ounces. In the New Testament, the term "shekel" refers to a coin which had the weight of 0.4 ounces.

Sheshbazzar - Jewish prince whom Cyrus allowed to lead the first return from the exile. Sheshbazzar may be another name for Zerubbabel.

Sidon - City in Phoenicia located on the Mediterranean sea coast. Sidon was visited by both Jesus and Paul.

Silas - A companion of Paul on his second missionary journey.

Simeon - One of the 12 sons of Jacob (Israel). Father and head of that respective tribe of Israel.

Simon of Cyrene - Stranger who was forced to carry Jesus' cross.

Simon Peter - One of the 12 apostles. Same as Peter. Also called Cephas.

Simon the Zealot - One of the 12 apostles.

Sinai - Or Sinai peninsula. Peninsula between the Gulfs of Suez and Aqaba. Sinai is sometimes used to refer to Mount Sinai, a mountain located on the peninsula.

Sodom - Old Testament city which was destroyed by God because of its excessive wickedness. Sodom was near the city of Gomorrah.

Solomon - Son of King David and Bathsheba who succeeded his father and became the third and final king of the united kingdom.

Song of Solomon - Poetical book in the Old Testament.

Stephen - One of the seven workers chosen by the apostles to help administer the work of the early Church. He was later the first Christian to be martyred.

Steward - One who is placed in charge of finances and property for another.

Succoth - 1. Palestine. A site several miles east of the Jordan River referenced in the Old Testament. 2. Egypt. The first place the people of Israel stopped during the exodus.

Sychar - City in Samaria where Jesus talked to the woman at the well. Probable location of Jacob's well from the Old Testament.

Synagogue - Either a Jewish place of assembly for worship or a Jewish community of worshipers. The concept of worship away from the temple most likely originated during the Babylonian Exile.

Synoptic Gospels - The three Gospels of Matthew, Mark and Luke which share common perspective, structure and content. Synoptic is from the Greek word "synoptikos," which means "seeing together."

Syria - Country north of Palestine. Antioch and Damascus were its major cities.

Tabernacle - Portable tent or temple used by the Israelites prior to the construction of Solomon's Temple.

Tamar - Canaanite woman who is listed in the genealogy of Christ.

Tarsus - City in Southeastern Asia Minor which was the home of the Apostle Paul.

Temple - Building or structure which is thought to be the dwelling place of some deity. More specifically, the name of the three successive temple buildings on Mount Moriah where the Hebrews worshiped God. The temple was originally constructed by Solomon, destroyed by Nebuchadnezzar, rebuilt by Zerubbabel and greatly remodeled and expanded by Herod. It was again destroyed in 70 A.D. by the Romans.

Testament - Old English word for covenant derived from the Latin word for "covenant."

Tetrarch - Roman ruler of a smaller district than a King would reign over. Originally the term was used for, "the ruler of a fourth part."

Thaddeaus - One of the 12 apostles. Also called Judas, son of James.

Theocracy - A state in which God is the ruler.

Theophilus - Person to whom the Gospel of Luke and the Book of Acts were addressed.

Thessalonians, I - Book in the New Testament. One of Paul's letters.

Thessalonians, II - Book in the New Testament. One of Paul's letters.

Thessalonica - City in Europe located in the Roman colony of Macedonia. Paul founded a church there and later addressed a letter to its congregation.

Thomas - One of the 12 apostles. Also called Didymus.

Tigris River - One of the two major rivers in Mesopotamia.

Timothy - Companion of Paul whom he referred to as "His child in the faith."

Timothy, I - Book in the New Testament. One of Paul's letters.

Timothy, II - Book in the New Testament. One of Paul's letters.

Titus - Gentile that Paul converted. He became a trusted companion and helper of Paul and later was the pastor of the church on the island of Crete. Book in the New Testament addressed to Titus.

Titus, Flavius - Roman emperor (79-81 A. D.) who captured and destroyed Jerusalem in 70 A.D.

Torah - Hebrew word for law which eventually became the title for the first five books of the Old Testament.

Trajan - Roman emperor during New Testament times.

Translation - A rendering of the Bible which is derived from the process of going back to the original language of ancient texts and translating each word into current language.

Tyndale's Bible - Bible translated directly from the original Greek and Hebrew manuscripts in the sixteenth century and considered more accurate than its popular predecessor, the Wyclif Bible.

Tyre - Major city in Phoenicia located on the Mediterranean sea coast. Tyre was visited by both Jesus and Paul.

Upper Room - Room on the second floor of a building where Jesus ate "The Last Supper," a Passover meal with his 12 apostles.

Ur - Land from where God called Abram. The land of Ur was located in southern Mesopotamia, in present day Iraq.

Uzziah - Ninth king (tenth ruler) of Judah during the divided kingdom.

Vanity - Emptiness or futility, the meaning in the Bible is not the modern use of the word. In the Hebrew text of Ecclesiastes, the Hebrew word is *"hebel"* which means vapor, or "hevel" which means breath was used.

Vespasian - Roman emperor during New Testament times.

Vitellius - Roman emperor during New Testament times.

Vulgate - Latin version of the Bible. Prepared by Jerome in the fourth century and used extensively for the next 1,000 years.

Wesley, John - Eighteenth century priest and theologian who underwent a profound experience after studying the Book of Romans. Wesley later brought about a spiritual revival in England and America.

Wyclif Bible - The first English Bible. It was translated from the Latin Vulgate in the fourteenth century.

Xerxes I - Persian king who married the young Jewish maiden, Esther, during the exile.

Yahweh - Hebrew name for God. From the Hebrew tetragram (four letters) YHWH.

Zacchaeus - Tax collector who climbed a sycamore tree in order to see Jesus.

Zacharias - Jewish priest who was the husband of Elizabeth and father of John the Baptist.

Zealot - One who has great zeal to maintain the Jewish faith. In New Testament times, a small political party that wanted to overthrow any political group opposing the Jews.

Zebulun - One of the 12 sons of Jacob (Israel). Father and head of that respective tribe of Israel.

Zechariah - 1. Fourteenth king of Israel during the divided kingdom. 2. Minor prophet who encouraged rebuilding of the temple during the return from the exile

Zedekiah - Nineteenth (twentieth ruler) and final king of the southern kingdom of Judah. Placed on the throne as a puppet ruler by Babylonian King Nebuchadnezzar; however, he rebelled, Jerusalem was destroyed and the Babylonian exile began.

Zephaniah - Book in the Minor Prophets of the Old Testament.

Zerubbabel - Jewish leader of the first exiles to return from Babylon. This group started rebuilding the temple but soon met opposition.

Zimri - Fifth king of Israel during the divided kingdom.

Zion - A broad term which sometimes refers to the city of Jerusalem, the hill upon which the temple was built or the Jewish religion.

NOTES

ANNOTATED BIBLIOGRAPHY
"Theologically Speaking" Sections

Chapter 3

1. W. J. A. Power, *The Book of Genesis: A Folk Theology* (Dallas, TX: Southern Methodist University, Perkins Journal, Volume 37, winter 1984, number 2); see p. 4.
2. Ibid., see p. 3.

Chapter 4

1. Lawrence Boadt, *Reading the Old Testament* (New York, NY: Paulist Press, 1984); see p. 165.

Chapter 5

1. Gerhard Von Rad, *Old Testament Theology, Volume I* (New York, NY: Harper Publishing Co., 1962); see p. 333.

Chapter 10

1. Luke Timothy Johnson, *The Writings of the New Testament: An Interpretation* (Philadelphia, PA: Fortress Press, 1986); see p. 172.
2. Ibid., see p. 151.
3. Ibid., see p. 223.
4. Ideas taken from a lecture on the Gospel of John by Dr. Virgil Howard, Professor, Perkins School of Theology, Southern Methodist University, Dallas, Texas.

Chapter 12

1. Ideas taken from a sermon preached by Dr. Fred Craddock, Professor of Preaching, Candler School of Theology, Emory University, Atlanta, Georgia.

Chapter 13

1. Luke Timothy Johnson, *The Writing of the New Testament: An Interpretation* (Philadelphia, PA: Fortress Press, 1986); see p. 207.

Chapter 14

1. Ibid., see p. 236.
2. Ibid., see p. 272.
3. Ibid., see p. 303.
4. Ibid., see p. 260.

NOTES

Chapter 1

1. T
2. little books
3. 66
4. Old Testament, New Testament
5. 39, 27
6. book, chapter, verse
7. There are two books named Timothy; I Timothy and II Timothy.
8. Pentateuch, Historical, Poetical, Major Prophets, Minor Prophets
9. Gospels, Church History, Paul's Letters, General Letters, Apocalyptic
10. T
11. The book itself, authority of the writer, church acceptance
12. Hebrew, Aramaic and Greek
13. Hebrew
14. Greek
15. T
16. T
17. LXX
18. Hebrew, Greek, versions
19. Dead Sea
20. Esther
21. cross reference
22. T
23. concordance

Chapter 2

1.   Mediterranean Sea
2.   Holy Land, Canaan, Promised Land, Land of Milk and Honey, Israel, Israel and Judah, Judea, Palestine
3.   Sea of Galilee, Dead Sea
4.   -1,292 feet
5.   2,600 feet
6.   70, 150
7.   Chinnereth, Gennesaret, Tiberias
8.   F
9.   Salt Sea, Arabah, Eastern, Asphatitis
10. T
11. Gaza Strip
12. Jordan River
13. 3
14. T
15. testament
16. 1,000
17. Old Testament
18. 4
19. II Kings, II Chronicles
20. Amos, sheep breeder

Chapter 3

1. beginning of time, 2,000
2. foundation
3. sinned
4. fellowship, sin
5. F
6. Ur, Mesopotamia
7. T
8. tithe
9. father, stars
10. 400
11. Abraham, Sarah
12. circumcision
13. T
14. Lot
15. Isaac
16. Jacob, Esau
17. Jacob, blessing
18. Israel
19. T
20. Israel
21. Joseph, slave
22. famine
23. 70
24. 1850
25. Judah, Messiah
26. Arab
27. Arabs, Moabites, Ammonites, Midianites, Edomites

Chapter 4

1. slaves
2. Egyptians did not like shepherds.
    Egyptians worshiped many gods.
    Hebrew slave population was large and disgruntled.
3. T
4. Pharaoh's daughter
5. 40, 40
6. Mount Sinai, burning
7. Egypt, Aaron
8. blood, frogs, gnats, flies, disease, boils, hail, locusts, darkness, death
9. T
10. firstborn
11. Passover
12. Holy Communion
13. silver, gold
14. Red Sea
15. quail, manna, water
16. T
17. golden calf
18. 4, 6
19. place, order
20. F
21. The Tablets of the Ten Commandments, manna, Aaron's rod
22. Levi
23. T
24. year, day
25. 40 years
26. constitution
27. Moses

Chapter 5

1. Joshua, military, spiritual
2. Jordan River stopped flowing
3. ceremony of circumcision
4. T
5. manna
6. F
7. F
8. Promised Land
9. spiritual, military, civil
10. 13, 300
11. T
12. Samson, strong
13. oppressed
14. anoint
15. Christ, Messiah
16. disobedient, sins
17. blessings
18. anoint
19. T
20. T
21. F
22. 3
23. Jerusalem
24. David's son would build the temple.
    The Messiah would come from David's family.
25. T
26. Solomon, second
27. T
28. 300
29. 1,000
30. T

Chapter 6

1. F
2. Rehoboam, Jeroboam
3. Judah
4. Israel
5. T
6. Judah, Jerusalem
7. Israel, Samaria
8. 209 years
9. 345 years
10. God
11. present
12. divided kingdom, exile, after the return from the exile
13. F
14. 1
15. wicked, Jezebel
16. Elijah
17. F
18. 28
19. T
20. Elisha, Jesus
21. prosperity
22. T
23. Messianic
24. Isaiah
25. Assyrian
26. T
27. Weeping
28. wickedness
29. 70, captivity
30. Nebuchadnezzar
31. overlord

Chapter 7

1. country, leader, temple, functioning priesthood, order of worship
2. Judah, Jews
3. synagogues
4. F
5. Egypt
6. 14
7. beginning
8. Daniel
9. T
10. plundered
11. Ezekiel
12. T
13. burned, walls, temple
14. Daniel
15. Cyrus
16. 42,360
17. Gentiles in Babylon, King Cyrus
18. desert
19. 550 miles
20. 4
21. 605, Nebuchadnezzar came to power
    535, foundation of the temple was placed
22. Darius I
23. Haggai, Zechariah
24. 20
25. Esther
26. destruction
27. Ezra, Nehemiah
28. priest, scribe
29. cupbearer
30. governor, walls
31. Malachi
32. Elijah, (John the Baptist)

Chapter 8

1. in thought
2. parallelism, speech
3. Job, Psalms, Proverbs, Ecclesiastes, Song of Solomon
4. Psalms, temple
5. David
6. 116
7. vinegar
8. none
9. wisdom literature
10. Why do the righteous suffer?
11. T
12. King Solomon
13. everything
14. a good name
15. youth
16. wise sayings, instructions for life
17. T
18. Wisdom
19. first
20. Lord
21. wisdom, understanding
22. You do not know what tomorrow will bring.
23. whale (fish)
24. T
25. foreign
26. everyone
27. Christ

Chapter 9

1. 4, intertestamental
2. Persian, Greek, Jewish Independence, Roman
3. Persia, return
4. T
5. good
6. Septuagint was made
7. F
8. Maccabeus
9. Hanukkah
10. Roman
11. F
12. Pharisees
13. Sadducees
14. copied the Law
15. experts in the Law
16. F
17. Apocrypha
18. LXX
19. personal relationship
20. 50
21. Luke
22. F
23. 4
24. Hebrews
25. Philemon

Chapter 10

1. good news
2. oral tradition
3. Matthew, Mark, Luke
4. view together
5. Jewish
6. 128
7. T
8. Greek
9. physician
10. F
11. 7
12. theological

Chapter 11

1. 40
2. Judah
3. 30 pieces of silver
4. Palestine
5. 5, Galilee
6. Samaria
7. 3
8. 100
9. for a census
10. Jerusalem
11. 20, 20
12. Jerusalem
13. Jordan River
14. wedding
15. T
16. Zacchaeus
17 Mount of Olives
18. Calvary, Golgotha
19. Garden of Gethsemane
20. synagogue
21. T
22. upper room
23. Bethany
24. 5 (including Mary Magdalene)
25. Lazarus
26. cousin
27. Peter - first, Judas Iscariot - last
28. John the Baptist

Chapter 12

1. Zacharias, Mary, Joseph
2. in a house
3. 12
4. John the Baptist
5. heavens, Holy Spirit (like a dove), God
6. Scripture
7. T
8. Mount
9. Blessed are
10. a boat
11. parables
12. F
13. 0, 4, 3
14. Peter, James and John
15. Moses and Elijah
16. F
17. 3
18. swine
19. controlled nature, cured people with demons, cured the human body, raised people from death
20. Mary
21. Bethany
22. The Last Supper
23. F
24. 2 - Pilate, 1 - Herod
25. Golgotha (Hebrew) or Calvary (Latin)
26. tomb sealed and guarded
27. 10
28. 40 days
29. T
30. The Great Commission

Chapter 13

1. Luke
2. 30
3. 12, Apostle Paul
4. James
5. Stephen, Philip
6. 2
7. Africa (North Africa), Europe
8. T
9. Holy Spirit
10. to the remotest parts of the earth
11. Pentecost
12. T
13. Peter, John
14. angel
15. T
16. Saul of Tarsus
17. Damascus, Jesus
18. basket
19. apostles
20. kill
21. Peter, Cornelius
22. clean, unclean, clean
23. Gentile
24. T
25. James, Peter
26. Barnabas, Saul
27. 8,000
28. John Mark
29. T
30. Silas, Timothy
31. calling Paul to Europe (Macedonia)
32. Philippi, Thessalonica, Corinth, Ephesus
33. F
34. 2,500 miles, 4 years
35. Jerusalem
36. Felix, Festus
37. Malta
38. house arrest

Chapter 14

1.   date, address, name
2.   grace, peace
3.   6
4.   third, Corinth
5.   F
6.   T
7.   Corinth
8.   18
9.   T
10.   problems, finances
11.   region, province
12.   Peter
13.   justification, faith
14.   Europe
15.   F
16.   Timothy
17.   T
18.   second coming
19.   Ephesians, Philippians, Colossians, Philemon
20.   Asia, west
21.   personal, circular
22.   church, reconciliation
23.   Europe
24.   on the river bank, to women
25.   F
26.   only letter of private nature in the Bible
27.   useful
28.   I Timothy, II Timothy, Titus
29.   T
30.   good soldier
31.   Crete
32.   8
33.   F
34.   practical aspects
35.   Babylon
36.   ½ a century
37.   II John
39.   F
38.   false teachers
40.   4, The Ultimate Triumph of
      Jesus Christ!